LOGIC, RHETORIC, AND LEGAL REASONING IN THE QUR'ĀN

Muslims have always used verses from the Qur'ān to support opinions on law, theology, or life in general, but almost no attention has been paid to how the Qur'ān presents its own precepts as conclusions proceeding from reasoned arguments. Whether it is a question of God's powers of creation, the rationale for his acts, or how people are to think clearly about their lives and fates, Muslims have so internalized Qur'ānic patterns of reasoning that many affirm that the Qur'ān appeals first of all to the human powers of intellect.

This book provides a new key to both the Qur'ān and Islamic intellectual history. Examining Qur'ānic argument by form and not content helps readers to discover the significance of passages often ignored by the scholar who compares texts and the believer who focuses upon commandments, as it allows scholars of Qur'ānic exegesis, Islamic theology, philosophy, and law to tie their findings in yet another way to the text that Muslims consider the speech of God.

Rosalind Ward Gwynne studied at Portland State University, the Middle East Centre for Arab Studies, Shemlan, Lebanon, and the University of Washington. She was a Fulbright Fellow in Yemen. She is Associate Professor of Islamic Studies in the Department of Religious Studies at the University of Tennessee.

ROUTLEDGECURZON STUDIES IN THE QURAN
Series Editor: Andrew Rippin
University of Victoria, Canada

In its examination of critical issues in the scholary study of the Quran and its commentaries, this series targets the disciplines of archaeology, history, textual history, anthropology, theology and literary criticism. The contemporary relevance of the Quran in the Muslim world, its role in politics and in legal debates are also dealt with, as are debates surrounding Quranic studies in the Muslim world.

LITERARY STRUCTURES OF RELIGIOUS MEANING IN THE QU'RĀN
Edited by Issa J. Boullata

THE DEVELOPMENT OF EXEGESIS IN EARLY ISLAM
The authenticity of Mulsim literature from the Formative Period
Herbert Berg

BIBLICAL PROPHETS IN THE QU'RĀN AND MUSLIM LITERATURE
Robert Tottoli

MOSES IN THE QURAN AND ISLAMIC EXEGESIS
Brannon M. Wheeler

LOGIC, RHETORIC, AND LEGAL REASONING IN THE QU'RĀN
God's arguments
Rosalind Ward Gwynne

LOGIC, RHETORIC, AND LEGAL REASONING IN THE QUR'ĀN

God's arguments

Rosalind Ward Gwynne

Routledge
Taylor & Francis Group
LONDON AND NEW YORK

First published 2004
by Routledge
2 Park Square, Milton Park, Abingdon, Oxon, OX14 4RN

Simultaneously published in the USA and Canada
by Routledge
270 Madison Ave, New York NY 10016

Routledge is an imprint of the Taylor & Francis Group

Transferred to Digital Printing 2009

Typeset in Sabon by LaserScript Ltd, Mitcham, Surrey

British Library Cataloguing in Publication Data
A catalogue record for this book is available from the British Library

Library of Congress Cataloging in Publication Data
A catalog record for this book has been requested

ISBN10: 0–415–32476–9 (hbk)
ISBN10: 0–415–55419–5 (pbk)

ISBN13: 978–0–415–32476–2 (hbk)
ISBN13: 978–0–415–55419–0 (pbk)

Publisher's Note
The publisher has gone to great lengths to ensure the quality of this reprint but points out that some imperfections in the original may be apparent.

CONTENTS

ACKNOWLEDGMENTS

I wish first to acknowledge my debt of gratitude to my professors of Arabic and Islamic studies, some sadly no longer with us, who sustained me through the long student years: Professors Noury al-Khaledy, Peter Abboud, Nicholas Heer, Farhat Ziadeh, Pierre Mackay, Marina Tolmacheva, Jere Bacharach, Walter Andrews, and George Makdisi.

I thank my colleagues in the Southeast Regional Middle East and Islamic Studies Seminar (SERMEISS), the American Oriental Society, and the American Academy of Religion (Study of Islam Section) for listening to and commenting upon initial presentations of some of the ideas presented in this study.

I thank my colleagues at the University of Tennessee, historian Thomas Burman and rhetorician Robert Glenn, for reading and commenting upon a draft of the book, as I thank the anonymous readers to whom the publisher submitted it. I thank logician John Nolt for answering my sporadic questions about matters of logic, at least once graciously alighting from his bicycle to ponder a particularly odd query. Mistakes and omissions are entirely my own.

I thank UT colleague David Dungan and Khalid Yahya Blankenship for the right books at the right time.

I thank the Department of Religious Studies at the University of Tennessee for its policy of arranging periodic research semesters for its faculty, as I thank my colleagues in the department for their support and encouragement.

I thank the editor of this series, Andrew Rippin, for his expertise in Qur'ānic studies. His prompt and thoughtful assistance solved my editorial problems while preserving my own particular approach to the scholarly issues.

And I thank my dear husband Robert for strength, companionship, hugs, computer support, and jazz.

INTRODUCTION

Toward the end of his long spiritual retreat, Abū Ḥāmid al-Ghazālī (d. 505/1111) composed a treatise in which he extracted from the Qur'ān five "scales" that would enable the believer infallibly to distinguish divine truth from falsehood. Together these scales constitute "the Just Balance", *al-qisṭās al-mustaqīm*, mentioned in Qur'ān 17:35 and 26:182, the instrument of known weights and impeccable provenance "that is better and fairer in the final determination" (Q 17:35). Ghazālī's book is also entitled *al-Qisṭās al-Mustaqīm*, and the five "scales" are five logical syllogisms.

Ghazālī had consciously grasped what most others had not: that the Qur'ān does not present its content as self-evidently significant but frames it in patterns of argument to show just how that material engages the hearer and the reader – how he or she is to ponder it, understand it and act upon it. Ghazālī demonstrated the use of the "scales" by recasting appropriate Qur'ānic passages into inference schemata, a technique that not only produces formally valid arguments but adheres more closely to the text than do many works of Qur'ānic exegesis (*tafsīr*). The principles of reasoning, explanation and justification are part of the *intelligibility* that the Qur'ān presents as characteristic of God's creation. The very fact that so much of the Qur'ān is in the form of arguments shows to what extent human beings are perceived as needing reasons for their actions and as being capable of altering their conduct by rational choice when presented with an alternative of demonstrated superiority. Choice is inevitable, but it is the wisdom and order built into creation that make choice at once a necessary and a meaningful act.

Inspired by Ghazālī's short treatise, the present work is a longer and much more detailed analysis of Qur'ānic argument. The text of the Qur'ān, closely examined, yields more than thirty varieties of explicit and implicit argument, elements of argument, techniques, and demonstrations. For ease of reference, each of these is stipulated to be an "argument." The present arrangement owes something to the discipline of classical rhetoric; yet the Qur'ān is not a forum. Arguments change direction and force when they are addressed not to one group of human beings by another human being but to the entire human race by God. God appeals to authority in his pronouncements, but the authority is his own, not that of a third party, as it would be were the same argument to proceed from the mouth of a human being. God argues by cause and effect, but the cause is himself as Creator of the order of nature. And God invites human beings to consider the evidence of his signs, but he shows that the scope of induction is not absolute by reminding them that their minds are limited, that they tend to forget and go astray, and that the conclusions of their specious reasoning often are not only untrue but invalid and hence absurd.

Now, by "Qur'ānic argument" I do not mean a jurist's or theologian's rearrangement of Qur'ānic passages to yield a conclusion not found in the text of the Qur'ān itself. Here "Qur'ānic argument" signifies the existence in the Qur'ān of full arguments with premises and conclusions, antecedents and consequents, constructions *a fortiori*, commands supported by justification, conclusions produced by rule-based reasoning, comparisons, contrasts, and many other patterns. These arguments occur within a single verse or sequence of verses; in the latter case due attention has been paid to the occasions of the revelations (*asbāb al-nuzūl*) in order not to be misled by any fortuitous contiguity of verses. With a few exceptions, I have not constructed arguments as jurists and theologians did, by combining verses separated by text and time. The exceptions are recurrent arguments such as the reasoning from material phenomena to the existence of a creator: not every premise or conclusion is restated every time. Augmenting one such passage with parallel passages from elsewhere in the Qur'ān is both a traditional and a scholarly method for clarifying the meaning.[1]

The fact that many Qur'ānic arguments can be analyzed by formal logic is in no way an assertion that Muḥammad was "influenced" by Greek or Hellenistic thought, or, for that matter, that Aristotle was a direct recipient of divine revelation.[2] Cogent argument is a product not only of formal logical training but of intelligence, language skills, and motivation, as anyone knows who has studied logic but lost an argument to someone who has not.

Because humans are capable of constructing rational arguments, mainstream Muslim scholars have not counted the presence of such arguments in the Qur'ān as part of its *i'jāz* ("miraculous inimitability") or proof of its divine origin. According to al-Bāqillānī (d. 403/1013), his Khurāsānī Ash'arite colleagues were "crazy about" that idea, "but the basis upon which they are constructing it is, in our opinion, unsound (*ghayr mustaqīm*)."[3] A modern opinion to the same effect was given to me by Dr. al-Sayyid Rizq al-Ṭawīl, Dean of the College of Islamic and Arabic Studies at al-Azhar University.[4]

Because of the rhetorical arrangement of components and the polyvalence of many Arabic words, particularly particles that serve as logical operators, it is not always immediately clear how an argument should be classified. I have identified arguments that can be cast into more than one form and presented the alternate forms. I have analyzed the arguments that have separate identities as rhetorical figures and distinguished their rhetorical and logical elements. As previously noted, I have, with help from the exegetes, made elements implicit in commonly abbreviated arguments explicit in order to recast the arguments in logical form. I have not used symbolic logic but have analyzed all arguments according to concepts developed by the ancient and modern logicians whose field is not symbolic logic but natural language, *logos*, from which "logic" took its name.

The first three chapters examine how the Qur'ān establishes the truths that serve as the premises of all Qur'ānic argument. Chapter 1 analyzes elements of the Covenant between God and humanity, the relationship that is the logical key to scriptural argument in Abrahamic religions. Chapter 2 explains two ways in which the Qur'ān validates the covenantal premises. First, it presents numerous divine signs as proof of the absolute power of God, Second, it recites events from sacred history, such as the sending of scriptures and prophets, as precedents from which God has not deviated and which are therefore binding upon humans. The concept of normative precedent (*sunna,* pl. *sunan*) was integral to the structure of pre-Islamic Arab society; the Prophet's contemporaries would have found it a uniquely effective argument. Chapter 3 examines *sunna* in its distinctive Qur'ānic form: the *sunna* of God.

Beginning with Chapter 4, we see how the Qur'ān uses Covenant, sign, and precedent as known truths to construct complex arguments both explicit and implicit. The chapter uses two separate modes of argument, rule-based reasoning and the logic of commands, to analyze the Covenant as a set of rules validating divine imperatives. Chapter 5 distinguishes "rules" from "laws" and shows how the Qur'ān translates divine rules and commandments into laws that apply to human beings but exhibit such juridical nuances as priority, equivalence, exception, and limitation.

Chapters 6 and 7 further expand the repertoire of argument by taking two "common topics" from the field of rhetoric and supplying examples of the multiple forms that each topic assumes in the Qur'ān. Chapter 6 analyzes arguments whose power of proof rests upon comparison with known things; it follows the theme of "comparison" in both its positive and negative manifestations, such as the consistent resemblance between God's prophets and the consistently invincible ignorance of their opponents. Chapter 7 deals with "contrast," a much more fundamental principle in that it begins with the difference between God and his creation. In it I show how arguments based upon contrast are indispensable for convincing skeptical humans to discriminate between belief and unbelief in order to make the decisions upon which their souls depend.

Chapters 8 and 9 enter the field of classical formal logic, taking up Ghazālī's and Najm al-Dīn al-Ṭūfī's analyses of arguments and applying them to a broader selection of Qur'ānic verses. Chapter 8 discovers examples in the Qur'ān of ten of the nineteen possible moods of the Aristotelian categorical syllogism. Chapter 9 examines Qur'ānic examples of conditional and disjunctive syllogisms as originally schematized by logicians of the Stoic school.

Chapter 10 uses several extended examples of debates between prophets and their interlocutors to demonstrate how the Qur'ān combines various forms of argument to support its teachings, illustrate debating technique and etiquette, and demolish the counter-arguments of the opposition. Chapter 11 presents the conclusions of this study of Qur'ānic argument and suggests directions for future research.

Here is a schematic outline of the arguments that appear in this book:

1 The Covenant
2 Signs and precedents
3 The *Sunna* of God
4 Rules, commands, and reasons why
  Does God work for a purpose?
  Rule-based reasoning

I believe that the reader will be surprised at how thick with argument the Qur'ān actually is. It has long been common practice to analyze the Qur'ān's historical and legal material, Biblical parallels and divergences, punishment-stories, rhetorical figures, vocabulary and grammar, data that bear on the life of the Prophet and other thematic selections – all indispensable disciplines. But after having previously concentrated upon some of the areas mentioned above, I found that analyzing Qur'ānic argument was like discovering a trove of hidden verses.

As often as Muslim thinkers cite Qur'ānic prototypes for purposes of argument, comparatively few works have been dedicated to analyzing Qur'ānic argument *per se*. Al-Suyūṭī (d. 911/1505)[5] notes that Najm al-Dīn al-Ṭūfī "singled the matter out for a treatise (*afradahu bi-al-taṣnīf*)"; he does not give the title, but it is *'Alam al-Jadhal fi 'Ilm al-Jadal*;[6] the Ḥanbalī author died in Hebron in 716/1316. In fact, less than half of that work is what we might call *tafsīr jadalī*. The first ninety-one pages are an introduction to juridical debate and forensic logic, including sections on questions and answers, inference (*al-istidlāl*), *qiyās*, and counter-arguments (*al-iʿtirāḍāt*). Ṭūfī then uses technical terms from those disciplines to analyze Qur'ānic argument, and he ends with sections on famous debates and witty exchanges which resemble debates "even though they may not come within their formal boundaries."[7] Suyūṭī fails to mention the source for much of his own material, Burhān al-Din al-Zarkashī's (d. 794/1391) encyclopedic *al-Burhān fi ʿUlūm al-Qur'ān*.[8]

Some books on Qur'ānic argument are simple handbooks meant to aid debaters in their disputations. *Kitāb Ḥujaj al-Qur'ān* by the Hanafī Aḥmad b. Muḥammad b. al-Muẓaffar al-Rāzī (d. 630/ 1233–34) consists of lists of verses, followed by brief explications and ḥadīth, which were to serve as proof-texts for debates over such topics as predestination, free will, and the Beatific Vision. In his *Kitāb Istikhrāj al-Jidāl min al-Qur'ān al-Karīm*, ʿAbd al-Raḥmān Ibn al-Ḥanbalī (d. 634/1236–7) also arranges the Qur'ānic arguments not by type or in Qur'ānic order, but by the points to be proven, such as the unicity of God and the prophethood of Muḥammad. In his final chapter, however, Ibn al-Ḥanbalī discusses the techniques used in the Qur'ān to confound the prophets' adversaries and the enemies of God. (I shall examine some of these debates in Chapter 12.) Suyūṭī mentions neither of these works.[9]

An interesting and far more sophisticated development of the genre can be found in works whose declared purpose is to prove the superiority of the Qur'ān over Greek logic. Thus the title of a book by ʿAbd Allāh b. al-Murtaḍā al-Yamānī, known as Ibn al-Wazīr (d. 840/1436, apparently unknown by Suyūṭī) is self-explanatory: *Tarjīḥ Asālīb al-Qurān ʿalā Asālīb al-Yūnān*. A modern work with many of the same concerns is *Manāhij al-Jadal fi al-Qur'ān al-Karīm* by Ibn al-Ḥanbalī's modern editor, Dr. Zāhir al-Almaʿī.[10] Dr. Khalīl Aḥmad Khalīl's *Jadalīyat al-Qur'ān* declares an interest in discovering the political ramifications of the Qur'ān's unifying effect as seen in the early Muslims' defeat of the Ethiopians, Byzantines, and Persians.[11] An excellent survey of both traditional and modern works in the field is Jane Dammen McAuliffe's indispensable "'Debate with them in the better way': the construction of a Qur'ānic commonplace."[12]

Though Qur'ānic reasoning underlies the immense structure of Islamic theology and law, relatively few books analyze the structure of Qur'ānic proofs. This is not to say that Muslim scholars were ignorant of Qur'ānic reasoning; on the contrary, they were so deeply imbued with it that it was not even second nature for them but first nature – *fiṭra*. For that very reason, I have taken the text of the Qur'ān itself as the primary source for this book. My analyses of arguments are supported, supplemented, and (no doubt) sometimes contradicted by material from exegeses and other sources but have not been formed by them in the first instance, except for that initial inspiration from Ghazālī.

A distinction is in order here. "Argument" is a multivalent term in English: when translated by the Arabic word *jadal*, it more commonly indicates "debate." There is, of course, a wealth of literature on that subject, and Qur'ānic precedents such as those cited in Chapter 10 are invariably invoked both to legitimate the procedure and to stipulate the etiquette that is to be observed. The Qur'ānic models are often obscured, however, by the preoccupation with forensics, that is, by the shift of focus from patterns of proof to techniques for the defeat of adversaries. In spite of the fact that of the twenty-nine mentions of *jadal* in the Qur'ān, all but three (Q 16:125, 29:46, and 58:1) condemn it,[13] works in the genre are so focused upon the elements of procedure – the techniques employed, the evidence cited, the winner, the loser – that only incidentally do some undertake logical analysis of Qur'ānic passages.

That, however, is the sole topic of this book.

1

THE COVENANT

When your Lord drew forth from the Children of Adam – from their loins – their descendants, and made them testify concerning themselves, (saying): "Am I not your Lord?" They said: "Yes! We so witness!" Lest you should say on the Day of Judgment: "Of this we were unaware!"

(Q 7:172)

When God created Adam, he put human beings in a unique relation to himself. He voluntarily limited his own absolute freedom to act upon his human creatures in ways they could not foresee; in return, they chose to acknowledge his power and – despite their own fallibility – accept the trust (*al-amāna*) that the heavens and the earth had refused (Q 33:72). What makes the relationship unique is the moral dimension, which depends upon the element of responsibility. Responsibility depends in turn upon the element of choice, or at least the perceived possibility of choice, which we shall define here as "uncoerced self-restriction." Otherwise the situation of human beings would have been identical to that of angels (Q 2:30 and 32), animals (Q 16:5), even grass and trees (Q 55:5): unmediated dependence upon God arising from the congenital absence of will. Because God chooses to perform actions that benefit humans, thus creating an obligation in the beneficiaries, the Qur'ān describes him with Names that are morally laudatory (*raḥmān, ra'ūf, ḥalīm, wahhāb*) far more often than with Names that can be construed as expressions of sheer, neutral power (*qadīr, qahhār, jabbār, ghālib*).

The relation between God and humanity is called the Covenant, and in my view it is the logical key to the entire structure of Qur'ānic argument. Virtually every argument in the Qur'ān expresses or implies one or more of the covenantal provisions, to be discussed in detail below. The pivotal covenant-passage is Q 7:172, the epigraph to this chapter. Just as Islam holds that no soul bears the burden of another's sin (cf. Q 6:164, 17:15, etc.), Q 7:172 depicts the Covenant not as a communal legacy but as an act by which every human soul individually accepts God as Lord. It has often been observed that the Qur'ān assumes its audience's prior knowledge of events in Judeo-Christian sacred history and the nature of God's dealings with humanity.[1] God has bound himself by his Covenant (*ʿahd, mīthāq, waʿd*) to behave consistently in a certain way, but his faithfulness to the Covenant can be proven only by experience, demonstrated over time and under a variety of circumstances. Otherwise, unsupported statements that God does not break his Covenant (e.g. Q 2:80) from an analytical point of view amount to simple assertions. Hence God not only creates and destroys, rewards, punishes, and forgives, but he also communicates that he has done so and gives his reasons. Without this communication there would be no sacred history, because sacred history consists of God's acts and words and human beings' response to them.

If we bear in mind the terms and continuity of the Covenant, we gain a new perspective on the questions long posed by scholars writing from Jewish and Christian perspectives: why are most Qur'ānic accounts of Biblical characters and events so allusive, discontinuous, and formulaic when compared with the versions in the earlier scriptures? Why do they sometimes differ?

Writing at mid-twentieth century, Abraham Katsh summarized some answers to these questions advanced over the years, noting that Abraham Geiger and R.B. Smith emphasized the Jewish element in the Qur'ān, Carl Brockelmann and Julius Wellhausen the Christian. Brockelmann ascribed the variation in material to ignorance on Muḥammad's part, while Charles Torrey wrote that Muḥammad's knowledge of Judaism was "intimate and many-sided."[2] Such criticism, past or present, apparently assumes that the only acceptable form for the Qur'ān is strict paraphrase or verbatim repetition, if indeed it can legitimately exist as scripture at all; and that the only acceptable status for Muḥammad would have been as either a Jew or a Christian.[3]

To Katsh's summary of scholarly approaches we add two more. The first is seen in Johann Fück's little article, "The Originality of the Arabian Prophet,"[4] where the author addresses the question of bias in research. He, too, assesses the work of earlier scholars, including some named above, as well as Tor Andrae, W. Ahrens, and Anton Baumstark. He concludes that neither the single-influence theory; nor the dissolving of Islam into elements from Judaism, Christianity, Manicheism, and paganism; nor assimilating prophethood to the functions of poet, soothsayer, and *ḥanīf*, will ever adequately explain the phenomenon that was Muḥammad.

> Once this point is understood, the question of possible prototypes, influences, and stimuli loses that decisive significance that it holds for a mechanistic conception of history. What is significant and worth knowing is how the Prophet employed the material provided him, how he altered it, selected from it, and rendered it amenable to his own purposes. That he did so more vigorously than perhaps any other religious hero in no way detracts from his originality. It belongs to the essence of all great men of the spirit to make generous use of material transmitted to them while impregnating it with new life.[5]

While the assumption that Muḥammad himself composed the Qur'ān is clearly not acceptable to Muslims, Fück's positive and appreciative tone is a healthy antidote to pseudo-scientific reductionism.

The second approach addresses the relation between the Qur'ān and its audience. Extremely productive for the present work, it is based upon the concept of *Deutungsbedürfdigkeit* – the need for exegesis – which John Wansbrough borrows from Erich Auerbach's *Mimesis*.[6] Auerbach contrasts the Old Testament with the *Odyssey*: the events of the *Odyssey* are "connected together without lacunae in a perpetual foreground; thoughts and feeling completely expressed . . .," whereas those of the Old Testament are "externalized" only to the extent "necessary for the purpose of the narrative, all else left in obscurity . . . mysterious and 'fraught with background.'"[7] As Wansbrough puts it:

> This is not merely to say that the content of scripture is enhanced by commentary, or that it may be made to bear any number of (complementary and/or contradictory) interpretations, but that the scriptural style is itself incomplete without commentary.[8]

This counters unfavorable comparisons of the Qur'ān with the Old Testament on grounds of the latter's supposed narrative completeness. Neither is a continuous chronicle, nor is it intended to be. Rather, the Old Testament presents the Covenant and the efforts made to fulfil or avoid it; the Qur'ān demonstrates that the Covenant remains in force, and that every generation must strive anew to understand it.

So intrinsic is it to the message of the Qur'ān, in fact, that the Covenant *as a discrete concept* does not have a clear profile in Islamic scholarship. As Bernard Weiss notes, "Covenant was not a subject on which Muslim authors deemed it necessary to write comprehensive and systematic treatises."[9] We shall see in the last section of this chapter that some exegetes treat the first passage containing the word *'ahd* (Q 2:27) in a way that might have developed the subject as a separate Qur'ānic science but in fact did not. Their commentaries on subsequent passages, especially those that contain the word *wa'd* ("promise"), are more concerned with the immediate context and with the occasions of revelation (*asbāb al-nuzūl*).[10] Later theological developments, especially the reaction against the Mu'tazilites, turned discussion away from any limitation – voluntary or not – upon the power of God, except in terms of such positive concepts as Divine Mercy: "God has prescribed mercy for Himself (*kataba 'alā nafsihi al-raḥma*)" (Q 6:12).

Humanity's first experience with the Covenant was not wholly successful, hence the ambiguity of Adam's status among the prophets. "We had already extended the Covenant to Adam before, but he forgot, and We found no firm resolve in him" (Q 20:115); ". . . thus Adam disobeyed his Lord and was misled" (Q 20:121). But God decreed only a temporary punishment, chose Adam, and guided him anew (Q 20:122). He extended his guidance to all. "If guidance comes from Me – and it will – then whoever follows My guidance will not go astray or fall into misery" (Q 20:123).

Adam was not only created but chosen. Qur'ān 3:33 places Adam with Noah, the family of Abraham, and the family of 'Imrān as having been chosen by God above all people. Should he not then have received the Scripture? Ibn Isḥāq (d. ca. 150/767) says that Adam had received fifty sheets of Scripture;[11] al-Ṭabarsī (d. 548/1153) says, on the basis of an apparently non-canonical tradition of Abū Dharr,[12] that he received ten. Al-Ṭabarī (d. 301/926) makes no attempt to minimize Adam's forgetfulness (Q 20:115). On the contrary, he glosses it with the word "abandon" (*taraka*) and quotes from Ibn 'Abbās the folk-etymology which derives the word for "human being" (*insān*) from the verb "to forget" (*nasiya*) used in this verse to describe the sin of Adam. A quotation from Ibn

Zayd (d. 182/798–99) and Ṭabarī's own summation are explicit on the point: Adam was weak, and the promise that he "forgot" was precisely the Covenant of God (*'ahd Allāh*).[13]

Later exegetical effort limits the scope of Q 20:115, apparently so as not to imply that Adam, as a prophet, could have betrayed the Covenant. Ṭabarsī quotes several glosses that discount any intention to sin, and he gives three possible interpretations of what it was that Adam forgot: (1) he forgot the threat of expulsion from heaven if he ate of the tree; (2) he forgot God's statement that Satan was his enemy; (3) he forgot the inference (*al-istidlāl*) that the prohibition was a generic prohibition (*al-nahy 'an al-jins*), mistakenly thinking that the prohibition extended only to the particular (*al-nahy 'an al-'ayn*).[14] This is as close as Ṭabarsī comes to Ṭabarī's conclusion that what Adam forgot was the Covenant of God.

Among the rewards that humans are to receive in return for keeping the Covenant are blessings, prosperity, power, and Paradise. God reminds Israel of his benefits to them: "O children of Israel! Remember the blessings I have given you: keep your Covenant with Me, and I will keep My Covenant with you. And fear Me" (Q 2:40). The precedent that he set with their predecessors will apply to the Muslims as well: "God has promised to those of you who believe and do righteous deeds that He will entrust power to them in the earth as He entrusted it to those before them ..." (Q 24:55). He adduces preceding scriptures as proof: "... A promise truly binding upon Him in the Torah, the Gospel, and the Qur'ān. And who is more faithful to His Covenant than God?" (Q 9:111). Humans are also assured that the Covenant will be kept in the future. "Whoever fulfills what he has covenanted with God – God will grant him a great reward" (Q 48:10). By the nature of the promise, conclusive proof can come only in the hereafter. The saved and the damned discuss it:

> Those of the Garden call to those of the Fire, "We have found that what God promised us was true; have you found that what God promised you was true?" They say, "Yes!" whereupon a crying [voice] proclaims between them, "God's curse is on the wrongdoers!"
>
> (Q 7:44)

Even the Devil admits that God keeps his promises. "Satan says, when the matter is decided, 'God gave you the true promise. I gave you a promise, and I broke it'" (Q 14:22).

Those whom Muḥammad has called to believe do so by declaring their own adherence to the Covenant:

> Our Lord! We have heard a caller calling us to the Faith: "Believe in your Lord!", and we have believed. Our Lord! Forgive us our sins, and grant remission for our evil deeds, and take us up among the pious. Our Lord! Bring us that which You promised us (*wa'adtana*) through Your Apostles, and do not shame us on the Day of Resurrection: You never fail to keep Your promise (*al-mī'ād*). And their Lord responded to them: "I will never let the work of a single one of you – male or female – be lost . . ."
>
> (Q 3:193–95)

I do not maintain that this or any other single passage in the Qur'ān is equivalent to the Mosaic Covenant-event on Sinai. On the contrary, the paradigmatic Covenant is not set out in one place, even though its elements are integral to the Qur'ānic idiom. I have already described the "referential" style of the Qur'ān, its apparent assumption that the hearers know the details of the Biblical stories. As F.E. Peters points out, the Prophet's hostile audience thought so, too, hence all the places in which they call him a "rehasher of old stories (*asāṭīr al-awwalīn*)" (Q 25:5).[15] Chronologically, the phrase *asāṭīr al-awwalīn* is found as early as Sura 68 (specifically in Q 68:15). In the Meccan Sura 46, the phrase is coupled with reference to the Covenant, where, at the end of three long verses commanding kindness to parents (Q 46:15–17), a disrespectful son ridicules his parents' belief in resurrection:

> "Fie on you! Do you two promise me that I shall be raised up after centuries have passed over me?" They ask God's help: "Woe to you! Believe it! God's promise (*wa'd Allāh*) is the truth!" But he says, "This is nothing but tales of the ancients!"
>
> (Q 46:17)

Even in the Meccan period, God tells the audience whom to ask if they do not know these things:

> And those whom We sent before you as apostles were only men whom We inspired. Ask the keepers of Scripture (*ahl al-dhikr*) if you do not know.
>
> (Q 16:43)

> Or is he not informed of what is in the Scrolls of Moses,
> and of Abraham, who fulfilled [his promises – *waffā*]?
> (Q 53:36–7; s. a. Q 53:38–62)

It is clear, then, that people were presumed to know not just the stories but the covenantal relation itself, and that if they did not know, they were to seek help from those who did. A list of all the suras that assume the existence of the Covenant, in that they relate God's proven bounties and his promises for the future to the virtuous actions of human beings, and his penalties to their sins, would omit fewer than a dozen: 114, 113, 112, 111, 109, 105, 97, and possibly one or two others. Allāh was already known to the audience; likewise, the nature of his relationship to humans was a pre-existing condition of which they needed to be not so much taught as *reminded*. As Toshihiko Izutsu has said:

> It is beyond doubt ... that the Qur'ān transferred this particular relationship between Yahweh and Israel into the very center of Islām and made it the basic form of the relationship between Allāh and the Muslims... The conception of religion as a covenant between two parties is indeed no less characteristic of the Qur'ān than of the Old Testament.[16]

Scholars have devoted immense effort to the study of the various sorts of treaties, covenants, oaths and other instruments designed to solemnize relationships between groups in the Late Bronze and Iron Ages, and how they affected the notion of Covenant as it appears in the Hebrew Bible. Obviously, some of these texts predated the Qur'ān by more than a millennium, yet one sort of external corroborating evidence of the existence and nature of such agreements has come from parallel phenomena in Arab culture. Thus P. Kalluveetil notes the similarity of Muslim Arabs' pacts of brotherhood with ancient Hebrew practices[17] and that the concept of the Hebrew *berit* included four types of Arab covenants, one of which was the *ʿahd*.[18] In their authoritative article "Covenant" in *The Anchor Bible Dictionary*, George Mendenhall and Gary Herion compare the related covenantal notions of gratitude and obligation with their counterparts in old Arab society[19] and note the existence of Bronze Age holdovers in later Arabic linguistic structures.[20] Their schema of a Late Bronze Era (LBE) covenant is based upon numerous examples, not all of which contain all elements of the schema. Likewise, some covenant-making events are less explicitly represented than others in the Qur'ānic formulation, but this is largely due to the fact that the original Covenant between God and humanity is understood to remain in effect.

Mendenhall and Herion list eight characteristics for an LBE covenant:

1 The covenant-giver is identified.
2 The historical relations are described reciprocally, setting out the benefits and the resulting obligations.
3 The stipulations of behavior are given, often in a legalistic "if ... then ..." format.
4 Provision is made for safekeeping of the document and periodic public reading.
5 A list of witnesses is given.
6 Blessings and curses for obedience and disobedience are described.
7 The covenant is ceremonially ratified, often by sacrifice of an animal.
8 If the covenant is actually broken, curses are imposed and punishment follows.[21]

Some may resist using the word for anything other than the Covenant between God and the children of Israel made on Mt. Sinai. Patricia Crone and Michael Cook, for example, refer to that which in Islam "occupies a position analogous to that of the covenant in Judaism." But they then draw a distinction with significant implications for Qur'ānic argument: they see Islam as possibly a development of the covenant with Abraham challenging the Mosaic covenant.[22] Bernard Weiss has also noted that, despite the importance of the Covenant in the Qur'ān, there is no "great covenant-making event in the life of the Muslim community ... no counterpart in the Muslim experience ... to the Sinai event."[23] Thus the Qur'ān's audience is not a chosen people excluding all others. "Muslims" are those who have kept the Covenant,[24] but that status is open to all, as all are included in the primordial but ahistorical "covenant of Sovereignty and Subordination" (*'ahd al-rubūbīya wa-'l-'ubūdīya*) made with all the offspring of the "children of Adam" in Qur'ān 7:172.[25]

Despite the Biblical use of the term, Mendenhall and Herion see the Abrahamic "covenant" (Genesis 15) as a phenomenon distinct from the Mosaic covenant, a "literary ideological motif" rather than an "historic enactment," because the religious community already existed at the time of writing. But regardless of the date of composition, the point of using the word is surely to establish the relation between Abraham and God as an "historic enactment" in its own right. To this sort of quasi-covenantal pact the authors have given the name "divine charter." They date the Abrahamic text as the second of three: the first is that of David (2 Samuel 7), which is not called a "covenant" (*berit*), and the third is that of Noah (Gen. 9:8–17), which is.[26]

Here are the characteristics of the "divine charter" set out in parallel format:

9 A deity bestows some special privilege, power, or status upon a human being, almost always a king, and his descendants in perpetuity.
10 There is no specific literary form.
11 It is a "unilateral divine promise ... it is God, not human beings, who are bound by oath."
12 It provides for witnesses, with Yahweh swearing "by himself."

Let us now examine the twelve conditions[27] as they apply to the Qur'ān, and especially to the earliest suras. The later covenantal developments that are relevant to the Qur'ānic presentation will be added as needed.

1 **The covenant-giver is identified.** If we accept the majority opinion that the first verse to be revealed was Q 96:1, "Read! In the name of your Lord Who created" (*Iqra' bi-smi rabbika 'lladhī khalaq*),[28] we note that the introductory command is immediately followed by identification of its source: the Lord who created humanity. In Chapter 4 I shall analyze the logic of Qur'ānic commands, including the sequence of command-authorization-definition that appears in the first revelation, and we shall see in greater detail that the opening of Sura 96 fulfills the first condition for creating a covenant in a way that the other early revelations do not.[29] In the primordial Covenant-passage (Q 7:172),[30] God identifies himself as Lord in a manner that enables humanity simultaneously to acknowledge that identification and accept the Covenant.

2 **The historical relations are described reciprocally, setting out**

the benefits and the resulting obligations. Although the command "Read!" addresses a single individual, the benefits recited – beginning with creation – have been granted to all human beings. This creates the obligation.

The first descriptions of the relations between God and human beings are "historical" in that God's past actions precede the obligations that they create. But more conventionally "historical" episodes were not long in coming and indeed occupy very large sections of the Qur'ān, in the form of stories of earlier prophets and vanished nations, divine precedents, and the sunna of God.[31] One of the best brief examples of the covenantal combination of history, benefits, and obligations comes in Sura 42 *al-Shūrā*:

> He owns the keys of the heavens and the earth: He extends sustenance to whom He will and restricts it; He knows all things. He has decreed for you by way of religion what he enjoined on Noah – and what We have inspired to you, and what We enjoined upon Abraham and Moses and Jesus: to uphold the Religion and not to separate ...
>
> (Q 42:12–13)

As Weiss points out, much theological argument turned upon whether or not humans could know of the existence of the Covenant without the sending of prophets. The Sunni consensus was, of course, that they could not, hence the commandment to believe in God "*and his prophet*" and to obey both of them.[32]

3 **The stipulations of behavior are given, often in an "if ... then" format.** There are hundreds of such stipulations in the Qur'ān. The Arabic language is capable of fine distinctions between conditional propositions: purely hypothetical propositions introduced by the word *in*, "if-and-when" propositions with *idhā*, and contrary-to-fact propositions with *law*, besides such operators as "whoever," "whenever," "wherever," and so on. In any of these conditionals, the protasis ("if-clause") or apodosis ("then-clause") may also be a command or commandment. These constructions are discussed in the section of Chapter 4 that deals with imperatives. Here is an example in which each "if-clause" (in this case a "when-clause") is followed by a "then-clause" that is a command, then by a description of the rewards to be earned:

> O you who believe! When (*idhā*) it is said to you: "Make room in the assemblies! then make room: God will make room for you." And when it is said: "Rise!" then rise: God will raise the rank of those of you who believe and have been given knowledge. And what you do God knows perfectly.
>
> (Q 58:11)

4 **Provision is made for safekeeping of the document and periodic public reading.** Mendenhall and Herion note two successive changes in this conception of the covenant that are relevant here. First, the "new covenant" mentioned in Jeremiah 31:31–34, which they date to shortly after the destruction of Jerusalem in 586 BCE, no longer applies to a body politic. Instead, says the Lord, "I will . . . write it on their hearts, and will be their God, and they shall be my people" (Jer. 31:33); this knowledge will no longer depend upon teaching but will be innate (Jer. 31:34).[33] Second, rabbinic Judaism refocused on written scripture with its emphasis on the Sinai covenant. All three covenantal stages have parallels in Qur'ānic textual history.

The Qur'ān describes itself as being on a Preserved Tablet (Q 85:21–22) and in a Protected Book (Q 56:77–78); thus the original is with God and cannot be lost or damaged, but humans after the death of the Prophet were clearly concerned to collect and preserve the text they possessed. Numbers of Muslims initially preserved the Qur'ān by memorizing it and passing it along to others; to that extent it was a public document from the beginning. Legends of Muḥammad's yearly verification of the text with Gabriel also exhibit the motifs of "safekeeping" and "periodic reading."

Attention has already been drawn to God's innate covenantal relationship with humanity as seen in Q 7:172. This verse is often explained by another, Q 30:30: ". . . the pattern (*fiṭra*) of God upon which He fashioned (*faṭara*) humanity; there is no change to God's creation."[34]

Applying the terms "document" and "written scripture" to the Qur'ān raises well-known questions about the form it was to take. Was it originally intended to be a "document," as implied by the terms "scrolls" (*ṣuḥuf* – Q 87:19) and (sometimes) "Book" (*kitāb* – Q 2:78, cf. Q 46:30)? Did the root *q-r-'* signify oral recitation or did it signify the reading of something written? The latter meaning – as a concept integral to the idea of Covenant – would lend weight to the traditions that describe the early gathering and collation of the written documents that contained parts of the Qur'ānic text.

5 **A list of witnesses is given.** The concept of "witness" is integral to the Qur'ān in both the religious and the legal sense. Qur'ān 73:15 may be the first verse in which Muḥammad is called *rasūl*; in that verse he is called *shāhid* as well: "We have sent you a Messenger as a witness to you" (Q 73:15). Qur'ān 85:3 swears "By witness and witnessed" as part of the introductory oath-sequence (see §11 and §12 below); and God is called "a witness to all things" in verse 9. This is not "a list of witnesses;" but early reference to the notion of witness without an actual list of witnesses seems appropriate if the original Covenant was still in effect.

Later suras add material to this covenantal category. In Sura 2, human consent and witness are affirmed:

> And when We took your covenant (*mīthāqakum*) not to shed each other's blood and not to turn each other out of your homes, you agreed to that while bearing witness.
>
> (Q 2:84)

Ṭabarī reports that Qatāda's (d. 117/735–36) interpretation of the twelve *naqībs* appointed among the children of Israel in Qur'ān 5:12 is that the twelve were witnesses.[35]

In God's covenant with the prophets,[36] both sides witness:

> "... Then a prophet comes to you confirming what you already have. Believe in him and support him!" He said: "Do you agree and take My covenant to that effect?" They said: "We agree (*aqrarnā*)." He said: "Then so witness! And I am a Witness with you."
>
> (Q 3:81)

For his part, God witnesses (*shahida*) in Q 3:18 that there is no deity but he. He witnesses what he has sent down, and the angels do so as well; but God is sufficient as a witness (Q 4:166, 48:28). In a number of locations (e.g. Q 10:29, 17:96, 29:52, 46:8), Muḥammad, too, is told to cite God as sufficient witness to the truth of the message.

Thus both God and men are witnesses. One of the most complete formulations comes in Q 6:19:

> Say: What is strongest by way of witness? Say: God is witness (*shahīd*) between you and me. And this Qur'ān was revealed so that by it I might warn you (*li-undhirakum*) and those whom it reaches. Is it true that you witness (*a-innakum la-tashhadūn*) that there are other gods with God? Say: I do not bear witness to that. Say: God is truly One, and I am not a party to associating others with Him (*barīʾun mimmā tushrikūn*).[37]

6 **Blessings and curses for obedience and disobedience are described.** Although the original punishment for violation of the covenant was dispersion of the Israelite "body politic," Jeremiah's new covenant spoke of forgiveness, not punishment.[38] Christianity placed the covenantal benefits in the life to come.[39]

Again, all three stages occur in the Qur'ān. But since so much of God's treatment of parties to the Covenant is history, and since there is no single, communal covenant-making episode during the lifetime of Muḥammad, the Qur'ān rarely shows a dramatic pause, as it were, between the time that the Covenant is solemnized and the first time that it is obeyed or violated.

One example can be found at the beginning of Sura 5 *al-Mā'ida*, verses 1–11. Verses 1 and 2 contain a long series of commandments dealing with proper conduct during the pilgrimage (*ḥajj*), particularly with regards to sacrificial animals, hunting, and reaction to other people's anti-Muslim feelings. Muslims are not to react but are to support each other: "Help each other in righteousness and piety; do not help each other in sin and aggression. And fear God: God is strong in punishment" (Q 5:2). Verses 3 and 4 continue with a detailed ban on unclean meats (except in cases of starvation); verse 5 describes the women whom Muslim men may marry. Each of these also ends with a punishment-formula. Other stipulations include performing proper ablutions (verse 6), justice and piety (8), and remembering God's favor (11). Blessings are mentioned in verse 9, curses in verse 10. In the middle comes a Covenant-passage:

> Remember God's favor (*niʿma*) to you, and the covenant (*mīthāq*) that He made with you, when you said, "We hear

and obey!" And fear God, for God knows what is in your hearts.

(Q 5:7)

We shall see below and in Chapter 3 to what extent God's destruction or dispersal of the vanished nations, who were cursed in this life and some of whose traces are still visible, is brought on by violations of the Covenant.

Islam, like Christianity and the Judaism of Jeremiah's "new Covenant," explicitly rejects the notion of collective punishment; thus reward for obedience and punishment for disobedience are tied to the acts of individuals, not communities. The formulae occur countless times in the Qur'ān, beginning as early as Sura 74. Verses 15 through 30 describe the sinner's haughty ingratitude to God and his contempt for the Qur'ān; verses 17 and 26–30 specifically describe his punishment as something that will happen in the future. As for other early suras, sin and its punishment are to be found in Qur'ān 68:7–16 and 35–45; 1:7; 73:12–18; 100:6–11; 107:1–7; 111:1–5; and 87:11–13. Virtue and reward are correlated in Q 68:34; 73:19; 103:2–3 (implicitly), and 87:9–10 and 14–15. Virtues are recited to a greater extent than these numbers indicate, however, because many of the verses which describe sins do so in terms of virtuous actions neglected, such as failure to pray or to feed the poor (Q 74:43–44).

To cite the virtue/reward and sin/punishment *topoi* in the later suras would be to cite most of the text. So pervasive are they that it is unnecessary to make a case for their existence. What must be remembered is that they are *covenantal* notions.

7 **The Covenant is ceremonially ratified, often by sacrifice of an animal.** Sacrifice is mentioned a number of times in the Qur'ān. The earliest is undoubtedly Sura 108 *al-Kawthar* 1–2: "We have given you abundance (*al-kawthar*), so worship your Lord and sacrifice (*wa-'nḥar*)." That is the only occurrence of the root *n-ḥ-r*; the act of slaughtering by cutting the throat (*dh-b-ḥ*) is used in the episode (Q 2:67–71) that gives Sura 2 *al-Baqara* its name. It is used for pagan sacrifices (Q 5:3) and also for what Abraham nearly does to his son (Q 37:102) before God provides an alternate sacrifice (*dhibḥ* – Q 37:107).

The principal words used in ritual contexts come from the ambiguous *n-s-k*, the first meaning of which appears to be "worship," which includes the secondary meaning of ritual sacrifice.[40] The secondary meaning had strong supporters among the apparently more concrete-minded early Muslims. Thus Ṭabarī discusses both meanings at length and eventually opts for the first, that it means all rites of the pilgrimage (*manāsik al-ḥajj*). Fakhr al-Dīn al-Rāzī (d. 606/1209–10) explicitly rejects the equation of *manāsik* with "sacrifices," saying that the confusion of meanings arose only because the broader "rites" includes the narrower "sacrifices;" otherwise "sacrifices" would have no place in the matter at all.[41] The main descriptions of Islamic sacrifice come in Q 2:196 and 22:32–7. Both contain derivatives of *n-s-k;* the first also has the term for sacrificial animals (*hady* – also Q 5:2, 5:97, and 48:25), and both contain the word *maḥill* – "place of ritual sacrifice" (also in Q 48:25).

Three passages using derivatives of *n-s-k* may be singled out for their covenantal implications. In Q 2:124–129, God covenants (*ʿahidnā*) with Abraham and Ishmael that he will make the House (sc. the Kaʿba) a safe meeting place and that they will keep it sacred. They accept the condition, praying:

> Our Lord, make us submissive to You (*muslimīn laka*) and our progeny a nation submitting to You (*ummat*^{an} *muslimat*^{an} *laka*) and show us our religious rites (*manāsikanā*) . . .
>
> (Q 2:128)

Qur'ān 2:200 combines the term *manāsik* with the covenantally important notion of *dhikr* – remembering (or mentioning):

> And when you have completed your rites (or "your sacrifices"), remember (or "mention" *fa-dhkurū*) God as you remember your fathers, or with a stronger memory (*aw ashadda dhikr*^{an}) . . .[42]
>
> (Q 2:200)

Qur'ān 6:162 follows a passage (Q 6:151–2) often compared to the Ten Commandments. The last of these is to fulfill God's Covenant (*wa-bi-ʿahdi 'Llāh awfū* . . .), and the intervening verses are also replete with covenantal elements: "My Straight Path" (153); the Book (154–57), the unity of faith (158–9), reward for virtue and punishment of sin (160), the Straight Path and the faith (*milla*) of Abraham (161). Only then does the text speak of sacrifice. "Say:

My prayer and my sacrifice (*nusukī*) and my life and my death are for God Lord of the Worlds" (Q 6:162). Exegetes are more willing to accept "sacrifice" as the equivalent of *nusuk* than of *mansak/ manāsik*: Ṭabarī simply glosses it with *dhibḥ*;[43] and Ṭabarsī quotes the philologist and grammarian al-Zajjāj (d. 311/923) to the effect that "*nusuk* is anything by which one comes closer to God, but the more prevalent is 'sacrifice;'" while a *nāsik* man is not one who sacrifices but one who carries out all the necessary rites.[44]

Mendenhall and Herion note that verbal oaths are usually absent from Late Bronze Era treaties because the ceremonial act of sacrifice renders them unnecessary.[45] Oaths are more prominent than sacrifice in the earlier suras, bringing them closer to the "divine charter" detailed in §9–12 below; but the presence of sacrifice in the later suras is substantial and, as we have seen, more than once connected with covenantal elements. F.E. Peters uses extra-Qur'ānic evidence to show that the sacrifice mentioned in Q 108:2 may be connected with Muḥammad's alleged participation in the rites of the goddess al-'Uzzā before receiving his prophetic call.[46] But he marshals even more evidence to show the extent to which the pre-Islamic Arabs had retained – or more likely recovered – aspects of their Abrahamic history and identity.[47] Thus it would seem at least as likely that any pre-Islamic sacrifice performed by Muḥammad was Abrahamic and covenantal as that it was polytheist.

The other ritual act mentioned in the Old Testament is circumcision. Josephus (d. ca. 101) and Sozomen (d. ca. 447) noted that the pre-Islamic Arabs already practiced circumcision, which they considered an Abrahamic rite.[48] Muslims, of course, consider it a religious duty despite the fact that it is never mentioned in the Qur'ān.

8 **If the Covenant is actually broken, curses are imposed and punishment follows.** The Qur'ān distinguishes between curse and punishment. Some exegetes preserve the distinction, while others tend to assimilate the two elements.

God's curses are mentioned more than three dozen times in the Qur'ān. Among others, God curses those who disbelieve (e.g. Q 2:88–89, 2:161, 3:87, 4:46, 5:78), who lie about God (Q 11:18), who are hypocrites or polytheists (Q 9:68, 33:61, 33:64, 48:6), and who commit murder (Q 4:93) or slander (Q 24:42). He curses Satan as well (Q 4:118, 15:35, 38:78). Where *l-ʿ-n* first occurs

(Q 2:88), Ṭabarī explains its meaning as "distancing" (*b-ʿ-d*) from God and his mercy, "expulsion" (*ṭ-r-d*), "humiliation" (*kh-z-y*), and "ruin" (*h-l-k*) but not as "punishment" (*ʿ-q-b, ʿ-dh-b*, etc.). Ṭabarsī repeats the concept but adds that "it has been said" that it means "sealing their hearts by way of punishment" (*ʿan sabīl al-mujāzāt*).[49] Rāzī defines the word at its second occurrence (Q 2:159) as having the original meaning of "distancing" (*ibʿād*) in the language "and, in the usage of the Revelation (*fī ʿurf al-sharʿ*), distancing from reward."[50]

Two passages may be interpreted to show that the curse is a result of violating the covenant and that it is distinct from the punishment. The curse is immediate, while the punishment will come on the Day of Resurrection:[51]

> God took the covenant of the children of Israel ... Because they broke their covenant, We cursed them and made their hearts hard: they change the words from their places, and they forgot part of what they were reminded of ... And from those who said "We are Christians" We took their covenant, and they forgot part of what they were reminded of; so We produced enmity and hatred between them until the Day of Resurrection. And God will make them aware of what they have done.
>
> (Q 5:12–14)

> Those who break God's covenant after adhering to it and cut what God has commanded to be joined and commit corruption in the earth – on them is the curse, and for them is the Evil Abode!
>
> (Q 13:25, cf. 40:52)

As we have seen, some violators of the Covenant have already been punished. The Qur'ān regularly cites evidence of God's wrath, most often the visible remains of vanished nations who sinned and were punished. The earliest allusion to this may be Q 68:15; Watt and Bell also list 53, 54, 69, and 89 among the early "punished-nations" suras.[52] Explicit curses are pronounced upon Pharaoh and his people (Q 11:99, 28:42), upon ʿĀd (Q 11:60), and upon Jewish violators (Q 4:46, 5:64), once by the tongues of David and Solomon (Q 5:78). The historical precedents represented by such stories will be discussed in the next two chapters.

God does not break his covenant.

> It is God's to command in the past and in the future. On that Day the believers will rejoice in the support of God: He supports whom He will, and He is the Powerful, the Merciful. The Promise (*wa'd*) of God – God does not break His Promise, but most people do not know that.
>
> (Q 30:4–6)

The verbal Covenant is a subset of the "words of God" (*kalimāt Allāh*), and the words of God are never changed (Q 10:64). The actions that God undertakes in accordance with the Covenant may be assimilated to his *sunna*, which, as we shall see in Chapter 3, likewise is never changed (e.g. Q 35:43).

Now let us consider the additional characteristics of the quasi-covenantal "divine charter" as outlined by Mendenhall and Herion:

9 **A deity bestows some special privilege, power, or status to a human being, almost always a king, and his descendants in perpetuity.**[53] The Qur'ān explicitly rejects the notion that faithfulness to the Covenant can be bequeathed; significantly, it is Abraham himself who asks whether his descendants will fill his position:

> [The Lord] said [to Abraham]: "I am making you an imam for the people." He said: "And my offspring (*wa-min dhurriyatī*)?" He said: "My covenant (*'ahdī*) does not apply to evildoers."
>
> (Q 2:124)

The class that *is* singled out for special responsibility, with its attendant privileges and status, is that of the prophets. The covenant with them mentioned in Qur'ān 3:81[54] is distinguishable from the one made with all humanity.[55]

10 **There is no specific literary form.** We have already noted that the Qur'ān contains no single passage cast in the literary form of the LBE covenant, but that it is rich in covenantal elements that humans are constantly urged to *remember*. This indicates that the Covenant between God and humanity was seen as remaining in place, obviating any need for verbatim restatement in the Qur'ān.[56]

The Qur'ānic memory-topos occurs as early as Q 74:49–56. Here are the relevant phrases, isolated and presented as a list for easier analysis:

a 49–51: What is wrong with them that they turn away from the Reminder (*tadhkira*)?
b 52: Each of them wants to be given written scrolls (*ṣuḥuf munashshara*)
c 54: It is a *tadhkira*
d 55: So whoever wills to do so will remember it (*dhakarahu*)
e 56: They will not remember (*yadhkurūn*) unless God wills.

This very early double occurrence of the word *tadhkira*, "reminder," with its related verbs all signifying both "remembering" and "mentioning" [sc. aloud], is the best evidence that, even in the very earliest revelations, the relation between God and man was understood as a continuous binding agreement, but one which the weaker party had forgotten. Among the early suras, variants on the root *dh-k-r* can be found in Q 68:51–52; 80:11–12; 53:29, 73:19, 89:23, 81:27; 77:5; 88:21; 89:23; and especially Sura 87, in which Muḥammad is told to

> remind/warn (*dhakkir*) [people], in case the reminder should benefit them (*in nafaʿat al-dhikrā*). He who fears [God] will remember (*sa-yadhdhakkaru man yakhshā*); . . . he will prosper who remembers (mentions) the name of his Lord (*wa-dhakara 'sma rabbihi*). . .; this is in the first Scriptures, the Scriptures of Abraham and Moses (*ṣuḥuf Ibrāhīm wa-Mūsā*).
>
> (Q 87:9–10, 15, 18–19)

Not only Muslims were urged to "remember" their relationship with God: the theme is prominent in both the Hebrew Bible and the New Testament. Otto Michel has noted

> [A] basic element in OT piety is that man remembers the past acts of God, His commandments and His unexhausted possibilities (Nu. 15:39–40; Dt. 8:2, 18). [Deuteronomy] especially develops a theology of remembering (Dt. 5:15, 7:18, 8:2, 18; 9:7 . . .) . . . All recollection serves to maintain the purity of faith.[57]

The Hebrew root used is *z-k-r*, cognate with the Arabic root *dh-k-r*. Mendenhall and Herion note that the root carries additional layers of meaning – "to swear," "invoke" – and that "its cognate is still used with this sense in modern village Arabic."[58] They also point out that the Greek *anamnēsis* in the Last Supper narrative lacks the multiple meanings carried by the Semitic root;[59] but both they and Michel find that in it and related Greek words (e.g. *mimnēskesthai* and *mneia*) the Hebrew substrate "may be constantly detected."[60]

> These things I have spoken to you, while I am still with you. But the counselor, the Holy Spirit, whom the Father will send in my name, he will teach you all the things and bring to your remembrance all that I have said to you.
>
> (John 14:25–26)[61]

The last two of the twelve LBE characteristics will be treated together.

11 **It is a "unilateral divine promise ... it is God, not human beings, who are bound by oath."[62]**
12 **It provides for witnesses, with Yahweh swearing "by himself."**

The concept of "witness" has been dealt with in §5 above.

God swears by himself that sinners will be punished (Q 15:92, 16:56), that he has sent apostles (Q 16:63), that what he has covenanted to people (*mā tūʿadūn*) is the truth (Q 51:22–23), and that those who choose disbelief can be replaced by better people than they (Q 70:40).[63]

Humans swear oaths to each other by God, but they can hardly swear oaths *to* God *by* God. In the Qur'ān, only the evil do so, apparently as a sign of perversity.

> They swear their strongest oaths by God that God will not resurrect those who die. On the contrary! It is a promise truly incumbent upon Him, but most of the people do not know.
>
> (Q 16:38)

The polytheists swear to God by God on the Day of Judgment that they have not been guilty of *shirk* (Q 6:23); but when confronted with evidence to the contrary, they admit it, swearing by their Lord that *that* is the truth (Q 6:30, cf. 46:34). Equally perverse, though not human, Iblīs swears to God by God's own power, after being granted permission to remain on earth: "By Your power, I shall mislead them all, except those among them who are Your sincere servants" (Q 38:82). Thereupon God vows to fill Hell with him and his followers.

God swears, but can he be said to swear oaths to human beings? Many of the early suras begin with or contain sequences of tremendous oaths, some quite long, followed by promises, threats, and descriptions of the Last Judgment – in other words, references to basic components of the Covenant. In her essay, "The Makkan sura introductions,"[64] Angelika Neuwirth arranges these suras in three groups:

1 Those that begin with phrases of the pattern *wa-l-fāʿilāt*: 100, 79, 77, 51, 37.
2 Those that refer to sacred places: 95, 90, 52.
3 Those that refer to "cosmic phenomena" and certain times of day and night: 93, 92, 91, 89, 85.

She uses Nöldeke's chronology to show that all are from the first Meccan period except Sura 37, which is from the second. Distinguishing what she terms "genuine oaths" from these "oath-clusters," she argues that the latter "exclusively serve as a literary device:" what genuine oaths and literary oaths have in common is that their "convincing force" depends upon a reference to "phenomena of a different, in most cases superior, kind."[65]

The primary functions of Neuwirth's three sequences are, respectively, "to depict a prototypical 'tableau' of the eschatological phenomena,"[66] "to arouse the listener's expectation towards the explication of a particular idea,"[67] and to convey a "sensation of an intimate personal relationship between the divine speaker and his human addressee" in which the latter is provided with "the language of liturgical services" appropriate to certain times of the day and night.[68] All these assertions she illustrates with sensitive analyses of the sequences and the contexts in which they are embedded. Without denying that the passages in question affect the hearer in the ways Neuwirth describes so minutely, we must ask a more basic question: why are these passages cast as oaths in the first place? What is it, exactly, that gives an oath its strength? Is it valid to call oaths sworn by humans invoking God "genuine oaths," while maintaining that oaths sworn in the Qur'ān by God are a literary device "completely devoid of any legal connotation"?

It is surely a more productive approach to treat these oaths as formulae that solemnize the Covenant.[69] As Neuwirth herself shows, every single divine oath-cluster in this group is the beginning of a sequence that ends with a more or less detailed picture of human fate when justice is rendered, either as retribution in the past or the Last Judgment in the future. The oath-clusters are solemn, unshakable undertakings by God that the relations between God and man, virtue and reward, sin and punishment, are the truth upon which all reasoning – indeed, all action – must be based.

But if oaths are part of the original Covenant, why are there still more oaths in a text that calls itself the "Reminder"? Are the two functions distinguishable? In fact, there is remarkably little overlap between the oath-suras and those suras that speak of the relation between man and God as something of which mortals must be reminded. Only three suras exhibit significant elements of both.[70] The earliest of these, by all reckonings, is Sura 77 *al-Mursalāt*, where both oaths and reminders come in the first seven verses. Sura 51, *al-Dhāriyāt*, has the oath cluster at verses 1–14, but the reminder-passage does not come until verse 55. Sura 52 *al-Ṭūr*, which some count earlier than Sura 51 and some later, begins with oaths sworn upon what Neuwirth calls "monotheistic emblems:" by Mount Sinai (verse 1), by a book inscribed in a parchment unrolled (2–3), by the House that is visited (4). After a vivid description of Paradise, Muḥammad is told, "Remind (*fa-dhakkir*)! By God's grace you are not a soothsayer, or a madman. Or do they say, 'A poet!'? …" (Q 52:29–30).

Thus only three out of fourteen suras contain both oaths and reminders, and only the earliest of the three suras has a reminder-passage as part of the oath sequence; in the other two, oaths and reminders are widely separated. The separation of oaths from reminders may be only an interesting coincidence, or it may signal that reminder-suras and oath-suras are addressed to two different groups of people. The first group needs only to be reminded that a covenant is in force, but the second will not understand the seriousness of the relationship unless it is bound with oaths.

Space does not permit analysis of all covenant-passages. Elements of the Covenant are integral to our arguments throughout this book and will constantly reappear, but here we shall consider only the first occurrence of the Covenant in the Qur'ānic text, how the idea is developed in the verses that follow it, and how it has been treated by certain exegetes.

Verse 27 of Sura 2 *al-Baqara* comes after a passage (Q 2:26) in which God is said not to disdain to use the example of a gnat or something greater to guide or lead astray whom he will, "but He leads astray only the corrupt (*al-fāsiqīn*)." Verse 27 then says, "Those who break God's covenant (*ʿahd*) after its ratification (*mīthāqihi*), and cut what God has commanded be joined, and commit corruption in the earth: those are the losers." A rhetorical question follows: How can anyone disbelieve when it is God who creates the living from the dead and who created the earth and the seven heavens? (Q 2:28–29). The scene is now set for transition into the story of the creation of Adam, the Fall, and the punishment of sinners (30–39). This is followed by another covenant-verse: "O children of Israel, remember the benefits that I have conferred upon you, and fulfill your covenant with me (*ʿahdī*) and I shall fulfill mine with you (*ʿahdikum*), and fear Me" (40). The audience are then adjured to believe in what has been revealed confirming that which they already have (41) and are given other commandments as well.

As Qurʾān 2:27 is the first occurrence of the word *ʿahd*, that is where most exegetes discuss the covenant. Ṭabarī notes that scholars differ over the possible identifications of *ʿahd*:

1 It is God's *waṣīya* to his creatures: his commands and prohibitions in his books and on the tongue of his Prophet. By their disobedience, they broke the covenant.
2 The verses refer to the unbelievers and hypocrites among the People of the Book. The covenant that they broke is that which comes in the Torah, including the acceptance of Muḥammad, whose coming they knew about but concealed.
3 In this verse, God is signifying all polytheists, unbelievers, and hypocrites, and the *ʿahd* is God's covenant with all of them indicated by his signs to them and his prophets with their miracles.
4 It is the *ʿahd* that God took from all Adam's unborn offspring when he asked "Am I not your Lord? And they said 'Yes, we testify to that' . . ." (Q 7:172). Their breaking of the Covenant is their failure to fulfill it.

Ṭabarī says that he prefers the second, which refers to Muḥammad's treatment by the Jews of Medina, but he then goes on to say that that can apply to all *kuffār*, and that sometimes a particular instance precedes the general description in the text and sometimes follows it.[71] This prefigures his interpretation of Sura 5:13 (see §8 above) and effectively erases any meaningful distinction.

Ṭabarsī says that *ʿahd Allāh* may refer to (1) the innate, God-given capacity to recognize evidence (*adilla*) of the unicity and justice of God and the evidentiary miracles of prophets; (2) God's commandment (*waṣīyat Allāh*) to his creatures through his Apostle ordering obedience and forbidding sin; (3) the Sinai event, including the (future) obligation to follow Muḥammad, to believe in the message that he would bring, and not to conceal it "and al-Ṭabarī chose this aspect;" (4) the covenant with the offspring of Adam before their birth, "and this is weak, because it is impossible that He should use as a *ḥujja* against his servants a covenant that they do not remember or know about . . ."[72]

Fakhr al-Dīn al-Rāzī finds both a general and a particular application, the general to all humankind, the particular to those who rejected prophets. He accepts the general for its superior applicability; he rejects Ṭabarī's second and fourth options, as he does the possibilities that *ʿahd* refers to God's pact with the prophets (e.g. Q 3:81) or that with the custodians of the Book (*al-ʿulamāʾ* – Q 3:187).[73]

Al-Suyūṭī's (d. 911/1505) early exegetes, through Qatāda, see in the verse merely a warning not to break the covenant, "for God hates that it should be broken, and makes promises and threats concerning it; and in certain Qurʾānic verses he offers an introduction to the subject, advice, sermon, and proof" (*taqdima wa-naṣīḥa wa-mawʿiẓa wa-ḥujja*)."[74]

In the vocabulary of argumentation and logic, the Covenant may be called the cosmic rule, the unshakable basis for the structure of moral reasoning that God requires of human beings. It validates divine commandments, defines the human condition, provides premises in categorical syllogisms, affirms or denies antecedents to yield known consequents, and supplies the criteria that distinguish better from worse and good from evil. We shall examine all of these applications in the coming chapters.

2

SIGNS AND PRECEDENTS

The first verses of the Qur'ān brought by the Angel Gabriel began with a command from God to the Prophet Muḥammad, "Read!" God then identified himself and testified to his own authority by citing two signs of his divine power: that he had created humanity and that he had given it knowledge.

> Read! In the name of your Lord Who created – created the human being from a clot of blood. Read! And your Lord is most generous, Who taught by the Pen – taught humanity what it did not know.
>
> (Q 96:1–5)

The divine signs in this passage validate a command from God.[1] The combination of Divine Command and Divine Sign defines the relationship between Creator and creature and the nature of a prophet's mission, whether it is Muḥammad's visit from the Angel Gabriel or the experience of Moses on Mt. Sinai (Q 7:143–147).[2]

Some of the Signs of God, such as his creation of the world, are single events; but others, such as his sending of prophets, are repeated many times. When God repeats an act, repetition confers upon the first such act the status of precedent. In this chapter, we shall also survey the notion of precedent in the context of both Abrahamic religious history, as it appears in the Qur'ān, and the Arabic language. In Chapter 3, we shall examine how the notions of Path and Precedent combine in the important pre-Islamic Arabian concept of normative precedent, *sunna*; and we shall see how the Qur'ān redefines and revalidates it as the *sunna* of God. In Chapter 4, we shall see that normative precedent and Covenant are, in a technical sense, "Rules." Rule-based reasoning, a key to legal logic, is the form of argument that assesses the legality of an act or the validity of a command by referring it to the applicable standard.

THE SIGNS OF GOD

A sign in itself is not an argument but a piece of evidence that supports various forms of argument, explicit or implicit. Signs appear in the Qur'ān as parts of syllogisms, historical precedents, parables, and other types of demonstration.

> "God makes the sun rise from the East, so you make it rise from the West!" Thus he who rejected faith was confounded.
>
> (Q 2:258)[3]
>
> Surely the same is in the Books of the earliest peoples. Is it not a Sign to them that the learned among the Children of Israel know it?
>
> (Q 26:196–197)
>
> Have We not made the earth a resting-place, and the mountains as stakes ... and gardens luxuriantly growing?
>
> (Q 78:6–16)
>
> Let the human being consider from what he has been created – from a gushing fluid, emerging from between the spine and ribs.
>
> (Q 86:4–7)

Muslim thinkers built an immense structure of theological and philosophical argument on the basis of such Qur'ānic evidence. The latter two passages, for example, are among those with which Ibn Rushd (d. 595/1198) opens his account of the logical bases of creeds advanced by Muslim theologians, *Manāhij al-Adilla fī ʿAqāʾid al-Milla*. Beginning with arguments for the existence of God, Ibn Rushd cites Q 78:6–16 as a proof in the argument from Providence (*dalālat al-ʿināya*), Q 86:4–7 as a proof in the argument from Creation (*dalālat al-ikhtirāʿ*). All arguments that are not either one or the other, he asserts, are combinations of the two types.[4]

Some Signs of God come in the form of words and scriptures, and some do not. In the Qur'ān, the created world and all it contains are signs; heaven, earth, and stars are signs; ordered phenomena are signs, and unprecedented cataclysms are signs as well.[5] The most common word for "sign" is *āya*: it and its plural *āyāt* appear some 382 times. *Aya* also came to mean "a verse of the Qur'ān" precisely because the Book of God and its constituent verses are signs of God. The next most common Qur'ānic term, *bayyina* (with its plural *bayyināt*) occurs 71 times. Others are *ālā'* (34, all but three in Sura 55), *burhān* (8), *sha'ā'ir* (4), *'alāmāt* (1), and *āthār* (1). Some entire suras, such as 54 *al-Qamar,* 55 *al-Raḥmān*, and 56 *al-Wāqi'a*, are essentially litanies of the signs of God.

Divine signs are evidence in the great argument that logically concludes in belief, but not every sign-passage contains an explicit argument. Thus Sura 96 establishes by implication the cause-and-effect relationship between God's signs and human belief in God. Other passages explicitly connect them. Beginning in verse 11 of the very early Sura 74 *al-Muddaththir*, God describes a man whom he has created[6] and showered with benefits – property, sons, an easy life – who yet remains obdurate, refusing to accept signs as evidence. "But then he wants Me to add to it! By no means! For he has been stubbornly resistant to Our Signs" (Q 74:15–16).[7] His refusal to believe is not just a sin but a failure of logic.

Humans may infer the sublimity of the Creator from his material creation; but if their view is to be complete, they must also see signs in the moral framework that gives it meaning. God could have refrained from creating humans or the world at all; after creating them he need not have paid any further attention to them; he could have created them in heaven or in hell as easily as on earth; but he did none of these things. On the contrary, to his creation that is the physical world he added further signs: the dimensions of caring, responsibility, and self-restraint. "Remember God's grace when you were enemies and He reconciled your hearts . . ." (Q 3:103). These aspects of the relationship between God and humanity are enshrined in the Covenant, and they also characterize proper relations among human beings.

> Among His Signs is that He created you from dust, and now you are human beings dispersed throughout [the earth]. And among His Signs is that He has created spouses for you from your own kind, so that you may find comfort with them; and He has created love and compassion between you. There are Signs in that for people who will reflect. And among His Signs is the creation of the heavens

> and the earth, and the difference in your languages and colors. There are Signs in that for those who know.
> (Q 30:20–22)

Creation is the first sign of divine power. It is all too easy, however, to allow the concept of "power" to shift to the negative side and mean only the power to destroy. When taken out of context, stories of divine punishment for sin are too easily reduced to the classic fallacy, the *argumentum ad baculum*: "Do this or I will hit you with a stick!" Punishment stories are prominent in the Qur'ān, but the purpose of punishment is to enforce the moral order embodied in the Covenant. It is not simply the negative counterpart of creation: no matter how much power can be inferred from the fact of physical existence, creation has no *meaning* without the moral order.

In that spirit, let us look at one of the traditional accounts, not of the first revelation but of Muḥammad's reaction to it. The event appears to have left the Prophet at the very least in a state of confusion. His wife Khadīja, however, and especially her cousin Waraqa b. Nawfal are depicted as having recognized what sort of phenomenon it was because they were well acquainted with the idea that God communicates with human beings. They paid close attention to the moral atmosphere of the event as well as to its verbal content, in order to guard against false prophecy, demonic possession or self-deception. Khadīja assured Muḥammad that his personal virtue precluded such things,[8] but she also tested the source of the revelation by proving that it did not occur in unseemly circumstances. Gabriel appeared to Muḥammad when he was sitting next to Khadīja, even sitting in her lap, but he disappeared when she removed her veil. She said, "O son of my uncle, rejoice and be of good heart, by God he is an angel and not a satan."[9]

A useful classification of divine signs by type is found in *Bell's Introduction to the Qur'ān*:

> For the purposes of exposition four usages or applications of the word may be distinguished: (1) natural phenomena which are signs of God's power and bounty; (2) events or objects associated with the work of a messenger of God and tending to confirm the truth of the message; (3) signs which are recited by a messenger; (4) signs which are part of the Qur'ān or of the Book.[10]

As the first revelation was in all probability a command validated by signs, I shall illustrate Bell's four categories with examples of that same construction:

1 Natural phenomena:

> Among His Signs are the night and the day and the sun and the moon. Do not worship the sun and the moon, but worship God Who created them, if it is He Whom you [truly] worship.
>
> (Q 41:37)

2 Messengers of God and events associated with their missions:

> [Jesus said] I have brought you a Sign from your Lord: that I make for you out of clay something like the shape of a bird, and breathe into it, and it becomes a bird, by God's permission. And I heal the blind and the lepers, and I revive the dead, by God's permission ... I have brought you a Sign from your Lord, so fear God and obey me.
>
> (Q 3:49–50)[11]

3 Signs recited by a messenger:

> We have sent to you a Messenger from among yourselves reciting Our Signs to you, and purifying you, and teaching you the Book and Wisdom, teaching you what you did not know. So remember Me (*fa-dhkurūnī*) and I shall remember you; and thank Me, and do not disbelieve in Me.
>
> (Q 2:151–152)

4 Signs that are part of the Book:

> *Alif, lām, rā'*: This is a Book whose verses (*āyāt*) are made firm, then set out in detail by One Wise and All-Knowing, that you should worship none but God ...
>
> (Q 11:1–2)

These four examples remind us that, while divine commands to individual prophets address specific tasks that are part of their prophetic mission, the primordial command to humanity as a whole can be reduced to a few imperatives: believe in God, fear God, worship God, remember God, thank God.

A very common pattern among sign-passages begins with a

recital of individual signs in which no word for "sign" appears, followed by the audience's reaction, positive or negative, to what then are collectively termed "signs." Thus in Sura 19 *Maryam*, the following incidents and prophets are cited: Abraham's call to his father to worship God and reject idols (41–49); Isaac and Jacob (49–50); God's call to Moses (51–53); Aaron (53); Ishmael (54–55); Idris (56–57); Adam, Noah with his Ark, Abraham, and Israel (58). No word for "sign" is mentioned until the end of verse 58: "Whenever the Signs of the All-Merciful (*āyāt al-Raḥmān*) were recited to them, they would fall down, prostrating themselves and weeping" (Q 19:58). Sura 6 *al-An'ām* mentions the sprouting and growth of seeds (95); the day, night, sun, moon, and the reckoning of time (96); and the stars as guiding beacons (97). The sequence ends with, "We have set forth Our Signs for people who know" (Q 6:97).

The entire short Sura 105 *al-Fīl* is clearly intended as a sign-passage, yet it contains no specific word for "sign". It cites the fate of the "People of the Elephant" as an indication of God's power to protect His sanctuary, but instead of single word for "sign", a full description serves the purpose.

> Have you not seen how your Lord dealt with the People of the Elephant? Did He not cause their plot to go astray? And He sent against them flights of birds loosing upon them stones of baked clay; thus He made them like a field of grain eaten away.
>
> (Q 105:1–5)

Too often, the audience's reaction to these Signs is to ignore them:

> And We have destroyed generations before you, when they did wrong: their apostles came to them with clear signs (*bayyināt*), but they would not believe. Thus do We requite a nation of sinners
>
> (Q 10:13).

Moses recites God's signs to Pharaoh: the earth spread out like a carpet with roads for ease of travel; rain from the sky producing a multiplicity of plants for food and pasture; creation, death, and resurrection (Q 20:53–55). "And We showed Pharaoh all Our Signs, but he denied and rejected them" (Q 20:56). It is characteristic that the prophets' unsympathetic audiences accept signs as evidence but demand signs other than the ones offered. Moses brings Pharaoh many Signs, each greater than the one before it (Q 43:48), but Pharaoh will accept none of them:

> Rather, I am better than this [fellow], who is contemptible and can hardly speak clearly. Why have bracelets of gold not been bestowed upon him, or angels come along with him in procession?
>
> (Q 43:52–53)

Finally, an uncommon but interesting sort of "sign" parallels some found in the Old Testament: not prophetic miracles but symbolic behavior carried out at God's command. In the Qur'ān, Zakariyya says, "'My Lord, give me a sign.' He said, 'Your sign is that you shall not speak to people for three nights, while being in sound health'" (Q 19:10). In a later revelation (Q 3:41), the same instruction is given but with further specification: "Your sign is that for three days you will not speak to people except by means of signs." This recalls a passage from the Old Testament:

> At the same time the Lord spoke to Isaiah, son of Amoz, saying, "Go and loose the sackcloth from your loins and take the shoe off your foot." And he did so, walking naked and barefoot. And the Lord said, "As my servant Isaiah has walked naked and barefoot three years for a sign and wonder upon Egypt and upon Ethiopia, so shall the king of Assyria lead away the Egyptians prisoners, and the Ethiopians captives, young and old, naked and barefoot, even with buttocks uncovered, to the shame of Egypt."
>
> (Isaiah 20:2–4)

The prophet Jeremiah is commanded to break a clay vessel to symbolize the destruction of Jerusalem (Jeremiah 19). The same sort of "sign" is found throughout the book of Ezekiel, notably 4:4–8, in which the prophet is instructed to lie for 150 days on his left side, then for 40 days on his right side, symbolizing the years of punishment to be visited upon Israel and Judah; and 24:15–27, in which Ezekiel refrains from mourning the death of his beloved wife "as a sign to the exiles that the news of the fall of Jerusalem would fill them with sorrow too deep for tears."[12]

PRECEDENT IN SACRED HISTORY

When we examine the Qur'ānic accounts of the prophets as examples of "normative precedent," we find another reason for the stories' relative brevity and allusiveness,[13] as well as the frequency of their repetition in series.[14] Human beings must be constantly reminded that the coming of a prophet is not unprecedented. God has consistently sent prophets to inform them of the existence of their Creator and to remind them of their covenantal obligation to him. Prophets bring good news and warnings, confirm previous revelations, witness their truth, and serve as examples – *imāms* – of righteous behavior (e.g. Q 2:124). The people who reject them either do not know God's custom of sending prophets or ignore messages that clash with their own man-made customs. In other words, the two sides reason from conflicting precedents.

Those who ignore the prophets justify their actions on the grounds that they are following the example of their forefathers and may not do otherwise. The word *ābā'* ("fathers") occurs 67 times in the Qur'ān, the vast majority in such contexts.

> They say, "We found our fathers following a certain religion (*'ala ummat^{in}*) and by following in their footsteps we are guided."
>
> (Q 43:22)

Not only do they cover sin with the mantle of custom, they claim divine sanction for it as well.

> Whenever they commit some scandalous act (*fāḥisha*), they say, "We found our fathers doing it", and "God has commanded us to do it" . . .
>
> (Q 7:28)
>
> Those who associate partners with God will say, "If God had willed, neither we nor our fathers would have ascribed partners, nor would we have forbidden anything at all!"
>
> (Q 6:148)

Sometimes the Qur'ān answers such arguments by pointing out that the forefathers lacked knowledge:

> When it is said to them: "Come to what God has revealed,

> and to the Apostle", they say: "What we found our fathers doing is enough for us." What? Even though their fathers knew nothing at all and had no guidance?
>
> (Q 5:104)

But the most telling refutation of the *mushrikīn* turns their own argument against them by identifying God as the very deity whom the earliest of their forebears worshipped:

> The Lord of the heavens and the earth and all that is between them ... There is no god but He. He gives life and death – your Lord and the Lord of your fathers from the beginning.
>
> (Q 44:7–8)

The prophets, of course, have had this argument on their side all along. Joseph says:

> I follow the religion (*milla*) of my fathers, Abraham and Isaac and Jacob. It was not for us to associate anything with God as a partner: that was part of God's grace to us and to all people. But most of the people do not give thanks.
>
> (Q 12:38)

A related *topos* is the sociolinguistic phenomenon that equates the familiar with the morally good, the unfamiliar with the bad. In Arabic, *maʿrūf* equals "known" equals "good," and *munkar* equals "unknown" equals "bad." A brief reflection will convince the reader that such equivalences are common in many, if not most, languages. Something that is "unheard of", *inouï, unerhört, inaudito*, is almost always bad.[15] One sign of the strength of Arab custom and precedent is that the respective positive and negative meanings of the Arabic words *maʿrūf* and *munkar* survived Islamization of the language, although Toshihiko Izutsu notes that the meaning of *maʿrūf* became more restricted: "proper", "in the right way", and, in legal passages, "through due formalities."[16]

The well-known Qur'ānic verbal formula is *taʾmurūna bil-maʿrūf wa-tanhawna ʿan il-munkar*:

> You are the best nation that has been brought forth for humanity: you command what is known [to be right] and

> forbid what is not known [to be right]; and you believe in God. If the People of the Book believed, it would be better for them. There are believers among them, but most of them are sinners (*fāsiqūn*).
>
> (Q 3:10, cf. 7:157, 9:71, 22:41, etc.)

Good people command the good (*al-maʿrūf* – the known, the customary) and forbid the evil (*al-munkar* – the unknown, the repugnant), while evil people command the evil and forbid the good (Q 9:67). A Muslim is to observe *al-maʿrūf* in matters of compensation for wrongful death (Q 2:178), bequests to relatives (Q 2:180), betrothal (Q 2:235), divorce (Q 2:228–229, 231–232, 236, 240–241; 65:2,6), executor's fees (Q 4:6,8), domestic relations (Q 4:19,25), relations with friends (Q 33:6), and governance of one's speech (Q 4:5, 47:21). Today, the colloquial Arabic[17] question "*Btaʿmil-li l-maʿrūf?*" is a virtually contentless request for a service or favor. Its meaning depends upon the physical setting and position of the two parties: "Would you mind doing what you know that you should do for me under these circumstances?" – open the door, help me with my packages, and so on. As my first Arabic teacher translated it, "Do the known thing."[18]

The root *n-k-r* has even more colorful and varied applications in Qur'ānic Arabic. Most illustrative for our purposes is the use of the root to describe the initial impressions made upon Abraham and Lot by their angel visitors. Though the prophets' capacity for spiritual discernment ultimately prevails, their first feeling in the presence of these strangers is one of deep unease. When Abraham roasts a calf for the guests, they do not eat; because of this clear breach of *sunna*[19] he "mistrusts" them (*nakirahum*) and "conceives a fear of them,"[20] and they must reassure him (Q 11:69–70). Al-Farrā' (d. 207/822/3) notes, "That is because the *sunna* of the time was that, if people came to them and were offered food and did not touch it, they thought that they were enemies or thieves."[21] Al-Qurṭubī (d. 671/1273) – though he does not use the word *sunna* – introduces a long discourse on the etiquette of hospitality in terms of precedent, crediting Abraham with being the first to add to the basic duty toward travelers mentioned in Surat al-Baqara (i.e. Q 2:177, 215).[22] And Abraham privately concludes, "They are strange people" (*qawm munkarūn*) (Q 51:25). Lot says as much to them openly (Q 15:62), whereupon they reassure him as well.

Munkar is also used to refer to the sin of the males among Lot's people (Q 29:29), who are sexually attracted to the angels and whom Lot must beg not to disgrace him in front of his guests (Q 11:77ff., 15:59ff., 54:33ff.). Lot's main argument against his people is that their sins are without precedent.

> Do you commit obscenity such as no one in the world ever committed before you? You approach men out of sexual desire in place of women! You are certainly a people who transgress all bounds!
>
> (Q 7:80–81, cf. 29:28–29, 26:165–166)

Again, the powerful duties and taboos of Middle Eastern hospitality are discernible in his reaction. When his people come rushing to see the newcomers, he knows that he alone cannot protect them. He is so afraid of being shamed in front of his guests that he offers the townspeople his own daughters,[23] only to be told, "We have nothing to do with your daughters. You know what we want!" (Q 11:78–79, cf.15:67–71, 29:33). Lot's people are unimpressed by his recital of their sins and do not bother to appeal either to other gods or to custom.

> "You commit obscenity such as no one in the world ever committed before you. Will you approach men, and commit highway robbery, and engage in repugnant practices (*al-munkar*) in your council?" But his people answered only, "Bring on the punishment of God, if you are telling the truth!"
>
> (Q 29:28–29)

The play between known and unknown, customary and "unheard of," is an important element in the disputes over precedent between the messengers of God and their stubborn audiences. The nations argue on the basis of their own customs, the prophets on the basis of the *sunna* of God, which is based on the Covenant. (See Chapters 3 and 1, respectively.) In Sura 23, for example, the chiefs of the opposition crisply sum up their objections to Noah and the message that he brings: he is only a mortal who seeks superiority over them; if God had wished, He could have sent down angels; they have never heard anything of the sort from their forefathers; he is insane (Q 23:24–25). The people of ʿĀd say to their prophet, "O Hūd! You have brought us no sign (*bayyina*), and we do not desert our gods at a word from you. We do not believe you!"

(Q 11:53). Arguments from historical precedent have nothing to do with them personally: "It is all the same to us whether you preach to us or not: this is only something that people did a long time ago, and we are not the ones who will be punished" (Q 26:136–138).

Interesting results are achieved when one interprets the uniqueness of Abraham's position in prophetic history as a function of precedent. Like the Prophet Muḥammad, Abraham is called a "good example" (*uswa ḥasana* – Q 60:4); he is also "an *umma* devoted to God" (Q 16:120). God says to Abraham, "I am making you an *imām*" (Q 2:124), and we shall see in the next chapter further evidence that one meaning of the word *imām* refers to the authority to set *sunna*. When, in the same verse, Abraham asks if the office of imam will be bequeathed to his descendants, God answers, "My covenant does not extend to wrongdoers." This general principle does not exclude Abraham's virtuous descendants, however. We see in following verses and elsewhere that God includes both Abraham and Ishmael in the covenant to purify His House "for those who circle around it, and those who take it as a retreat, and who bow and prostrate themselves" (Q 2:125, cf. 22:26); and Abraham leaves to his sons and grandson Jacob the legacy of worship of the One True God (Q 2:132–133). God says of Abraham, Isaac, and Jacob, "We made them *imāms*, guiding according to Our Command, and We inspired them to do righteous deeds, establish prayer, and pay alms; and they served Us" (Q 21:73, cf. Q 14:39–40). These verses do not merely express individual devotion but describe the establishment of a structure of faith based upon normative precedents set by those with the authority to do so.

Abraham's pagan interlocutors advance the argument from custom for continuing in their idolatry:

> "What are these statues to which you are devoted?" They said, "We found our fathers worshipping them." He said, "You and your fathers both have been in manifest error."
> (Q 21:52–54, cf. 26:71–77)

An *imām*'s every action might be taken as *sunna* and emulated whether he intended it or not, unless care were taken to distinguish a private or particular act from a binding precedent. Abraham's argument with his father Azar over the new monotheism is such a case. Most early Muslims had to suffer the guilt of the twin offenses of disobeying their fathers and rejecting their fathers' religion, as serious a matter for the fledgling Islamic community as it had been for the earlier peoples. Abraham's example must have struck very close to home. Abraham begs his father not to take idols for gods (Q 6:74); not to worship things that cannot hear, see, or act (Q 19:42); and to avoid God's penalty (Q 19:45). Azar replies in wrath, "Do you turn away from my gods, Abraham? If you do not desist, I shall stone you! Leave me [and stay away] for a good long time!" (Q 19:46). Abraham replies that he will pray God to forgive his father (Q 19:47, cf. 60:4), but that while praying, he will turn away from his father (*aʿtazilukum*) and his false gods (Q 19:48). A later revelation distinguishes the principle by which Muslims are to be guided in such cases from Abraham's personal predicament, which resulted in part from his sensitive nature:

> It is not for the Prophet or those who believe to pray for forgiveness for the polytheists – even though they are their relatives – after it has become clear to them that they are of the Fire. Abraham's prayer that his father be forgiven came only because of a promise he had made to him; when it became clear that he was an enemy of God, he parted company with him. Abraham was truly tender-hearted and forbearing.
>
> (Q 9:113–114)

There is a difference of opinion over who promised what to whom in this verse. Ṭabarsī quotes Ibn ʿAbbās, Mujāhid, and Qatāda to the effect that Azar had promised his son Abraham that he would follow his son's faith, while Ḥasan al-Baṣrī says that Abraham promised Azar to ask God's forgiveness for him (cf. Q 19:47, 60:4) on condition that he embraced belief. The crucial question was this: could Abraham's action be a precedent for asking forgiveness for one who died an unbeliever despite the opportunity to believe? Specifically, would Muḥammad be permitted to ask forgiveness for his uncle and foster father Abū Ṭālib? Najm al-Dīn al-Ṭūfī allows only the interpretation cited first by Ṭabarsī – that it was the father who broke his promise. In the kind of conditional syllogism that we shall examine at length in Chapter 9, he notes that the "conditional relationship" (*al-sharṭiyya*) is correct, that if one polytheist can be interceded for, then all can. "And this consequent is valid, but the antecedent – the possibility of Abraham's asking for forgiveness for his father – is absolutely invalid; thus God answered by making the distinction."[24]

The situation of Moses is more complex than that of Abraham. He has supporters as well as enemies among both his own people and the people of Pharaoh, but Moses's people have been cut off by exile from those who might have handed down proper precedent. A new source of authority is required. "We brought Moses the Book after We destroyed the earlier generations, [to give] signs to the people, and guidance and mercy, that they might pay heed" (Q 28:43). The fact that his people have a unique but invisible relation with God (Q 2:40, 2:47; 5:20, and many others) makes Moses's task harder, not easier, because he must not only set precedent but first convince his people that he has the authority to do so. In the passage for which Surat al-Baqara is named, God orders the Children of Israel to sacrifice a cow; but they quibble at length about just which cow is meant, how old, what color, which particular cow because they are all alike, and so on. Finally they say, "'You have brought us the truth.' Then they slaughtered her, but they very nearly did not do it" (Q 2:67–71).

Many of Moses's difficulties with the Children of Israel arise from the fact that they have been living for generations within the ancient, sophisticated and polytheist culture of Egypt, with its vivid iconography. They are out of touch with the source of sound precedent in their own ancestral religion and are easily tempted to construct idols like those around them. After safely crossing the Red Sea with the help of God, the Children of Israel come among an idolatrous people. "O Moses, make us a god like the gods they have!" (Q 7:138), but Moses refuses. Far more dangerous to group identity is the episode of the golden calf (Q 7:148–153; 20:85–97). The mysterious "Sāmirī" who brings the calf out of the fire knows the Israelites' weakness on the subject of idols and normative precedent, and – apparently joined by others since the plural verb is used – he exploits it: "They said, 'This is your god, and Moses's god as well, but he has forgotten'" (Q 20:88). The Samiri is reversing one of the arguments *for* belief in the One God with which we began the present section:

> The Lord of the heavens and the earth and all that is between them . . . There is no god but He. He gives life and death – your Lord and the Lord of your fathers from the beginning.
>
> (Q 44:7–8)

For Pharaoh, precedent, authority, and power are identical: since he is Pharaoh, he is also god. "He gathered [his men] and proclaimed 'I am your lord most high'" (Q 79:23–24, cf. 26:29, 28:38). He can only interpret Moses's conduct as an attempt to seize power. "Have you come to us to turn us away from what we found our fathers doing so that you may be great in the land? But we do not believe you!" (Q 10:78, cf. 20:57, 26:35, 28:19, 40:26). The fact that Moses is from a subject people is a *prima facie* case for denying him credibility (Q 23:47). Pharaoh has clear ideas about the appropriate signs of divine authority: showers of golden bracelets and processions of angels (Q 43:53). Before producing his miraculous signs, Moses vainly appeals to history and precedent, attempting to convince Pharaoh that the "Lord of the Worlds" about whom Pharaoh has asked him (Q 26:23) is in fact "your Lord and the Lord of your fathers from the beginning" (Q 26:26).

Christ Jesus son of Mary (Q 3:45) appears in the Qur'ān as one in the succession of apostles to the Children of Israel (Q 3:49), but aspects of his life are without precedent. Jesus the prophet is also Jesus the miraculous child, born of a virgin (Q 3:47), who speaks in the cradle (Q 5:110, 19:29–33). One of his extraordinary signs is the forming of clay birds that are given life, then fly away (Q 3:49, 5:110). Other manifestations of Jesus's extreme compassion are his miracles of curing the blind and the leper and reviving the dead (Q 3:49, 5:110). In the same spirit, in the sequence (Q 5:112–115) for which Sura 5 *al-Mā'ida* is named, Jesus even tests the forbearance of God when, at his disciples' insistence, he asks God to send down a table set with food. This God grants, but not without warning that those who disbelieve after being given such an extraordinary sign will be visited with an unprecedented punishment, "a punishment such as I have never inflicted upon anyone in the worlds" (Q 5:115).

Where the Christians of the Qur'ān go wrong is in the precedents which they choose to follow. They imitate the old disbelievers in worshipping Christ instead of God (Q 9:30) and in raising their holy men above their proper station (Q 9:31, cf. 9:34–35). Monasticism is their own invention, not something prescribed for them by God (*mā katabnāhā 'alayhim* – Q 57:27); and it is worth noting that the word used is *ibtada'ūhā*, from the same root as the later word for "heretical innovation", *bid'a*. The "unknown" is still repugnant: one of the marks of those who disobey Jesus's message is that they do not forbid each other to commit *munkar* (Q 5:78–79).

Still, the Christians had been authorized by God to set new

precedents by making certain changes in the previous dispensation. Like all prophets, the Qur'ānic Jesus confirms the existing Law, but, more significant for this discussion, he is authorized to change some of it:

> [I come] confirming the Torah that I have in my hands, and in order to declare permissible to you some of what was forbidden to you; and I have brought you a sign from God, so fear God and obey me.
>
> (Q 3:50, cf. 5:46, 61:6)

The disbelievers will still be punished (Q 3:55–56) and the believers rewarded (Q 3:57). Polytheism – including trinitarianism – is still a sin (Q 5:73–74). The Qur'ān, however, cites no particular things which have been made permissible. Exegetes have generally understood the passage as an allusion to dietary laws.[25] Muqātil (d. 150/767–68) says that it refers to "meats and fats and anything with claws and fish" but does not include the Sabbath. "So they rose against it and it was removed from them in the Gospel."[26]

Examples of Divine Sign and Divine Precedent are so common in the Qur'ān that it is easy to lose the context and forget that the wonders of the physical world and the succession of historical events are cited to support *arguments*. The prophets' audiences, however, were quite aware of that fact. In sixth and seventh-century Arabia in particular, the notion of precedent – of *sunna* – possessed a peculiar intensity. When *sunna* contradicted the message brought by the Prophet, it was stronger than any other force; but when it became a part of that message, it explained God's observance of the Covenant in terms the Arabs could understand. The *sunna* of God could not but prevail over the *sunna* of human beings. We are now ready to examine *sunna* as it appears in the Qur'ān.

3

THE *SUNNA* OF GOD[1]

The pre-Islamic Arabs had their own notion of precedent, expressed in the concept of *sunna*. While it is often argued that they had no real sense of history, the Arabs were very concerned with genealogy, custom, and the deeds and repute of their tribe; and much of their conduct was governed by the "binding precedent" (*sunna*) set by their forefathers. The poet Labīd (d. ca. 30/650 or 41/661) spoke in his *muʿallaqa* of

> ... a tribe whose forefathers set an example for them
> And every people has a precedent and one who sets it (*sunna wa-imāmuha*).[2]

The concept of sunna is far more complex than can be conveyed in a one-word translation. The English word "precedent," with its legal significance, is most acceptable for our purposes. Michael Morony's description of sunna is clear, useful, and brief:

> The use of exemplary precedent as the basis for Islamic custom came most directly from the concept of *sunna* (Ar.) among tribal Arabs. It came from the way tribal leaders intentionally set binding precedents that their relatives and descendants were to follow. Such *sunna* was specific to each group, expressed its values, and regulated the details of its life. The concept of *sunna* also contained a feeling of social responsibility for an act that set a precedent; a person was held accountable for acts imitated by others. Everything done by Muḥammad ... set examples for Muslims to follow.[3]

Morony's formulation is based largely upon that of M.M.

Bravmann,[4] which is in turn an exhaustive critique of some of the ideas of Joseph Schacht.[5] From these layers of scholarship have emerged several points that clarify the concept of sunna. First, the precedent, the sunna, was an example which was meant to be imitated and which was set intentionally for that purpose by one who had the authority to do so.[6] Second, the one who established the sunna was responsible for the acts of those who later imitated him.[7] Third, the addition of derivatives of the root *m-ḍ-y*, such as in the phrase *sunna māḍiya* or the sentence *maḍat al-sunna*, indicates that the sunna had become binding, that it had "passed into obligatoriness," not that it had been in effect in the past.[8] Fourth, once a sunna was established as binding, it was virtually unbreakable.[9]

What is odd about the treatments of both Schacht and Bravmann is how little they cite the Qur'ān, passing from pre-Islamic usage to the problematic area of Prophetic Tradition while virtually ignoring the examples of sunna in the Qur'ān itself. In his zeal to deny an early date to the concept of "the sunna of the Prophet," Schacht does not cite a single Qur'ānic instance of the word sunna in either of his major monographs. That he is aware of it as a Qur'ānic concept can be seen in his description of the letter of ʿAbd Allāh b. Ibāḍ (late first c. A.H.) to the caliph ʿAbd al-Malik b. Marwān (r. 65–86/685–705):

> The term is used always in conjunction with a reference to the Koran, and it does not refer to the authoritative acts of the Prophet, and hence definitely not to traditions. The *sunna*, the norm to be followed, comes directly from Allah, and the '*sunna* of the Prophet' consists in following the Koran.[10]

More surprising is how little attention Bravmann pays to the Qur'ānic passages in which the word appears. His citation of Q 8:39/38 at the end of his discussion of the phrase *maḍat sunnat al-awwalīn* is the only Qur'ānic instance of the word that he cites in his own voice. The others are in quotations from al-Shāfiʿī (d. 204/820), Ibn Hishām (d. 218/834), and al-Bayḍāwī (d. 685/1286),[11] but Bravmann does not pursue these references. He does cite Q 5:35/32, an example of God's sunna that will be discussed below; but that verse does not contain the word *sunna*. Perhaps the great problems inherent in the study of hadīth have distracted scholars from the distinction between hadīth and sunna, though even Schacht has observed, "*Sunnah* and traditions are of course not really synonymous."[12] An examination of sunna as it occurs in the Qur'ān can serve as a needed check upon the too-easy tendency to identify sunna only with Prophetic Tradition or with the practice of the Medinan community. This chapter, then, will examine the neglected topic of *sunnat Allāh*.

I pointed out in the Introduction that one of God's arguments may be formally identical with its human counterpart and yet exhibit a dramatic change in force and scope because it comes from God. Among humans, sunna is an exemplary precedent, set by someone of authority, which is binding upon followers of lesser status and later date. The sunna of God as it occurs in the Qur'ān, like the sunna of human beings, incorporates the concept of setting precedents and something like the concept of obligation. But these obligations and precedents in God's sunna apply, not to human beings, but to God himself. God is obligating himself to do what he has said he will do, and to continue doing consistently until Judgment Day what he has always done. However, in so far as such a description implies limits on the powers of the Deity, it resembles doctrines rejected in the debates on predestination. Thus it is more productive to characterize Qur'ānic occurrences of *sunnat Allāh* as objective explanations by God of how the Divine Will operates: intentionally, necessarily, and consistently.

Sunna, in fact, seems to be the only satisfactory way to convey *why* God does what he does. The Law is for human beings; the Covenant (*ʿahd, mīthāq*) binds man and God; but if God were to violate his part of the bargain, there would be no other power to enforce it. As is true of so many pairs of concepts, then, the notions of cause and effect in God are one. One is left with the reality that God does what he does because he has always done what he does. "I am Who I am" (Exodus 3:14).

By their very nature, appeals to sunna and other sorts of precedent imply argument: they are evidence marshaled against adversaries who refuse to be convinced. Sunna – a precedent intentionally set, authoritative, and unvarying – amounts to a *rule* in the procedure known as "rule-based reasoning," to be discussed in Chapter 4. The assertion in Q 35:43 that there is no change in God's sunna is followed in verse 44 by an argument *a fortiori*: "Have they not traveled in the earth and seen what the end was of those before them, though they were stronger ...?" That is, if God can bring an end to those stronger than Quraysh, he can certainly terminate Quraysh as well. Arguments *a fortiori* are treated in Chapter 6.

The word *sunna* occurs 14 times in the Qur'ān, its plural *sunan* twice. Sunna is annexed grammatically to the word *Allāh* eight times, four times to "the ancients (*al-awwalīn*)," once to "those before you," and once to "the prophets We have sent before you." One refers to "Our *sunna*," and in another sunna is the indefinite subject of a sentence. More than one of these elements may be present in the verse or in the immediate context (e.g. Q 33:62). The first part of Table 3.1 lists all sunna verses; the second part, below the double dotted line, groups the four earliest verses together, for ease of comparison. As always, authorities disagree over which verse was the first to be revealed.[13]

Table 3.1 demonstrates that all sunna-loci in the Qur'ān show sunna as something to be understood with reference to the past. At least one of the four words signifying the past (*awwalīn, maḍā, khalā*, and *qabl*) occurs in all the verses. Furthermore, four of our eleven verses use the words *tabdīl* or *taḥwīl* or both to assert that God's past sunna will not change in the future; and five passages (those containing verses Q 8:38, 15:13, 18:55, 33:38, and 40:85) state or imply that what was done to past deniers will be done to future ones. That leaves only two late revelations, Q 3:137 and

Table 3.1 Sunna verses

	sunna	*sunan*	*Allāh*	*awwalīn*	*maḍā*	*khalā*	*qabl*	*tabdīl*	*taḥwīl*	*Total*
3:137		x				x	x			3
4:26		x					x			2
8:38	x			x	x					3
15:13	x			x		x				3
17:77	x (2)						x		x	4
18:55	x			x						2
33:38	x		x			x	x			4
33:62	x (2)		x (2)			x	x	x		7
35:43	x (3)		x (2)	x				x	x	8
40:85	x		x			x				3
48:23	x (2)		x (2)			x	x	x		7
35:43	x (3)		x (2)	x				x	x	8
15:13	x			x		x				3
40:85	x		x			x				3
18:55	x			x						2

4:26, which neither mention nor allude to the immutability of the divine sunna. By the time these verses were revealed, such an implication must have inseparable from the meaning of the word.

Because of the way the Qur'ān is arranged, much of the exegetical material concerning sunna is found in the commentaries on Sura 3:137, the first occurrence of the word in the text but one of the last to have been revealed. Using a broad array of exegetical opinion, we shall examine the first three sunna-passages in order of text, two of the first four in order of revelation, and a passage revealed concerning the Prophet's controversial marriage to Zaynab bint Jaḥsh. Finally, we shall examine at length the story of Cain and Abel, a sunna-passage that does not contain the word sunna at all.

The first passage is said to have been revealed "as a consolation to the believers for the killing and wounding that afflicted them on the day of Uḥud."[14]

> *Sunan* have gone before you (*qad khalat min qablikum sunan*): travel through the earth and see what was the end of those who rejected truth. This is a clear statement to people, a guidance and a good sermon to the God-fearing.
> (Q 3:137–138)

It displays some contextual anomalies, in that the word is not in *iḍāfa* but in the indefinite nominative plural (*sunan^{un}*), with no clear antecedents or consequents that might serve to define it. There are advantages for the reader in this, as the exegetes have had to add more clarifying material than would have been necessary had the first usage been as self-evident as, for example, Q 40:85.

Where the word is grammatically linked to others than God, as here where it is unascribed, sunna is sometimes construed as actions by human beings and sometimes as God's actions towards them. Mujāhid (d. 104/722) glosses the initial phrase as "alternation (*tadāwul*) of unbelievers and believers in good and evil,"[15] using the same root that appears slightly farther on: "Such days as those [i.e. Uḥud] We bring to people by turns (*nudāwiluhā bayn al-nās*) . . ." (Q 3:140). Muqātil b. Sulaymān (d. 150/767) refers the word not to what people did but what was done to them. He equates these sunan with the punishment of the vanished nations, cited to "frighten these peoples [of today] . . . so that they will reflect and affirm the oneness of God."[16]

Ṭabarī, too, begins by explaining that these sunan are things that God has done in the past to such as the people of ʿĀd and Thamūd: exemplary punishments that were carried out against them (*mathulāt sīra bihā fīhim*) for denying their prophets. Likewise, the fact that God sometimes allows the victory to fall to Muḥammad's enemies (*idāla*, cf. *nudāwiluhā*) should not be misinterpreted by those temporary victors.[17] Toward the end of the entry, Ṭabarī gives as an alternative synonym "the example [or 'pattern'] followed" (*al-mithāl al-muttabaʿ*) and says, quoting Labīd, that the one who establishes it is called *imām*. Finally, he quotes Ibn Zayd to the effect that *sunan* are *amthāl*.

Ṭabarsī begins with philological derivation. He glosses sunna as "the way that has been established so that it will be imitated (*al-ṭarīqa al-majʿūla li-yuqtaḍā bihā*)," quotes Labīd, and derives the meaning of the root *s-n-n* from the idea of "continuing in a certain direction (*al-istimrār fī jiha*)." A sunna, then, is a continuing procedure:

> When He (may He be exalted) shows what He does to the believer and the unbeliever in this world and the next, He shows that that is His habit (*ʿāda*) with His creatures.[18]

He, too, construes the plural (*min qablikum*) as being addressed to those defeated at Uḥud. As for the content of those sunan, he quotes al-Ḥasan (sc. al-Baṣrī, d. 110/728) and Ibn Isḥāq (d. 150/767) that the word refers to the exemplary punishments of the vanished nations who denied their prophets. Other possible synonyms for sunan are *amthāl* (Ibn Zayd) and *umam* (al-Mufaḍḍal, d. 146/763). An unattributed suggestion is that sunan means *ahl sunan*; and al-Kalbī (d. 146/763) suggests that the meaning is that "Every nation has had in effect a *sunna* and a *minhāj*: when they followed them, God was pleased with them."

The next occurrence of sunna in the text is also very late chronologically, but it has the fewest negative aspects of all the sunna-passages. It is not accompanied by a vanished-nations passage, and the proportion of divine punishment to divine mercy in the immediate context is very low.

> God wishes to make clear to you and guide you [by or to] the *sunan* of those before you (*wa-yahdiyakum sunana lladhīna min qablikum*); and to turn to you [in mercy], and

> God is all-knowing, all-wise. God wishes to turn to you, while those who follow their desires wish you to turn far away [from Him].
>
> (Q 4:26–27)

Muqātil b. Sulaymān reads it in light of the verses that precede it (Q 4:22–25), which concern the prohibited degrees in marriage: the sunan are "the laws (*sharāʾiʿ*) guiding those believers who came before them in the matter of prohibition on the grounds of relationship by blood and by marriage."[19] Ṭabarī quotes no authorities but limits his interpretation in the same way, referring it to marriage customs of believers and their prophets who observed the prohibited degrees.[20] Al-Zamakhsharī (d. 538/1144) expands the meaning of the phrase:

> God wants ... to guide you to the ways (*manāhij*) of the prophets and virtuous people who came before you and the paths (*ṭuruq*) which they followed in their religion, so that you may imitate them.[21]

Ṭabarsī, far more detailed than Ṭabarī on sunna-passages, notes that two things are said about *sunan alladhīna min qablikum*, namely, that God guides you in the footsteps of those before you so that you may gain what is advantageous in their conduct, and so that you may be vigilant in avoiding the [other] things they did.[22] In a passage clearly inspired by the jurist al-Jaṣṣāṣ (d. 370/980–981), Rāzī gives three opinions as to the meaning of the verse, of which the second and third are covenantal in tone: (1) that all the marriage laws immediately preceding the verse applied to all religions; (2) that the benefits of following God's commandments are the same, even if "the laws and the responsibilities" (*al- sharāʾiʿ wa-al-takālīf*) are different; (3) that God guides you to the sunan of those before you so that you may avoid what is false and follow the truth.[23]

The first occurrence of the phrase *sunnat al-awwalīn* follows a long passage about Meccan opposition to Muḥammad.

> Say to those who disbelieve [that] if they desist, what they did before will be forgiven them; and if they return to it, the *sunna* of the ancients has gone before (*wa-in yaʿūdū fa-qad maḍat sunnatu ʾl-awwalīn*). And do battle with them until there is no more temptation to impiety (*fitna*)

> and religion is entirely God's; and if they cease, then God sees what they do.
>
> (Q 8:38–39)

Ṭabarsī fully addresses the problem of grammatical ascription, pointing out that "the *sunna* of the ancients has gone before" really means "the *sunna* of God in [His treatment of] your ancestors and His custom in [causing] the victory of the believers have gone before (*maḍat sunnat Allāh fī ābā'ikum wa-'ādatuhu fī naṣr al-mu'minīn*)." It is God's sunna, but "He ascribed the *sunna* to them because it proceeded against them." By way of parallel, he cites the passage in Sura 17 that follows a description of the disbelievers' efforts to deter Muḥammad:

> Their purpose was to scare you off the land to expel you from it; if that had happened, they would have stayed on after you only a short while. That was the *sunna* of those apostles whom We sent before you, and you will not find any change in Our *sunna* (*sunnat man qad arsalnā min qablika min rusulinā wa-la tajid li-sunnatinā taḥwīl*)
>
> (Q 17:76–77)

The sunna is ascribed to the prophets "because it proceeded at their hands; then He said 'You will find no change in Our *sunna*,' ascribing it to Himself because it is He who carries it out."[24]

What was the first sunna-passage heard by the Prophet's audiences? According to most traditional Muslim authorities,[25] the very first revelation containing the word is Q 35:43, in which the word occurs three times, twice in the phrase *sunnat Allāh*.

> They [sc. Quraysh] swore their strongest oaths by God that if a warner (*nadhīr*) came to them, they should be better guided than any nation; but when a warner came to them, it only increased their aversion on account of their arrogance in the land and their plotting of evil; but the evil plot will catch only the plotters. Are they looking at anything other than the *sunna* of the ancients (*fa-hal yanẓurūn illā sunnat al-awwalīn*)? You will not find any change to God's *sunna* and you will not find that God's *sunna* is ever turned aside (*fa-lan tajid li-sunnat Allāh tabdīl wa-lan tajid li-sunnat Allāh taḥwīl*). Have they not

> traveled in the earth and seen what was the end of those before them, though they were stronger? ...
>
> (Q 35:42–44)

Of the two *sunnat Allāh*-verses that are candidates for primacy of revelation, Q 35:43 is the more complete in that it contains all the characteristic elements (see Table 3.1): it mentions *sunnat Allāh* twice and *sunnat al-awwalīn* once; and it explicitly denies change in this *sunna* by using both formulae, *tabdīl* and *taḥwīl*, the only *sunna*-verse to do so. Thus those who first heard this passage heard how Quraysh broke their oaths to God, rejected the prophet they had sworn to accept, and plotted against him. Whether "the *sunna* of the ancients" refers to the ancients' conduct, their resulting punishment at God's hands, or both, it leads into a passage that puts the living, hostile Quraysh in the same imperiled category as those vanished peoples whose visible traces reminded the living of God's inexorable punishment. The argument thus combines the covenantal elements of oaths and punishment for breaking them with the indigenous Arab concept of sunna.

None of these elements appears in the text here for the first time, so the commentators add only contextual details. Ṭabarī again refers to punishment of Muḥammad's people for rejecting God, but he adds an observation that resonates with the Covenant: retaliation against them has been made lawful (*uḥilla bihim min niqmatī*) on the grounds of their polytheism and rejection of the Prophet, as it was made lawful in the past under similar circumstances. He quotes Qatāda to the effect that *sunnat al-awwalīn* means *ʿuqūbat al-awwalīn* (the punishment of the ancients); and to the statement that there is no change to God's *sunna*, he adds the comment "because there is no averting His decree" (*li-annahu la maradda li-qaḍāʾihi*).[26] Ṭabarsī reproduces these points at somewhat greater length in a clear though not verbatim borrowing from Ṭabarī. His contribution is to gloss three words for "change:" *tabdīl* means "putting something in another's place;" *taḥwīl* means "putting something in a place other than the one it was in;" and *taghyīr*, frequently used to gloss the other two, means "making something different from (or "contrary to" – *ʿalā khilāf*) what it was."[27]

Other aspects of the adversarial context are worth noting as well. The Anglo-Iraqi N.J. Dawood has chosen Sura 18:55 as the earliest *sunna*-verse to be revealed. While his choice seems anomalous, it is certainly rich in elements of argument:

> In this Qur'ān We have explained for humanity every kind of example (*mathal*) but man is the most contentious of creatures (*akthara shay*^{in} *jadal*^{an}). Nothing has prevented people from believing, now that the guidance has come to them, and from asking forgiveness from God, unless it is [that they are waiting] for the *sunna* of the ancients (*sunnatu 'l-awwalīn*) to come to them, or for their punishment to come before their eyes. We only send the Apostles to give good tidings and to warn; but the disbelievers dispute, using what is wrong in order to destroy the Truth, and take My Signs – and the very fact that they have been warned – as a joke.
>
> (Q 18:54–56)

Verse 54 sets the agenda as being specifically one of evidence and argument. Humans are all too disposed to argue, but their grasp of proper procedure is faulty. They refuse to respond to verbal persuasion, thus drawing upon themselves a threat based on past examples (verse 55); they argue on invalid premises or by fallacious reasoning; and they trivialize what is vitally important (Verse 56). The passage is part of an important sequence of arguments that will be treated at length in later chapters; but we must note here that the entire context of this discussion of sunna is expressly one of argument, refutation, and proof.

Sura 33:36–38 was revealed in an acutely controversial situation, one that has drawn most unfavorable attention from non-Muslims: the Prophet's marriage to Zaynab bt. Jaḥsh, the divorced wife of his adopted son Zayd b. Ḥāritha:

> It is not for a male or female believer, once God and His Prophet have decided something, to have a choice in the matter, and whoever disobeys God has taken a path that is clearly wrong. You said to someone whom God and you had favored: "Keep your wife and fear God." You were hiding in your heart what God was going to reveal, for fear of the people, but God has a greater right that you should fear Him . . .[28] God's will be done (*wa-kāna amr Allāh maf'ūl*). There is no difficulty for the Prophet in what God has obligated him to do, according to God's *sunna* among those who have gone before (*sunnat Allāh fī 'lladhīna khalaw min qabl*). And the command of God is a set decree (*qadar*^{an} *maqdūr*^{an}).
>
> (Q 33:36–38)

The first concern of the text is to set rules and priorities: God and the Apostle's decision prevail over human choice, obedience over disobedience, fear of God over fear of public opinion. Arguments based on priority are legal arguments, to be dealt with in Chapter 5. The passage also associates sunna with the phenomenon of divine command (*amr*). As we shall detail in Chapter 4, a command functions as a logical quasi-proposition which must be justified by supporting evidence. Verse 38 also defines this particular example of God's sunna as an example of *qadar* ("divine decree"), in one of the few places in the Qur'ān where *qadar* refers, not simply to a measure of something (e.g. rain, cf. Q 23:18), but to a concept whose later theological implications gave rise to the controversy over predestination and free will.

The concept of sunna can be expanded by finding and examining other occurrences of words common to the sunna-contexts, such as *tabdīl, awwalīn, khalā*, and *maḍā*, and then (even more cautiously) words from these secondary contexts along with potential synonyms, especially those suggested in the exegeses. A very modest effort yields two more verses that resonate with those already cited. Qur'ān 10:64 assures the hearers that "There is no change in the Words of God (*la tabdīla li-kalimāt Allāh*)" [sc. that the friends of God will receive glad tidings in this world and the next]; and Q 43:8 warns, "So We destroyed [people] stronger than these in power [sc. for mocking prophets]; thus the example of the ancients has gone before (*maḍā mathal al-awwalīn*)."

Let us now consider a Qur'ānic passage that depicts the process of establishing a *sunna*, the episode in Q 5:27–32 concerning the sons of Adam. Although the word sunna does not appear in the passage, its elements are present and were so understood by the exegetes.[29] Beginning with the bare Qur'ānic text, we shall proceed to material from some standard *tafsīr*s, then follow the reasoning further to examine how sunna becomes *sharī'a*, as exemplified in al-Jaṣṣāṣ's *Aḥkām al-Qur'ān*.

The episode begins when Adam's two sons offer a sacrifice: "... It was accepted from one but not from the other, who said to his brother, 'I shall certainly kill you'" (Q 5:27). The threatened brother says:

> I intend that you shall be punished for my sin and your sin (*ithmi wa-ithmika*), so that you will be among those in the Fire. That is the punishment of those who do evil.
>
> (Q 5:29)

His brother then kills him, but the killer's shame and regret become acute when a crow comes and scratches up dirt to hide his dead brother's naked body, while he himself has not shown even minimal human consideration for the remains:

> "O woe is me! Have I failed even to be like this raven and hide my brother's shame?" And he began to regret. For that reason, We decreed for the Children of Israel that whoever takes a life for other than killing another human being or [spreading] corruption in the earth, it shall be as though he had killed all human beings, and whoever saves a life (*aḥyāhā*), it will be as though he had saved all people. And Our Apostles came to them with clear signs, yet many of them even after that still commit excesses in the earth.
>
> (Q 5:31–32)

Not only is Cain's murder of Abel (to use the Biblical names) the first killing in the world, Abel's death is the first death. The Qur'ān clearly points out the implications of these unprecedented facts: murder is not only a personal offense but a societal one, as saving a life is both a personal and a societal virtue. The exegetes differ over the meaning of the second part of the equation: does *aḥyā* mean counseling others not to kill, or does it mean saving people whose lives are threatened by fire, drowning, and the like? The next two verses (Q 5:33–34) lay out the canonical punishments and who is to be exempt, though they do not specifically mention murder as deserving the supreme penalty, only fighting against God and His Apostle and spreading corruption in the earth. Verses 33–34 may well have been revealed at a different time from the preceding verses, yet the juxtaposition of two verses which speak of "corruption in the earth" (Q 5:32 *fasād fī al-arḍ*; 5:33 *yasʿawna fī al-arḍ fasād*^{an}) virtually assures that the second will be construed as an explanation of the first.[30]

As usual, the Qur'ānic details of the murder and burial are sparse, so some exegetes fill in with material from the Bible and elsewhere. Muqātil's version of the murder and burial is two and one-half pages long and full of colorful details. He gives two reasons why Abel's offering was taken while Cain's was not. Their mother Eve's pregnancies were always with twins, a boy and a girl. Adam declares his intention to marry Abel's twin to Cain and vice versa, but Cain refuses, preferring his own sister because she is more beautiful. Adam then proposes that each bring an offering to God: the one whose offering is taken by the fire will marry the girl. Adam then goes away to Mecca. Cain brings as offering the worst of his harvest, "cankered wheat with tares in it," while Abel brings "the best of his sheep, along with butter and milk." So Cain both disobeys his father and makes a contemptible offering to God, hence his rejection.

Muqātil has Abel remonstrating with Cain for quite a long time, "until the middle of the day," to no avail:

> And at the end of what Abel said to Cain [came the following:] "If you kill me, you will be the first to be condemned to misery[31] and the first of my father's offspring to be sent to the Fire; and I shall be the first martyr to enter Heaven."[32]

Although nowhere does the word sunna appear, the force of Abel's argument clearly comes from the onus which would attach to the family and to Cain himself if the latter were to establish a bad sunna.

God's lesson in burying the dead affords Muqātil opportunity for an equally vivid bit of story-telling. Cain does not know what to do with his brother's corpse, so he carries it around for three days, until God sends a crow to teach Cain how to bury his brother. First, the crow kills another crow; then it digs a hole in the dirt with its beak, takes the leg of the dead crow in its beak and drags it to the hole, dumps it in, and finally fills up the hole with dirt, Cain watching all the while. When Cain has learned his lesson and buried his brother, God sends fear upon him, "because he was the first whom He frightened so that he fled away." A voice from the sky asks Cain where his brother is, and his reply echoes the Biblical one: "Am I a keeper over him? Let him go where he wants." The voice cries out that all Cain's limbs bear witness against him, and says, "Where can you be safe from your Lord? My God says, 'You are cursed in all the land.'"[33]

The criminal's flight takes him to the seashore, where he kills birds to eat by beating them to death, the origin of the ban on eating animals killed in that way. Yet another evil results from the crime. "The tame animals and the birds and the wild animals did not fear each other until Cain killed Abel." All had lived together around Adam, but after Cain's crime, the birds took to the air and the animals to the mountains and thickets.

> And from that day, the earth became angry with the disbeliever; hence the [dead] disbeliever is squeezed in the earth until his ribs collapse in on each other, while the believer's grave widens to the point that its two sides cannot be seen.[34]

Beyond drama, however, the story raises issues of covenant, precedent, and law. Muqātil does not apply sunna to the "equation" verse (sc. Q 5:32) but interprets it in terms of equivalence of penalties: a killer is killed if he kills one person as he would be if he killed all. If the victim's nearest male relative (*walīy*), who has a right to revenge, pardons the killer, the pardoner is rewarded with Heaven as he would be if he pardoned all.[35]

Ṭabarī prefaces his account with an assertion that this revelation came to Muḥammad to recite against the Jews who intended to raise their hands against him, so that they might know the consequences; and to illustrate the contrasting fates of those who kept the covenant and those who broke it, those who obeyed God and those who disobeyed. He adds vast amounts of detail and quotes variant interpretations, but matters which Muqātil construes as sunna Ṭabarī usually interprets in terms of obedience and disobedience to God. Still, it is possible to see from Ṭabarī's selective quotations that some early exegetes were concerned with the status of divine law in the period after Adam and Eve were expelled from Eden but before any crime had been committed. The concern with who was the first to perform a particular action and the interpretation of law as arising after the commission of a blameworthy act – or a praiseworthy one, for that matter – is informed by the concept of sunna. Ṭabarī quotes three versions of a *hadīth*: "No person is killed unjustly without some blame (*kifl*) for it falling upon the first son of Adam; that is because he was the first to practice murder (*dhālika bi'annahu awwal man sanna al-qatl*)."[36]

When it came to burying the corpse, there was no human practice for dealing with the dead, because until then there had been no dead; yet a "proper" procedure in some sense of the word clearly existed, because Cain recognized it when he saw it. "He said, 'Woe is me! Was I not able even to be like this crow and hide my brother's naked corpse?'" (Q 5:31). Ṭabarī describes the practice of burying the dead with the phrase *sunnat Allāh*: "The one of the two who killed his brother did not know God's *sunna* with regard to the custom (*'āda*) concerning the dead, and he did not know what to do with his murdered brother." So God sent the crow to teach him.[37]

It is worth reiterating that Ṭabarī has both a narrow and a broad use of the word sunna. What he means here is presumably "the example which is followed," as when he uses the word for such pagan practices as Jāhilī marriage customs; but he also construes "God's *sunna*" as his punishments of the vanished nations, a designation which places it in the realm of law – Command, Prohibition, Promise, and Threat – as Ṭabarī asserts that it was given to Adam *after* his exit from the Garden. Unlike earlier commentators who may have envisioned a period before the coming of God's sunna when evil was good,[38] Ṭabarī apparently sees no time when the Divine Order did not constitute the law of the earth, even before the coming of the prophets and the revelation of the first Book.

One more analysis of the passage will be offered to illustrate the concept of God's sunna as an important component of his Covenant with human beings and as predecessor to the full-blown *sharīʿa*. It comes from the second volume of al-Jaṣṣāṣ's *Aḥkām al-Qurʾān*, an early example of a genre with characteristics of both *tafsīr* and *fiqh*.[39] Arranged in Qurʾānic order, they combine the concerns of exegesis with those of law; like Ṭabarī, Abu Bakr Aḥmad al-Rāzī, called al-Jaṣṣāṣ (d. 370/980–981), was a jurist. The valuable material in his *Aḥkām* is rather awkwardly patched together, with long legal disquisitions and cross-references appended to the first mention of a topic, so that fully one-third of the book is devoted to the first two suras. Nor is every verse treated, only those with clear legal applications. The later work of the same title by Abu Bakr Muḥammad ibn al-ʿArabī (d. 543/1148) shows some of the same limitations; but by the seventh/thirteenth century, the genre had evolved into a full-blown *tafsīr*, as seen in *al-Jāmiʿ li-Aḥkām al-Qurʾān* of Abū ʿAbd Allāh Muḥammad al-Qurṭubī (d. 671/1273).

Jaṣṣāṣ is not particularly interested in the details of previous covenants, and he comments on only two of the sunna-verses. When it comes to violations of God's law that are also capital crimes, however, Jaṣṣāṣ the jurist is very much concerned. Five large pages of tiny print are required for the story of Cain and Abel, and another seven for the definition and punishment of "those who wage war against God and the Prophet and spread corruption in the earth." Does killing equal murder in all cases? Jaṣṣāṣ admits that one interpretation of Q 5:28, attributed to al-Ḥasan and

Mujāhid, that the verse requires non-resistance against someone who intends to kill one "is rationally possible" (*jā'iz fi al-'aql*) but that in any case it is abrogated, possibly by the laws of the previous prophets and possibly by that of "our Prophet, whom God bless and preserve," in Q 49:9, which deals with strife among Muslims. The author shows by his extensive treatment of the other alternative that he considers the verse far more likely to be a ban on aggression than a ban on self-defense; he cites many *ḥadith* in support of the right to defend oneself.[40]

Jaṣṣāṣ devotes an entire chapter to the sunna of proper burial. He rejects a version of the Cain and Abel story attributed to al-Ḥasan which held the killer and victim to be not Adam's immediate offspring but later Israelites. "If that were the case," points out Jaṣṣāṣ, "they would have known about burial from the fact that it was a customary procedure (*bi-jarayān al-'āda fīhi*) before that, and it is the origin of the *sunna* in burying the dead;"[41] in support he cites Q 80:21 and 77:25.

As a Ḥanafī, he finds support in the "equation-verse" (Q 5:32) for the validity of *qiyās*. Of the equation between killing one and killing all he says:

> Certain aspects [of interpretation] have been cited for it. One is that it expresses the magnitude of the burden. The second is that on him [sc. the first killer] lies the equal of the sin of everyone who kills, because he established the practice of murder and made it easier for others, thus he is like a participant in it.[42]

He cites the *ḥadīth* used by Ṭabarī concerning the share of Adam's son in all murders, then quotes a better-known one that is also canonical:

> Whoever establishes a good *sunna* has its reward and the reward of him who acts according to it until the Day of Resurrection, and whoever establishes an evil *sunna* bears its burden and the burden of him who acts according to it until the Day of Resurrection.[43]

Jaṣṣāṣ's observation that the first killer made killing a *sunna* and so became a quasi-participant in every murder is quoted nearly verbatim by al-Ṭabarsī, who attributes it to the Mu'tazilī theologian Abū 'Ali al-Jubbā'ī (d.303/916).[44] Although Jaṣṣāṣ rarely cites by name any source later than the imams of law and *ḥadīth*, the attribution of the passage to al-Jubbā'i is probably reliable, as he was one of Ṭabarsī's principal sources; and since al-Jubbā'ī is reported by some sources to have been a Ḥanafī,[45] it would not be surprising if the Ḥanafī al-Jaṣṣāṣ were to quote him.

The verses dealt with in this section have implications beyond their roles in the Qur'ān. At the very least, references to sunna in the early Islamic texts must be re-evaluated in light of the fact that there are not two possible alternatives but three: the sunna of the Prophet, the sunna of the early community, and the sunna of God.

In human terms, sunna, "binding precedent," is set *mindfully and authoritatively* by a *particular* person who *intends* that his act should be imitated and who *bears responsibility* for the acts of those who do so. *Sunna* in pre-Islamic Arabia can be seen as an effort to establish a moral enclave within the amoral, impersonal, and irreversible flow of Time. Because Time moves in only one direction, being the first person to do or say a particular thing carried a weight that, good or bad, was inescapable. No act could be counteracted and no word could be revoked. The only socially effective way to deal with that fact was to invest the concept of the unprovoked word or unprecedented deed with a moral significance so grave as to ensure that few would dare to incur such a responsibility.

Islam placed on human beings new responsibility for their own actions, but it also freed them from bad old sunan and revalidated acceptable ones – including the institution of sunna itself – by substituting divine and prophetic sunna for human sunna, the law of God for the law of man. The Covenant was not new, being the trust which human beings had accepted from God when the angels refused it (Q 33:72–73), and which Adam forgot but God reconfirmed (Q 20:121–122). But it was new to most of the Arabs, and it marked the beginning of *taklīf*, the state of being under God's commandment. More fundamentally, Islam changed the human perception of reality by rejecting the old view of nature as impersonal and the pagan gods as entities themselves subject to time and fate. Instead, it placed the entire universe with its unidirectional flow of time under the power of God, thus investing all action, all manifestation, and all of the unseen as well with a moral significance that could not be escaped even in death. Especially not in death, since death marked not only the end of one's acts but the end of one's opportunity to repent for them. Nothing was left but the Last Judgment and the Garden, or the Fire.

Failure to observe sunna remained a serious breach of socially approved conduct, but it might now also be a sin, possibly one involving eternal punishment. New sins now existed in Arabian society, and new crimes; and an act that would once have rendered the actor an outlaw, such as preferring religious ties to family ties when the two conflicted, might now be reinterpreted as an act of virtue. This change is surely the source of the old exegetes' feeling that the world before the Covenant in general, and during the Jāhilīya in particular, differed from Islam in a way that was radically perverse. The role of the prophet was to be always at odds with the non-believing society, and his position could not be a "virtuous" one when virtue was defined by such a society. Only a system of virtue rooted in the transcendent could make such socially non-conforming behavior a desirable model to heed or imitate.

4

RULES, COMMANDS, AND REASONS WHY

In this chapter we shall begin to see how the Qur'ān combines elements of the Covenant, signs, precedents, divine *sunna*, and other basic precepts to produce formally complete arguments that enable believers to apply religious principle to practice: to believe, act, abstain, choose, judge, and enforce in the ways prescribed by the Covenant. Argument-schemata rooted in classical logic and rhetoric will appear in later chapters, but this chapter analyzes arguments using two methods borrowed from modern logic: rule-based reasoning and the logic of commands. When incorporated into the "metaphysics of morals" and used to classify human actions as they relate to divine law, these two techniques can both analyze and influence conduct in that they first evaluate the premises underlying an act of moral or legal reasoning, then assess the validity of the reasoning process, and finally judge the result as not just valid or invalid but as right or wrong.

To introduce the themes of justification and validitation integral to these forms of reasoning, I begin by examining a few of the hundreds of verses in which God sets out reasons for his acts and decrees. I then discuss the aspects of rule-based reasoning relevant to Qur'ānic argument, then analyze the phenomenon of divine command, which is both the major example of rule-based reasoning and the proper sphere for discussion of God's commands and deeds.

DOES GOD WORK FOR A PURPOSE?

One of the classic topoi of Islamic theology is the question of whether or not God's actions can be said to have a "cause" (*ʿilla*). For a number of reasons, Muslims of varying theological persuasions rejected the idea that God could be questioned about "why" (*li-mā*) he acted in one way and not another. Muʿtazilite theologians, for example, held that God existed wholly in eternity, an existence which did not permit motion, change or knowledge of particulars. Why God chose in the first place to create, to reward, and to punish was, in such a theological view, not only an unanswerable but an unaskable question, in that it implied that God's actions were caused by something outside himself. Traditionalist thinkers, *ahl al-sunna*, also considered such questions unaskable, but for different reasons: they were improper and irreverent, a heretical innovation that violated Qur'ān 21:23: "He is not to be asked about what He does: it is they who are to be asked."[1] As will become clear in the discussion of the logic of commands, disputes over the "motives" of divine commands arose from failure to distinguish between two separate notions: the logical requirement that valid commands be justified and the theological conclusion that to justify a divine command was in some way to limit the Divine Will. One can understand ordinary Muslims' exasperation with the theologians who refused to concede that God works with wise purpose, given the plain fact that there are vast numbers of Qur'ānic passages whose function is precisely to explain to human beings just why God commands what he commands.

Not only God's commands to humans but his own actions are very often paired with his reasons for doing them. Why does he send books and prophets?

> We gave Moses the Book after We destroyed the earlier generations [to give] insights to human beings, and guidance, and mercy, that they may be mindful.
>
> (Q 28:43)

> We have sent down to you the Book with the Truth, so that you may judge among the people according to what God has shown you.
>
> (Q 4:105)

Why did God not create perfect people in perfect societies?

> If God had willed, He would have made you one people, but [he did not] in order to test you in what He has brought you, so strive with each other in all the virtues ...
>
> (Q 5:48)

How can we know that God is both powerful and merciful?

> Say: 'Do you see? If God were to set night eternally over you until the Day of Resurrection, what deity other than God would bring you light? Do you not hear?' Say: 'Do you see? If God were to set daylight eternally over you until the Day of Resurrection, what deity other than God would bring night in which you might rest? Do you not see?' From His mercy He has made you the night and the day so that you might rest in it and might seek His grace, and perhaps be thankful.
>
> (Q 28:71–73)

Why was the Qur'ān revealed a few verses at a time?

> Those who disbelieve say 'Why was the Qur'ān not revealed to him all at once?' [It has been revealed] in this way so that We may strengthen your heart, and We have spoken it in a slow, orderly manner. They cannot come to you with an example (*mathal*) for which We have not brought you the Truth and the best explanation.
>
> (Q 25:32–33)

Why did God reveal the Qur'ān at all?

> We have sent down the Book to you with the Truth, confirming the Scripture already in existence and keeping it safe ... So judge between them by what God has revealed, and do not follow their desires, and beware of them lest they seduce you away from some of what God has revealed to you ... Is it a judgment from the time of ignorance (*jāhilī*) that they want? Who is better than God as a judge for people whose faith is certain?
>
> (Q 5:48–50)

RULE-BASED REASONING

Given the command to judge according to the Qur'ān, and given that the Qur'ān contains numerous governing principles – Covenant, *sunna*, commandment, example – how does one determine which one applies to the situation at hand? How does one know its range of applicability? Its limitations? If a number of principles apply, which one has priority? How does one determine what is a rule and what is not?

The method best suited for answering these questions is called *rule-based reasoning*. In its narrower sense, it is a form of logic applied to "rules" in the field of law; thus it lies at the heart of one of the most important disciplines in the Islamic intellectual tradition. More broadly, it is indispensable for examining many of the factors that influence human behavior, social interaction, and judgment. Rule-based reasoning is not reducible to deduction or induction and may be said to precede both, in that the very validity of a logical operation is evaluated by referring to rules. A basic text in the field is *The Logic of Choice* by the legal philosopher Gidon Gottlieb,[2] a study which borrows important points from Georg Henrik von Wright's *Norm and Action*.[3]

What is a "rule"? Von Wright uses a broader term than does Gottlieb – "norms" – and identifies three major types:

1 rules (e.g. the rules of games or grammar)
2 prescriptions or regulations, including commands, permissions, and prohibitions (e.g. the laws of the state)[4]
3 directives or technical terms (e.g. the means to be used for a certain end)

To these he adds three important minor groups that share characteristics of more than one main group:

4 customs (social habits that combine aspects of rules and prescriptions)
5 moral norms (see below)
6 ideal rules (prescribing not what one should *do* but how one should *be*: e.g. generous, truthful, temperate)

I pointed out in the Introduction that certain arguments change direction and force when they proceed from God and not from a human being. Without delving into these changes, von Wright shows in a number of places that he is aware of them. In trying to determine whether his "moral norms" are "rules," "customs," or "prescriptions," he says that the third is the choice of those who believe that moral norms are the commands of God to men. These prescriptions are "not only of a very special *kind*" but "must, perhaps, be thought of as prescriptions in a special *sense* of the term" because of their supernatural source. After comparing this to the teleological view, he concludes that moral norms are *sui generis*, not because they "form an autonomous group of their own" but because they "have complicated logical affinities to the other main types of norm and to the value-notions of good and evil."[5] Gottlieb's brief typology of rules[6] is based upon von Wright's more nuanced system of classification.[7] It is confusing that von Wright's narrowest term, "rules," should be Gottlieb's broadest, incorporated in the indispensable term "rule-based reasoning." Here I shall use the word in Gottlieb's sense and focus on the process rather than pursue the distinctions between different types of rule.

How does a rule work? Rule-based reasoning is not deductive. While the final stage of the argument may contain a deduction, the crux comes not in the actual process of reasoning but in the preliminary "classification of particulars," that is, identifying the field of choice among possible governing principles, choosing the proper rule to be the major premise, then choosing and ascertaining the truth of the relevant facts to make up the minor premise.[8] Rule-based reasoning is not inductive, because induction is based upon observation of particulars, and inferences so based are not conclusive, only more or less probable. By contrast, conclusions in legal or moral decisions are based not on empirical evidence but on legal or moral rules, which have nothing to do with probability.

> In other words, it is not possible to *apply* a rule inductively, irrespective of the manner in which that rule may be derived ... While inductive reasoning is designed to govern inferences about matters of fact, reasoning relying on rules is designed to guide decisions and judgments ...[9]

Whatever the structure of the original rule-sentence, it must be restatable in the following form: "In circumstances X, Y is required/permitted."[10] If it cannot be so restated, it cannot serve as a guide for inference. This deceptively simple form is the product of four "structural characteristics ... necessary for the rule to function as a rule ...

1 an indication of the circumstances in which the rule is applicable;
2 an indication of that which ought, or may, or must be, or not be, concluded or decided;

3 an indication of the type of inference contemplated, whether under the rule it is permitted, required, or prohibited;[11]
4 an indication that the statement is indeed designed to function as a rule or inference-warrant."[12]

Let us apply these criteria to a neutral example from an area that both Gottlieb and von Wright hold to be governed by rules: language. In the Arabic language, when a noun is the direct object (*maf'ūl bihi*) of a transitive verb, it must go into the accusative case (*al-naṣb*). Restated in Gottlieb's pattern, it shows the four structural characteristics.

1 the rule applies when a transitive verb has a noun-object;
2 the noun-object goes into the accusative case:
3 use of the accusative case is required;
4 for correct diction, the rules of Arabic grammar must be followed.

A so-called "exception to the rule" in fact indicates that another rule has prevailed over the expected one. In our grammatical example, a non-accusative ending on a direct object at the end of a line of poetry is permissible by poetic license, where preserving metre and rhyme is a rule that apparently supersedes the grammatical rule. I say "apparently," because a commentator will still note that the word is "in the position of the accusative (*fi maḥall al-naṣb*)" but that its ending has been changed to fit the rhyme.[13]

Gottlieb has even suggested that, because all words and linguistic concepts are used according to rules (or "microrules"), rules are a prerequisite for communication.

> If words are rule-particles, so to speak, then every form of human communication may well be a type of normative activity which displays some of the characteristics of reasoning with rules.[14]

This reminds us that when ancient peoples encountered foreigners with whom they could not communicate (*barbaroi, 'ajam*), they did not recognize the foreigners' strange utterances as language at all, because they appeared to obey no known rule.

Is the Covenant a rule? It is *par excellence* a "governing principle," but given its complexity, we should first see the Covenant as a "moral norm" *sui generis* in von Wright's sense. It defines the field of moral behavior in terms of the relationship between man and God and between good and evil; it instructs ("directs") its human adherents how to achieve the reward for good and avoid the punishment for evil; and it both generates and validates ("prescribes") many individual sub-rules, in accordance with Gottlieb's observation that some rules precede other rules.[15] For practical purposes, therefore, despite the existence of countless sub-rules, the Covenant is a single rule and is so treated in the Qur'ān. Using Gottlieb's four elements, we may summarize it as follows:

1 Circumstances: The Covenant governs all relations between human beings and God, with corollary implications for human beings' relations with each other.
2 Conclusion: Humans shall adhere to the Covenant.
3 Type of inference: Adherence to the Covenant is obligatory. Sub-rules may apply to those who have never heard the word of God (Q 9:11) or are temporarily incapable of observing one or more of its conditions (Q 2:173), but even those are ultimately governed by the primordial covenant of Qur'ān 7:172: "Am I not your Lord? (*a-lastu bi-Rabbikum*?)"
4 Status as rule: Reward for adherence and punishment for non-adherence indicate that the rule is intended to be a rule.

The rule may be restated as follows: "In the relationship between human beings and God, humans are required to adhere to the Covenant".

As an example of a Covenant-based sub-rule, let us re-examine the notion of the *sunna* of God, here assimilating it to a single practice, not to a complex code like the Covenant. We have seen that in the Qur'ān itself the phrase *sunnat Allāh* is often found in the neighborhood of the punishment stories. When, like most exegetes, we equate *sunnat Allāh* with the practice of punishing disbelieving peoples, it may be restated as a rule: "In circumstances where a people disbelieve, God will certainly punish the disbelievers."

How does this interpretation of God's *sunna* function as a rule when measured against Gottlieb's four structural characteristics?

First, the circumstance is indicated under which the rule will be applied: human unbelief, defined as failure to believe in God in spite of the primordial Covenant, and in spite of ample evidence and opportunity for believing.

Second, the conclusion or decision is indicated: unbelievers will be punished.

Third, the type of inference is signaled: punishment proceeds inevitably, a character-tag which connotes necessity and requirement.

Fourth, the *sunna*-passages are designated as rules in at least three ways: by definition ("binding precedent"), by demonstration of past punishments ("Travel in the earth and see ..."), and by projection into the future ("You will find no change in God's *sunna*.")

As an example of a rule that governs human relations and offers more than one possible course of action, let us consider a verse on divorce.

> When you divorce women, and they fulfill the term of their waiting-period, either take them back on equitable terms (*bi-ma'rūf*) *or* set them free on equitable terms; but do not take them back to injure them, (or) to take undue advantage; if any one does that; He wrongs his own soul. Do not treat God's Signs as a jest, but solemnly rehearse God's favours on you, and the fact that He sent down to you the Book and Wisdom, for your instruction. And fear God, and know that God is well acquainted with all things.
> (Q 2:231)

Taking just one part of this complex rule, I shall restate it as follows: "When a husband who is considering divorce decides to take his wife back, he may do so provided that he treats her equitably and does not intend to harm her."

1 Circumstances: A man considers divorcing his wife.
2 Decision: He decides not to divorce her.
3 Type of inference: This decision is permitted, provided that his intention is to treat her equitably and not to harm her.
4 Status as rule: If the man fails to observe this rule, he will bring punishment upon himself, because he is ignoring what God has sent down for his instruction.

The Covenant then, is the rule that God observes in dealing with his creatures, not because of any external obligation but because he has committed himself to behave consistently and predictably. He will invariably reward belief and virtue, punish unbelief and sin, turn toward those who turn toward him, and send prophets to inform humans of what they need to know in order to achieve salvation. From the point of view of argument, it is this invariability and predictability that give the Covenant the status of rule upon which structures of reasoned argument can be raised. Indeed, most Qur'ānic rule-passages mention only the action and its reward or punishment; the other two steps in rule-based reasoning are understood and therefore omitted.

The elements of rule-based reasoning will reappear many times in this study, and so I shall not add further examples here. What the reader must bear in mind is that the word "rule" as used in this book is a technical term and "rule-based reasoning" a branch of logic. But another element now enters the discussion: many "rules" in the Qur'ān are expressed in the form of commands.

THE LOGIC OF COMMANDS

God's primordial mode of speech in the Abrahamic faiths is that of command, so that the study of divine command is in a sense co-extensive with the study of revelation. God's very acts of creation are commands: "Let there be light" (Gen. 1:3); "He created [Adam] from dust, then said to him 'Be!' and he was" (Qur'ān 3:59). Many of the terms that express the relationship between God and human being – "Lord" and "servant," "Creator" and "creature," "King" and "subject" – are extracted metaphorically from contexts in which it is expected and appropriate for one human being to issue orders to another. For God, then, to issue orders to humans is not only correct *a fortiori*, it is *right*. Any other mode of address is, as it were, a metaphor for the primary mode.

In fact, command may be the primary mode of *all* speech. In his evocative *Language and Magic*, Toshihiko Izutsu has written:

> The imperative is a very remarkable linguistic device for designating the action or event desired in so straightforward and compulsory a way that the mere mention of the action or event in that form is generally sufficient to bring about its immediate realization. Besides, the second person of the imperative consists, in a great many languages of the world, of the bare word-stem or something that approximates it, a fact which speaks strongly in favour of the chronological priority of this form to most other linguistic modes of expression ...[16]

Recognizing commands as a province of logic seems counter-intuitive to anyone who has been taught to construe arguments from authority or power as *ipso facto* fallacious. Fortunately, a whole literature exists on the subject. My primary source is Nicholas Rescher's *The Logic of Commands*;[17] references to one of his principal sources, von Wright's *Norm and Action*, have already appeared in this chapter.

The first step in analysis is to distinguish a true command from a construction that uses the imperative mood of the verb to make another kind of statement altogether. Imperatives in the Qur'ān are used to challenge ("Produce a *sura* like it [the Qur'ān]!" Q 10:38); to reproach ("Do not beg for mercy on this Day, for you will not be helped by Us!" Q 23:65); to condemn ("Taste the punishment of the Fire!" Q 8:50); to call for help ("Pour down to us water or anything that God has given you by way of sustenance!" Q 7:51); to pray ("Guide us on the Straight Path," Q 1:6); and to create ("To anything which We have willed, We but say the Word 'Be' and it is," Q 16:40).[18] Conversely, a locution may be a command even when it contains no imperative verb: "Forbidden to you are your mothers, and your daughters, and your sisters ..." (Q 4:23); "We have enjoined man to treat his parents kindly ..." (Q 46:15).

Commands proper are what Rescher calls "orders, directives, injunctions, instructions, prohibitions,"[19] and what von Wright calls "prescriptions."[20] These in turn must be subdivided into commands to perform specific actions ("Rise and warn!" Q 74:2) and commands to achieve or realize a certain state ("For your Lord's sake, be patient!" Q 74:7).[21] Finally, a distinction is usually drawn between a command and a commandment: the former has its source in a person, the latter is a "sourceless" moral imperative.[22] The Muslim view, of course, is that moral imperatives are not "sourceless" at all but issue from a divine source; that is what makes them moral, and what makes them imperatives.

Is a command the same as a rule? Rescher quotes the positivist Carnap to the effect that moral rules *are* imperatives: "[T]here is only ... stylistic difference between 'killing is evil' and 'do not kill.'"[23] Gottlieb quotes Wittgenstein's assertion that following a rule is the same as obeying an order, but as a legal philosopher he disagrees with him, on the grounds that one who is given an order need not worry about the motives of the person in charge, while one who applies a rule must worry about both its purpose and its particular application.[24] Islamic thought can be seen as harmonizing the two points of view. Over the years it came to distinguish fundamental moral principles (*uṣūl*) from the laws that embodied them (*furūʿ*) but never lost sight of the fact that both ultimately proceed from the same source: the Qur'ān.

This brings us back to Rescher who, though he explicitly rejects the equation of "moral imperatives" with "commandments," admits that the logic is the same.[25] The author of a valid command must have some entitlement or authority for giving the command in the first place, "some status ... that puts him in a position to exact compliance or at least elicit cooperation."[26] There must also be a good reason for the command – it must be "rational, sound, or sensible,"[27] providing "a rational and reasonable answer to the question 'why?'"[28]

In a number of senses, as we have seen, God cannot be asked to justify his commands or indeed provide motives for his acts at all: "He is not to be asked about what He does; it is they who are to be asked" (Q 21:23). This is not to say that God acts capriciously or inconsistently; as we have seen, he both binds himself by the Covenant and explains his reasons for commands. But human beings may not second-guess the Deity, whose power and authority are absolute: "O people, it is you who need God: God is self sufficient ..." (Q 35:15). The Divine Name *al-ghanīy* signifies the attribute of transcendent self-sufficiency: God does not need any created object ("All that is in the heavens and the earth belongs to Him: He is truly self-sufficient ..." – Q 22:24), as he does not need people to carry out His commandments ("Whoever engages in *jihād* does so for his own sake, for God is free from all need for created things" – Q 29:6).

But human beings cannot so easily be discouraged from asking questions, particularly not the question "Why?" Certainly the Qur'ān could be cited as encouraging humans to seek knowledge of God (e.g. Q 16:43, 21:7), and one Qur'ānic passage in particular gave hope to those who inquired boldly:

> O you who believe! Do not ask about things which would hurt you if they were explained to you. But if you ask about them when the Qur'ān is being revealed, they will be explained to you – God will forgive them, as God is forgiving and patient. People before you asked those questions, then fell into disbelief because of them.
>
> (Q 5:101–102)

COMMANDS IN THE EARLIEST REVELATIONS

Using Rescher's two criteria for the validity of a command – that the author must have some sort of authority over the recipient, and that there must be a good reason for the command – let us analyze certain passages held by various authorities to be the earliest revelations. In this way, we can ignore accounts of the circumstances of revelation and still find support for the early date of some passages and the later date of others based solely upon the presence or absence of ordered arguments and the corresponding levels of urgency they must have conveyed to the first hearer.

The weight of tradition supports the view that the first word of the Qur'ān to be revealed was a command: *Iqra'*! "Read!" or "Recite!" (Q 96:1).[29] If this is the case, then the Qur'ānic text contains an order not preceded by apparatus establishing the authority of the source of the command. It is true that this one-word primordial command is followed immediately in the text by a clause which establishes the authority of the Speaker: "In the name of your Lord Who created – created man from a clot of blood;" but it is significant that some accounts of the first occasion of revelation indicate a hiatus between the order and the justification, which contributed to Muḥammad's initial confusion. He is said to have answered the bare command "Read!" either with protests of his inability to read (*Mā anā bi-qāri'*) or with questions about just what it was that he was to read (*Mā aqra'? or Mā dhā aqra'?*)[30] before being given the text. A human being's logical need to identify the source of any command before obeying it is vividly illustrated by this and other traditions that describe Muḥammad's fear and confusion upon receiving the first revelation. His wife sought guidance from her literate Christian cousin Waraqa, who explained the phenomenon using a concept that we have already examined: precedents from Judeo-Christian sacred history.[31] Whatever status one grants to the historicity of Prophetic Tradition, Muḥammad's need to know the source of the order before following it is not only perfectly natural but logically necessary.

For ease of analysis, we present Q 96:1–5 in schematic form, labeled by verse number:

(1) a command: "Read!" (*iqra'*)
(1) an authorization: "In the Name of your Lord" (*b-ismi Rabbika*)
(1) a definition: "Who created" (*alladhī khalaq*)

(2) an expansion on the previous definition: "Created the human being from a clot of blood:" (*khalaqa 'l-insāna min 'alaq*)

(3) a repetition of the initial command: "Read!" (*iqra'*)

(3–5) three more definitions: "And your Lord is most generous, Who taught by the Pen, taught the human being what he did not know" (*wa-rabbuka al-akram alladhī 'allama bi-l-qalam, 'allama 'l-insāna mā lam ya'lam*).

In sum, the first verse of Sura 96 contains in five words a command, an authorization for the command, and a functional definition of the author of the command. Verse 2 clarifies the authority of the author of the command in verse 1. Verse 3 repeats the initial command "Read!"; and verses 3–5 follow up the command with three more definitions of its author. In covenantal terms as set out in Chapter 1, the source of the revelation is identified as the covenant-giver, whose benefits to humanity include its very existence and its reception of knowledge following initial ignorance. Humanity's resulting covenantal obligations are as yet unspoken, except for the command to "Read!" issued to a single human being. Thus in these first twenty words revealed to the Prophet Muḥammad were present the elements of authority: divine command, authorization, identification, and Covenant, a combination of logic and sacred history.

Ibn Kathīr (d. 774/1373) notes that al-Bayhaqī (d. 458/1066) relates a *ḥadīth* in *Dalā'il al-Nubuwwa*, repeated by al-Bāqillānī (d. 403/1013), that the *Fātiḥa* was the first revelation, but that sound opinion supports the priority of *Iqra' b-ismi rabbika alladhī khalaq*.[32] Al-Suyūṭi gives four candidates for the first revelation: Sura 96 *al-'Alaq*, Sura 74 *al-Muddaththir*, Sura 1 *al-Fātiḥa* with the *basmala*, and the phrase *bismillah al-raḥmān al-raḥīm* by itself.[33] The *basmala* is an authorization, so two of Suyūṭī's four versions hold that the Qur'ān *began with* the necessary authorization. If we analyze Sūra 96 with the *basmala* at the head, here is the resulting order of argument by verse-number:

(0) an authorization: "In the Name of God" (*b-ismi Llāh*)

(0) a definition: "the Compassionate, the Merciful" (*al-raḥmān al-raḥīm*)

(1) a command: "Read!"

(1) another authorization: "In the Name of your Lord"
(1) a definition: "Who created"
(2) an expansion on the previous definition: "Created the human being from a clot of blood"
(3) the command repeated: "Read!"
(3–5) three more definitions: "And your Lord is most generous, Who taught by the Pen, taught the human being what he did not know."

Now the name *Allāh* in the *basmala* precedes *Rabbika*; this arrangement makes the first use of *Rabb* an equational – that is, a one-for-one – definition of *Allāh*. The equation of *Rabb* with *Allāh* and the functional definitions of *Rabb* as creator, benefactor, and teacher, are well-suited to have inspired Muḥammad (after the initial shock) with confidence and a sense of familiarity. Both *Allāh* and *Rabb* were already known as divine names in pagan Mecca. The *basmala* strengthens the force of the command and introduces the name *Allāh*, but it adds no new element to the four (divine command, authorization, identification, covenant) present in the first twenty words of Sura 96.

If the *Fātiḥa* was the first revelation, then the Qur'ān began with the authorizing *basmala*. When we schematize it as we did Sura 96, it consists of:

(1)[34] an authorization: "In the Name of God"
(1) a definition: "the Compassionate, the Merciful"
(2–4) an expression of praise to Allāh followed by four synonymous definitions: Praise be to God Lord of the worlds (2), the Compassionate (3), the Merciful (3), Master of the Day of Judgment (4).
(5) a declaration of allegiance and dependence: "It is You Whom we worship and You Whom we ask for help."
(6) a petition for aid in achieving the goal, worded as an imperative: "Guide us on the Straight Path."
(7) a definition of that goal expressed both positively and negatively: "The Path of those whom You have blessed, not those with whom You are angry or those who have gone astray."

The structure is as tight and logically developed as that of Sura 96, but it moves in the opposite direction. Which party takes the initiative? In Sura 96, God addresses the Prophet and humanity; in the Fātiḥa, humanity addresses God. In other words, the Fātiḥa seems to refer to a relationship already established, not to be itself the formula that establishes the relationship. The hypothesized primacy of the imperative mood[35] lends support to the idea that it was God's command in Sura 96 that initiated the contact; while the authorization, definitions, and petition in Sura 1 are appropriate for a human being addressing a known deity, using the imperative mood as prayer: "Guide us!" For various reasons, few authorities accept the Fātiḥa as the first revelation. But because of the presence of the familiar name *Allāh* in the *basmala* and the elements of authorization and definition, and despite its reversal of the arrangement of Q 96:1–5, my own analysis cannot rule it out entirely on the basis of content.

Another candidate for primacy of revelation is Sura 74 *al-Muddaththir*.[36] After the *basmala*, it begins with a vocative, "O you who are wrapped in a mantle" (Q 74:1), followed by a command, "Rise and warn!" (2). More commands follow: "Magnify your Lord!" (3); "Purify your garments!" (4); "Shun all abomination!" (5), and so on. In light of the previous discussion, we should expect the imperatives to be accompanied by text establishing their authoritative status. Such references begin to appear in verse 8, but the transition is oblique and allusive: the verses do not speak of God's power or benefits but of a time "when the trumpet is sounded; on that day will be a Day of Distress" (8–9). Then they mention God's creation of a human who is ungrateful, stubborn, and haughty, and who will be punished as a result (11–25).

As an argument the passage is comparatively diffuse. There is no authorization for the series of commands except the *basmala*. The Lord (*Rabbaka*) is mentioned in verses 3 and 7 but not otherwise identified or defined. He describes his own actions in verses 11–14 using the first person singular: "Leave me alone with him whom I created alone, and to whom I granted extensive wealth and sons in his presence, and made his way smooth." The wording, however, is not that of a functional definition of *Rabb*, particularly when compared to the definitions in Sura 96.

Insofar as the imperatives in Sura 74 are directed at Muḥammad alone, they are commands and not commandments. But the sura does not close before a commandment – a generalized moral imperative – is imparted: "But no, this is surely an admonition, so let who will, remember it; but none will remember it except as God wills. He is surely the Lord of Righteousness and the Lord of Forgiveness" (Q 74:54–56). The command to remember may therefore be called the first commandment; that it was a command to *remember* is of utmost covenantal significance. In all, however, the sura seems not to be the first step in re-establishing a Covenant long forgotten but an elaboration upon human duties, failures, and punishments as judged by a Covenant that exists in full force.

Let us test the thesis that the first revelation is likely to contain command, authorization, and definition by applying it to three anomalous candidates for primacy of revelation. In his *Aḥkām al-Qur'ān*, Ibn al-ʿArabī[37] quotes and rejects a statement attributed to ʿAlī b. Abī Ṭālib that the first passage to be revealed was Q 6:151. The verse begins, "Say: Come, I will recite to you what your Lord has forbidden you: do not associate any entity with Him; be good to your parents; do not kill your children for fear of poverty ..." Once again, a Muslim source advances a command-passage as the first to be revealed. The initial commands (verses 151–153) are followed by a definition of the Book according to the benefits inherent in it (154–157): no greater sin exists than to call it false and turn away (157). Only at the end of the sura is the Author of the commands and the Book fully defined: he is Lord of the Worlds (162), he has no partner (163), he is Lord of all things, to whom all will return (164), he has made men his vicegerents on earth, and he is quick to punish and also forgiving and merciful (165).

The fifteen verses contain numerous other covenantal elements, such as the sacredness of life (verse 151), human capacity to adhere to the Covenant (152), mercy for doing so (155, tenfold in 160), punishment for failure to do so (157–159, 160), revelation of the Book to the Prophet Moses (154) and more broadly to two previous "communities" (*ṭā'ifatayn*) (156), and the rejection of polytheism by Abraham (161). It was surely its rich array of covenantal proofs that led some (including ʿAlī?) to conclude that this passage was the first to be revealed. But there is a more likely reason for the presence of these arguments: most accounts place verse 151 in the middle of a connected passage whose immediate beginning is a discussion of permitted and forbidden foods and whose context is a long demonstration of how to argue against Jews and polytheists. In short, Q 6:151 is not the beginning of anything.

Two European authors, Sir William Muir in his *Life of Mahomet* (1858–1861, with later revisions) and *The Coran, its Composition and Teaching* (1878), and the "socialist" Hubert Grimme[38] in his *Mohammed* (1895), used then-current theories about the nature of religious experience and scripture in offering their candidates for first revelation.

Muir's view of the Prophet and the Qur'ān is quite complex. In his opinion, Sura 103 *al-ʿAṣr*, one of the oath-suras, is the earliest; the other oath-suras date from the same period; and they are the words of Muḥammad and not of God.[39] Among them he includes the *Fātiḥa*, whose "petitions (though probably adapted subsequently to public worship) contain perhaps the germ of frequent prayer at this early period."[40] Some (e.g. Sura 95) use the first person plural. "The Oracle sometimes begins now to come direct from the Deity, speaking as 'We' and to Mohammad as 'Thou.'"[41] Apparently influenced by the Romantic view of religion as essentially an emotional or aesthetic experience, Muir sees a "harmony" between Muḥammad's "troubled world within" and the desolate landscape of Mt. Ḥirā', by which "the impulsive and susceptible mind of Muḥammad was wrought up to the highest pitch of excitement." Descriptions of nature are marked by "wild, rhapsodical language, enforced often with incoherent oaths."[42]

But does this in fact describe Sura 103? The first verse of the sura is an oath ("By Time" or "By the Sun turning" – *wa-'l-ʿaṣr*). Oaths are an element of the Covenant and were discussed in Chapter 1. Verse 2 defines the human condition ("humankind is in a state of loss"); verse 3 introduces an exception to that definition, in the form of a list of the saved ("those who believe, do good deeds, counsel each other to Truth, and counsel each other to patience"). The oath and the two definitions constitute a sober description of the human state without and within the Covenant, not a "wild rhapsody." Even if one associates the first suras with an emotional crisis experienced by the Prophet, Sura 103 seems an unlikely vehicle, as it is quite rational in tone. God is not mentioned at all, except in the *basmala*. If Islam originates from a re-establishment of the Covenant, Sura 103 is an inadequate basis, as it assumes more than it expresses. Finally, despite the psychological complexities that he introduced into the discussion, Muir had to revert to Sura 96, the choice of the majority, to explain adequately the beginning of Muḥammad's prophethood and of Islam. "Henceforth, he spoke literally *in the name of the Lord* ... every sentence ... prefaced by the divine command, 'SPEAK' or 'SAY'" (*qul*)[43] lest there appear to be any human influence in the message.[44]

Hubert Grimme chose Sura 111 *Tabbat* (or *al-Lahab* or *al-Masad*), according to Watt and Bell,[45] on the basis of "doctrinal characteristics." The sura is a curse upon "Abū Lahab," usually identified as an uncle of the Prophet, and upon his wife. A curse may be construed as a command or request to a superior power, but here that power is not identified, nor its relation to the one uttering the curse, nor the transgression that has earned the curse. Aside from the (presumably later) *basmala*, God is not mentioned at all. The only thing vaguely doctrinal about the sura is the wish in verse 2 that Abū Lahab's wealth not profit him in the face of the curse, an implication that earthly wealth is not a sign of virtue. By this theory, the virtual absence of doctrine makes Sura 111 the most "primitive" sura, beyond which others could only "evolve." Such a curse coming unheralded into his consciousness might well have fueled Muḥammad's reported fears that he was insane or afflicted by *jinn*. On the basis of content alone, however, and in the absence of precedent, context, or any other frame of reference, it is difficult to see how Sura 111 could have been construed as a revelation from God.

Once the power, authority, and authenticity of the Source of revelation have been established, all subsequent commands from that Source, however laconic, are logically valid. "O you who believe, fulfill your obligations" (Q 5:1). But even so, there are very few imperatives without either implicit contextual justification or explicit textual justification. It would seem that God does not order his creatures to do something in a way that ignores their desire to know why they must do it. Only occasionally is there an anomalous command whose relation to Divine Power is not clear without exegesis. Such is Qur'ān 2:104: "Oh you who believe, do not say *rāʿinā* ('listen to us') but say *unẓurnā* ('look upon us' or 'take care of us') and listen; and the unbelievers will have a painful punishment." The prohibition is expanded and explained in a later revelation, where the Jews are shown saying the word "twisting their tongues and attacking the religion" (Q 4:46). Exegetes describe the word as unpleasantly close to a Hebrew curse, or as having been deliberately mispronounced by the Jews to produce a repugnant meaning ("he is stupid" or "our evil one"), or as having had a bad connotation in the Jāhilīya, or as showing the same kind of disrespect for the Prophet as did raising one's voice above his (cf. Q 49:2). It may simply express preference for a neutral word over a word with specifically Islamic content, as *ḥadīth* enjoin believers to say *ʿinab* (grapes) instead of *karm* and *fatā* (youth) instead of *ʿabd* in non-religious contexts.[46] In any case, there is no explanation in the immediate context for ordering that the word not be used.

COMMANDS, COMMANDMENTS, AND PURPOSE

One of the chief activities of Islamic jurists and theologians has always been to decode the divine commands in Scripture and determine to whom they are addressed. Which divine imperatives were directed at people in general and which at a particular group? Which commands applied to Muḥammad alone and which were "categorical imperatives?" Which directives were absolute in their scope and which were qualified or restricted? Which were true commands and which were, in effect, only suggestions?

To answer these questions, Muslim thinkers combined Qur'ānic verses which had related content but were separated by textual order and period of revelation. They added historical glosses from what was known or conjectured of the occasion of revelation; and they supplemented revelation with *sunna* and other methods acceptable to their own schools of thought (*madhāhib*). Knowledge of the typology of divine command was a branch of the discipline known as "the foundations of religion" (*uṣūl al-dīn*). As Tāshköprüzādeh puts it in his section on "General and Particular" (*ʿāmm wa-khāṣṣ*): "The subjects of this science are part of the science of *uṣūl*, and whoever masters them will easily recognize them in the verses of the *Furqān*."[47]

Commandments by definition do not require a designated audience, because they apply to all. "O people, worship your Lord, Who created you and those who came before you, thus may you learn righteousness" (Q 2:21). "Do not associate any other deity with God, lest you be thrown into Hell, reproved and banished" (Q 17:39). Also not difficult to analyze are passages that clearly designate the recipients with a phrase such as "O you who believe"[48] and have the command in the plural: "O you who believe, remember God often, and glorify Him morning and evening; it is He who sends blessings upon you ..." (Q 33:41–43). "O Children of Israel, remember the favor that I have bestowed upon you, and that I have preferred you above all peoples; then guard yourselves against a Day when no soul will avail another in any way" (Q 2:122–3).

More complex are commands that apply only under certain conditions, or only to subgroups of the larger groups addressed. Some subgroups are by their nature temporary and potentially include all persons: travelers, debtors, pilgrims, those who are temporarily ill or infirm or in danger. Other subgroups, particularly gender groups, are permanent. Passages of limited applicability may begin with a command to perform a certain act, then enumerate conditions that modify the scope of that command:

> The punishment of those who wage war against God and His Apostle ... is execution, or crucifixion, or the cutting off of hands and feet on opposite sides, or exile from the land ... except those who repent before they come under your power ...
>
> (Q 5:33–4)

Qualified commands may begin with the qualifying conditions themselves:

> If you are afraid that you will not deal justly with the orphans, marry women of your choice, two or three or four; but if you fear that you will not deal justly with them, then only one, or what your right hands possess. Thus you are more likely not to stray from justice.
>
> (Q 4:3)

As can be seen from these citations, many exceptive constructions are found in legal arguments. These have a separate section in Chapter 5.

From an exegetical point of view, determining the scope of grammatically singular commands is far more difficult. Singularity adds another step to the task of identifying the target of the command, namely, determining whether the singular is generic or specific. When the possible conditions of a command are multiplied by this new factor, the number of potential interpretations increases proportionally. Fortunately for the exegetes, the proportion of singular to plural imperatives – of commands to commandments – is small, and the context clear.

Easiest to analyze is the singular command preceded by a vocative phrase designating the recipient: "O Abraham, turn away from this. The decree of your Lord has gone forth, and a penalty is coming for them" (Q 11:76). "O Apostle, proclaim what has been sent down to you from your Lord; if you do not, you will not fulfill His mission ..." (Q 5:67). More cryptic but still scarcely open to dispute are the descriptive allusions to the Prophet found in the openings of Suras 73 and 74. "O you who are enfolded in garments: rise [to pray] at night, except for a bit of it – half of it, or subtract a bit or add a bit ..." (Q 73:1–4). "O you who are wrapped in a mantle: rise and warn ..." (Q 74:1–2).[49]

Even when not preceded by a vocative, second-person singular commands from suras revealed to the Prophet before he began his public preaching might also be construed as directed at him alone, especially when they refer to his personal life; but it appears that very early on exegetes explained the commands as generalized moral imperatives and not solely as private orders from God. Thus the commands at the end of Sura 93 *al-Ḍuḥā* follow and parallel clear references to the actions of God in the Prophet's own life:

> Did He not find you an orphan and shelter you? And He found you straying and guided you, and found you poor and enriched you. Therefore, the orphan – do not oppress him; the beggar – do not drive him away; the bounty of your Lord – proclaim it.
>
> (Q 93:6–11)

Clear as this might seem, Mujāhid (d. 104/722), for one, made it more general, explaining the order to "proclaim it" not in terms of obedience to divine command but as a social act, as when a benefactor's good deed is publicized "so that he will adopt it as *sunna* and do similar things."[50] Abū Naḍra[51] saw it as part of the general moral principle of thanking the benefactor, *shukr al-munʿim*. Whatever the case, all explanations work to justify the command and thereby validate it, and none suggests that it was not directed at the Prophet.

Not all contexts are consistently singular or plural; the Qurʾān famously shifts back and forth between the two. Qurʾān 17:22–25 says:

> Do not take (masculine singular) another deity along with God ...Your (m.s.) Lord has decreed that you (masculine plural) are to worship none but Him ... Do not say (m.s.) a word of contempt to them ... Your (m.p.) Lord knows best what is in your hearts (m.p.)
>
> (Q 17:22–25)

Verses 26 through 30 are singular, 31 to 35 plural, 36 to 39 singular, and 40, which is the final verse in the sequence, plural. Given that the content of the sequence is clearly a series of commandments, the alternation of singular and plural here creates no obvious problems of compliance for believers.

Ambiguity may occur, however, when a singular order is enclosed within a plural context, such as when one member of a group is singled out to perform an action that certain existing conditions have made necessary. For an example, let us examine the first occurrence in Qur'ān 2:282 of commands in the singular, namely, the directive ordering the debtor to dictate the terms of the debt to the designated scribe, who is to record the debt and not refuse. The context is plural in that at least three individuals are involved; but when debtor, creditor, and scribe are spoken of together, there is no doubt which of the three is being commanded to dictate and which to write. That would seem to be simple enough when viewed as an argument justifying a command to a person in a particular role; however, a problem comes when we try to assign the relator pronoun *-hu* to one of its two possible antecedents.

> ... Let the debtor dictate, fearing God his Lord and not subtracting anything. If the debtor is mentally deficient, or infirm, or unable to dictate himself, let his guardian [or "let him to whom the debt is owed"] dictate fairly (*fal-yumlil walīyuhu bi-l-ʿadl*) ...
>
> (Q 2:282)

If the possessive *-hu* is construed as applying to the incapacitated debtor, the construction is that it is the debtor's guardian (*walīyuhu*) who is to dictate the terms of the debt. But when the pronoun is construed as applying not to the debtor but to the debt, the resulting interpretation is that it is not the guardian of the incapacitated debtor but the one to whom the debt is owed (*walīyuhu*) – that is, the *creditor* – who is to dictate the terms of the debt to the scribe.

The legal implications of this second interpretation are serious when one considers that nowhere is it specified that the scribe should record in the presence of both parties, only that the terms should be dictated faithfully, in the fear of God. This may have been necessary to facilitate long-distance commerce, but it could lead to a situation in which a creditor dictated the amount of debt owed by an incapacitated debtor who had no competent person present to represent him. Not only would this afford an opportunity for violation by an unscrupulous creditor no matter how many oaths he took, but such a consequence would also be contrary to God's stipulated purpose for decreeing that a record be kept. No better illustration could be found of the difficulties latent in even the most clear-sounding command. That is how a divine command may be Law without yet being *a* law. (The same verse will be further analyzed in Chapter 5.)

Finally, let us examine what is undoubtedly the most common singular imperative in the Qur'ān, the word *qul*, "say," which, according to 'Abd al-Bāqī's concordance, is repeated 332 times. Anyone who has threaded his/her way through an early *isnād* or a second-hand account of a debate is familiar with the ambiguity of the verb *qāla* in language which had not yet developed a consistent means of distinguishing direct from indirect speech or signaling a change in speakers. The Qur'ānic problem of levels of discourse is slightly different: how can a command to say a particular thing also be part of that which is to be said?

When it is God who is instructing Muḥammad in what he should say to refute the unbelievers, *qul* is necessary to the sense of the sentence, and the context is clear:

> And they say "The Fire will not touch us except for a certain few days." Say "Have you taken a promise from God, Who will never break His promise, or are you saying about God something you know nothing about?"
>
> (Q 2:80)

The problem is more acute when *qul* comes at the beginning of a sura, as it does in Suras 72, 109, 112, 113, and 114. Early exegetes inserted *yā Muḥammad* after *qul*[52] but do not appear to have concerned themselves with the logical problem of distinguishing the utterance from the command to utter it. In a passage which itself is not free from *qāla* -induced complexities, the grammarian Ibn Khālawayh (d. 370/980–1) solves the problem by interpolating yet another *qul*:

> *Qul* is an imperative. And if someone asks and says, "When the speaker says, 'Say "There is no god but God,"' you have to say, 'There is no god but God' and not add *qul*; so what is the reason for keeping the imperative *qul* in all of the Qur'ān?", the answer is that the meaning is understood to be "Say, O Muḥammad, 'Say He, God, is One'" (*qul yā Muḥammad qul huwa Llāhu aḥad* ...) and "Say, O Muḥammad, 'Say I take refuge in the Lord of the

> People;'" and the Prophet (S) said [it] as Gabriel dictated it to him from Almighty God. And Muḥammad b. Abī Hāshim informed us, from Thaʿlab, from Ibn al-Aʿrābī, who said, "It was said to a Beduin, 'What have you memorized from the Qur'ān?' and he said, 'I have memorized the suras of *al-qalāqil*,' that is, those that begin with *qul*." And in the text of Ibn Masʿūd it is "He, God, is One" without *qul*.[53]

In sum, while human beings may not be entitled to demand explanations from God, they are entitled to know their relation to him. Accordingly, Qur'ānic commands and commandments are usually accompanied by explanations of the results God will produce when his orders are obeyed, or of the circumstances which create the obligation to perform a certain action or achieve a certain state. In other words, God's commandments come with answers to the question "Why?" This demonstrates that God does not command human beings to do meaningless things for arbitrary reasons, a point consistent with the assertion that God has not created human beings in vain as indeed he does not do anything in vain:

> It is not in play that We created the heavens and the earth and what is between them. If We had wished to adopt a pastime, We should have taken it from Our own Presence (*min ladunnā*), if We were to do it at all.
>
> (Q 21:16–17)
>
> Did you think that We had created you for no reason and that you would not return to Us?
>
> (Q 23:115)

We have seen how the Covenant, the rule that defines the overall relationship between humanity and God, in turn generates sub-rules that govern particular actions, transactions, states, and relationships between human beings and God and among human individuals and groups. While the last two sections of the present chapter have focused upon a single type of sub-rule explaining the operation of divine command, and the previous chapter analyzed the rule of divine consistency embodied in the *sunna* of God, the next chapter will examine arguments whose *forms* are usually associated with the language of legal scholars but whose *content* may be anything from rules of etiquette to rules whose violation will bring eternal damnation.

5

LEGAL ARGUMENTS

Rules are not laws. A rule precedes a law in that it groups a set of circumstances, acts, and inferences according to the following schema: "In circumstances X, Y is required/permitted."[1] We have seen that both the Covenant as a whole and the individual components thereof fit the description of "rule" better than that of "law." In fact Mendenhall and Herion take care to point out that the "norms" for future behavior set out in §3 of their prototypical Covenant are to be distinguished from "laws," with which they are often confused.[2] Their "norms" (like those of von Wright) thus correspond to our "rules." By classifying the sorts of verses found in works of *aḥkām al-Qur'ān* and *uṣūl al-fiqh* as "rules" and not "laws," one is able to use rule-based reasoning to examine arguments in the Qur'ān from a perspective broader than that of the Islamic or any other single system of legal reasoning. Translating the word *ḥukm* as "rule" in its technical sense may indeed give a fresh perspective on that genre of scholarly works known as *aḥkām al-Qur'ān*: "Qur'ānic rules."

My aim in this chapter is to examine how the elements of rules – circumstance, conclusion, scope, and applicability – shape arguments whose clearest models are found in legal thinking. Unlike books on positive law, which are arranged by subject, this chapter on legal arguments (like all chapters in the book) is arranged according to the principle upon which each type of argument operates: reciprocity or recompense; priority, equivalence, or limitation; distinction or exception. We shall also examine what Aristotle called "non-artistic proofs" – laws, witnesses, contracts, torture, and oaths – which he classed not as logic but as a branch of rhetoric, and of which some are clearly analogous to legal arguments based on the Covenant. Finally, we shall examine the legal aspects of those speech acts known as "performative utterances" – "performatives" for short.

It must be emphasized that what is presented in this chapter is a small sample of the legal material found in the Qur'ān, and that short examples have been preferred to long ones.

RECIPROCITY AND RECOMPENSE

Reciprocity

The principle of reciprocity is the basis of the Covenant. It first occurs in the second of the eight covenantal elements,[3] which is also the first to mention both parties to the Covenant. Many of the Qur'ān's strongest arguments for pious behavior are those which show God and human beings engaged in reciprocal acts that produce mutual esteem and support, as well as concomitant obligations. One of the principal ways in which the Qur'ān argues for reciprocity is by using identical terms to describe the mutual obligations of the two parties:

> O Children of Israel! Remember My favor which I bestowed upon you, and keep My Covenant as I keep yours. And fear Me.
>
> (Q 2:40)

> O you who believe! If you will support God He will support you and give you a firm footing.
>
> (Q 47:7)

> ... God will bring a people whom He loves and who love Him ...
>
> (Q 5:54)

The fact that obligations are reciprocal, of course, does not always mean that the actions of both parties are identical:

> We have granted you abundance. Therefore worship God and sacrifice.
>
> (Q 108:1–2)

Humans can hardly "grant abundance" to God in return, nor does God need their "support" (as in Q 47:7, above) or obedience (e.g. Q 3:97, 14:8, 29:6, 47:38), nor will he be harmed in any way by their failure (Q 3:176–177, 47:32). Thus al-Qurṭubī (d. 671/1273), after citing numerous interpretations of God's command to the children of

Israel, "Keep My Covenant and I will keep yours" (Q 2:40, above), says that it includes all of his commands (*awāmir*), prohibitions (*nawāhi*), and commandments (*waṣāyā*), including "the mention (*dhikr*) of Muḥammad (*ṣallā Allāhu ʿalayhi wa-sallam*) that is in the Torah and elsewhere;" and that God's Covenant with them is that he will cause them to enter Paradise. He adds:

> I say: The keeping of the Covenant that is required (*maṭlūb*) of these is also required of us ... And their keeping of the Covenant of God is a sign (*amāra*) of God's keeping the Covenant with them for no [prior] cause (*la ʿillata lahu*): rather, it is [an act of] Grace (*tafaḍḍul*) from Him to them.[4]

The negative relationship between God and sinners likewise is sometimes expressed as a function of reciprocity:

> They are plotting a scheme, and I am plotting a scheme. So grant the unbelievers a delay: deal with them gently for a while.
>
> (Q 86:15–17)

> It will be said: "On this Day We forget you as you forgot that you would meet this Day of yours. Your resting place is the Fire, and you have no supporters!"
>
> (Q 45:34)

That relations between human beings are also ultimately governed by the Covenant is most clearly illustrated by the Qur'ānic concept of charity. It is a three-sided relationship: one person gives to another for God's sake, and God rewards the giver.[5]

> Whatever benefits you pay out are for your own souls, when you spend desiring only the Face of God. The benefits you give will be given back to you, and you will not be wronged.
>
> (Q 2:272, cf. 8:60)

In a similar schema, God's protection, guidance, and benevolence to the orphan Prophet are presented as the source of the Muslim's corresponding obligation to care for orphans and not turn away the indigent (Q 93:6–11).

Argument based upon the covenantal rule of *quid pro quo* extends to the relations between humans as well, where true reciprocity is required, whether in contracts (Q 2:282), alliances (Q 9:7), war (Q 2:191, 2:194), peace (Q 8:61), or social relations:

> When you are given a greeting, give a better greeting or return the same one: God takes account of all things.
>
> (Q 4:86)

In fact, the longest verse in the Qur'ān is the one that sets out the conditions for a legal contract (Q 2:282). I have already examined two aspects of this verse in Chapter 4 as examples of command and justification; but since "Contracts" have a separate identity in argument as the third of Aristotle's five "non-artistic proofs," they are treated below in this chapter.

The formula of negative reciprocity also describes hostility among human beings, but it is usually paired with examples of the positive reciprocity that is its antidote. For example, the passage in Sura 2 on the proper conduct of battle specifically articulates the principle of reciprocity, alternating between positive and negative formulations:

> And fight in the path of God those who fight you, but do not commit aggression:[6] God does not love the aggressors. And kill them where you find them, and expel them from where they expelled you, for *fitna*[7] is worse than killing. And do not fight them at the Sacred Mosque unless they fight you there; but if they fight you, then kill them: such is the recompense (*jazā'*) of those who disbelieve. But if they desist, God is forgiving and merciful ... The sacred month for the sacred month, and there is retaliation in kind (*qiṣāṣ*) for [violation of] sacred laws. And whoever acts aggressively against you, act aggressively against him in the same measure as his aggression against you; and fear God, and know that God is with the God-fearing.
>
> (Q 2:190–192, 194)

In my translation, each repeated English word indicates a repeated Arabic word. The passage has always been a challenge to exegetes, in that "aggression" is first forbidden, then – seemingly – commanded. Qurṭubī explains the apparent paradox as follows:

"And whoever acts aggressively against you, act aggressively against him" is an agreed-upon generality, whether [carried out] directly, if possible, or by means of arbitrators. People have differed over the matter of legal equivalence (*mukāfa'a*), whether [the second] can be called "aggression" or not. Whoever says, "There is no metaphor (*majāz*) in the Qur'ān" says "The equivalent (*muqābala*) is aggression, but it is permitted aggression (*'udwān mubāḥ*)" ... And whoever says that there is metaphor in the Qur'ān calls it "aggression" by way of metaphor and equating the word with what is similar to it .[8]

Recompense

Arguments from "reciprocity" shade into arguments based upon "recompense" (*jazā'*, *ajr*). The distinction is that "reciprocity" applies to the relation between one agent (divine or human) and another, "recompense" to the relation between an action and its reward or punishment.

> ... Whatever you spend in the cause of God will be repaid, and you will not be wronged.
>
> (Q 8:60)

> Whoever performs a good deed will have ten like it; whoever performs an evil deed will be punished only with its equivalent; and they shall not be wronged.
>
> (Q 6:160, cf. Q 27:89–90, 28:84)

Many passages include both reciprocity and recompense, both agent and reward:

> The recompense for an evil deed is an evil deed like it; but whoever forgives and reconciles will have a reward from God; for God does not love those who do wrong. And those who prevail after being wronged cannot be blamed in any way.
>
> (Q 42:40–41)

It is the sixth section of the prototypical Covenant that describes blessings for obedience and curses for disobedience; the eighth imposes those curses when the Covenant is actually broken. Here one may place the dozens of descriptions of Heaven and Hell and of the deeds that earned them, as well as passages that incorporate the "vanished nations" *topos*, where the ruins of previous civilizations that may be seen on the earth in this life are pointed out as evidence of divine recompense. Two short passages that combine explicit covenantal and punishment *topoi* will suffice as illustration.

> Those who fulfill God's Covenant (*ʿahd Allāh*) and do not break the pact (*mīthāq*) ... and fear their Lord ... and pray ... will achieve the Abode – gardens of Paradise which they shall enter ... And those who break God's Covenant after it has been compacted ... will have a curse upon them and the most evil Abode ...
>
> (Q 13:20–25)

> Say: "Travel in the earth and see just what the fate was of those who denied [the Apostles]." Say: "To whom belongs all that is in Heaven and Earth?" Say: "To God! He has written mercy [as a condition binding] upon Himself (*kataba ʿalā nafsihi al-raḥma*)."
>
> (Q 6:11–12)

Here, too, are the rules of proper requital for those acts defined by Revelation as crimes punishable in this world:

> O you who believe! [Equality in] retaliation (*al-qiṣāṣ*) is prescribed for you in cases of murder: the free for the free, the slave for the slave, the female for the female. He who is given a certain dispensation by the murdered man's brother should be prosecuted in the accepted way (*bi-al-maʿrūf*) and should compensate him in the best way (*wa-adāʾ ilayhi bi-iḥsān*): that is an alleviation from your Lord and a mercy. One who transgresses after that will have a painful punishment.
>
> (Q 2:178)

Thus the Covenant is present in human affairs, in that the laws which govern them arise from rules expressed as divine commandments. In Islamic law it is not only the criminal and the victim who must be conscious of divine scrutiny, but also the legal scholar and the judge, who translate the rules of the Qurʾān into the law of the land.

PRIORITY, EQUIVALENCE, AND LIMITATION

The Qur'ān as God's final revelation also sets the absolute criteria for arguments based upon comparison and contrast. While those rhetorical "common topics" will be found in the next two chapters, here we discuss their legal counterparts.

Priority

Difference and degree are facts in God's creation, even among the ranks of those in Heaven (Q 17:21, cf. Q 46:19). The Qur'ān instructs believers in the priorities of what already exists and guides them in assessing new situations according to these eternal priorities.

God is to be feared above human beings (Q 9:13), a rule that must be observed by the Prophet as well (Q 33:37). God and his Apostle (and, by implication, the community of believers) are to be set above everything else, including one's own family if they are not believers (Q 9:23–4). "The Prophet is closer to the believers than they are to each other (or "to their own souls" – *anfusihim*), and his wives are their mothers" (Q 33:6). A deed should please God and the Apostle before anyone else (Q 9:62). Relationships among humans follow an order of priority as well. One's relatives are closer to one than are other believers (Q 8:75, 33:6), but one must also treat friends fairly (Q 33:6). Muslims are to be preferred over unbelievers as friends and allies (e.g. Q 3:28), as spouses (Q 2:221), and as custodians of the mosque (Q 9:17–19). That strict observance of these priorities was not always easy is attested by the fact that even the Prophet was reproached for lapses of judgment: "... You feared the people, when it was more fitting that you should fear God ..." (Q 33:37; s.a. Q 80:1–10).

If means are of this world, ends are of the next, and the two must not be confused. Those who were the first to fight and spend in the cause of God have a higher rank than those who did not do so until later, though all are promised a good reward (*al-ḥusnā*) (Q 57:10), another instance of the law of recompense. Obedience and reasoned speech are more fitting (*awlā*) than fear when revelations come that speak of the necessity to fight (Q 47:20–21). Armed struggle is not the worst thing that can happen in this world. *Fitna*[9] is more serious than killing (Q 2:191, 2:217). "Blocking the path of God" and preventing access to the Sacred

Mosque are worse than fighting (Q 2:217). Justice must be preserved even if it means witnessing against oneself or one's own family (Q 4:135), but it is also justice to assume the best of others and not accuse them without witnesses (Q 24:12).

Equivalence

Declarations in the Qur'ān that certain actions are legally equivalent allow the believer – under certain conditions – variety and flexibility in complying with many Qur'ānic imperatives while observing both the letter and the spirit of the Law. Legal equivalence may also work the other way, determining that a doubtful action is in fact the equivalent of one that is expressly prohibited. The Qur'ānic model of legal equivalence clearly grants ordinary Muslims authority to make reasoned decisions concerning their own everyday practice (*'ibādāt*), as it grants jurists scope for solving difficult questions concerning interactions between two or more parties (*mu'āmalāt*).

The Prophet's role is partly defined as being God's surrogate on earth, thus strengthening his position and the obligation to obey him: twenty-six times people are commanded to "Obey God and the/His Prophet." That obedience to the second equals obedience to the first is stipulated in Q 4:80: "Whoever obeys the Apostle has obeyed God." Likewise, an oath to Muḥammad is an oath to God, with corresponding punishments for violation and rewards for fulfillment (Q 48:10).

One of the best-known functions of equivalence in the Qur'ān is the setting of compensation for a religious duty (*'ibāda*) that for some good reason a Muslim has had to miss. Whoever cannot fast because of a journey or illness is to make it up later; one who has the means may pay to feed one or more poor people, though fasting is better (Q 2:184–185). Likewise one who is prevented from finishing the pilgrimage may fast, feed the poor, or sacrifice, depending upon his means (Q 2:196).

Equivalence is invoked to explain the enormity of the sin of Cain:

> Because of that, We decreed for the Children of Israel that whoever kills a person – unless it is for murder or for spreading corruption in the earth – it is as though he killed all people, and whoever saves a life, it is as though he let all humanity live.
>
> (Q 5:32)

The penalties for murder and mayhem are their judicial equivalents, but alternative penalties exist as well.

> In that matter We have decreed against them a life for a life and an eye for an eye ... but whoever forgoes the retaliation by way of charity, it counts in his favor as an act of expiation ...
>
> (Q 5:45, cf. 16:126, 42:40–43)

The lives taken must be equivalent[10] – "the free man for the free man, the slave for the slave, the woman for the woman" – but the brother of the victim may request alternative compensation (Q 2:178). An even more elaborate set of equivalent compensations is available to a believer who kills another believer by mistake (Q 4:92).

Reasoning on the basis of equivalence applies as well in lesser matters than murder. If no scribe is available to write a contract, an item may be left as security (Q 2:283, also below). If the witnesses to a will are impeached, others may be advanced by the parties who stand to lose if the testimony is false, and all are to be bound with oaths (Q 5:106–108). If four witnesses cannot be produced to support a charge of adultery, oaths may be used by both sides (Q 24:4–9). And calculating equivalence in difficult questions of dower, financial support, and divorce occupies Muslim jurists to this day.[11]

One might expect to find under this rubric the Qur'ānic examples of equality before the Law (e.g. the first part of Q 2:228) and before God (e.g. Q 33:35) so often adduced as evidence for equal treatment of women in Islam. But strictly speaking, these are *identical* rights, not *equivalent* rights: they are granted by a single commandment to both males and females. Here we are concerned with assertions that two unlike or unequal things are to be considered equivalent. Thus a woman's share of inheritance (Q 4:11) and her testimony in contracts (Q 2:282) may be only half those of a man, but they are the *legal* equivalents in that they fulfill the Law equally. The same is true for the requirements of modesty in dress and deportment that are so much more burdensome for the woman than for the man (Q 24:30–31). Slave status brings inequalities among women as well: a slave woman's punishment for "indecency" (*fāḥisha*) is half that of a free woman (Q 4:25).

Limitation

One of the clearest legal concepts in the Qur'ān is that of limitation. There is, in fact, a Qur'ānic term for "limits," *ḥudūd*, which occurs fourteen times, always in the plural. "Limits" characterize fasting in Ramadan in terms of abstention from food and drink during daylight hours, and from marital relations during mosque retreats (Q 2:187). They define proper conduct of the spouses in marriage, divorce, and remarriage (Q 2:229–230, in which the word is used six times, 58:4, 65:1). Two *ḥudūd*-verses come at the end of the passage on proper division of inheritance; they promise Gardens for those who observe God's limits (Q 4:13) and the Fire for those who do not (Q 4:14). The remaining two verses describe those who do not know God's limits (the Beduins – Q 9:97), and those who do (the believers – Q 9:112).

Although the word has become a synonym for the severe canonical punishments, that equivalence is the result of juristic reasoning. Qur'ānic usage is only implicit. As Qurṭubī puts it,

> These rules (*aḥkām*) are God's *hudud*, so do not cross them ... *Ḥudūd* are barriers (*ḥawājiz*); and *ḥadd* is prevention (*manʿ*). That is why they call iron *ḥadīd*: because it prevents the weapon from reaching the body. And the doorman and the jailer are called *ḥaddād*, because [they] prevent the one in the house from leaving and the one outside from entering. God's *hudud* are so called because they prevent the inclusion of that which is not of them and the exclusion of that which is. Hence they are called *ḥudūd* in reference to sins, because they prevent those who have committed them from returning to something similar ...[12]

Thus by synecdoche the word came most commonly to mean not God's legal limits but the punishments for transgressing them.

> When God tried Abraham by means of commands (*kalimāt*) which he fulfilled, He said to him, "I am making you an *imām* for the people." He said, "And my descendants as well?" He answered, "My Covenant does not extend to wrongdoers."
>
> (Q 2:124)

Just as God's Covenant with Abraham had a limit (Q 2:124), his forgiveness has a limit as well. "God does not forgive having partners associated with Him, but He forgives whom He will for what is less than that ..." (Q 4:47, cf. Q 4:116). God will not go so far as to accept apostasy (e.g. Q 9:74), deathbed conversions (e.g. Q 4:17–18, cf. Q 63:11), pleas of ignorance after the apostles have come (Q 4:165), or the exercise of personal opinion in a matter that has already been decided by God and the Apostle (Q 33:36).

Behavior that is legal in itself becomes illegal when it goes beyond a certain limit.

> Those who preserve chastity, except with their spouses and those whom they own, are not to be blamed. But whose desires go beyond that – they are the transgressors (*al-ʿādūn*).
>
> (Q 70:29–31)

If there are limits on human behavior, there are corresponding limits to human responsibility. Punishment is limited to the extent of one's evil deeds (Q 28:84), and one person will not be charged with another's sins (Q 6:52, 10:41) or burdened beyond his or her capacity to comply.

> Say: Should I seek other than God as my Lord, when He is Lord of everything? Each soul draws upon itself only what it earns, and no one bears another's burden ...
>
> (Q 6:164, cf. Q 17:15, 23:62)

DISTINCTION AND EXCEPTION

The Qur'ān devotes many verses to instructing the hearer in legal as well as spiritual discernment. Although the legal arguments based on distinction and exception are not always readily distinguishable from each other, the textual examples fall roughly into two groups. Those arguments classed here as instances of "distinction" hold that two apparently similar acts or phenomena are in fact distinct: they do not come from the same source, do not apply to the same groups, or are simply stipulated as distinct by God for reasons which he may or may not explain. In those arguments classed as examples of "exception," the things excepted are in fact of the same genus as those from which they are excepted but are governed by some intervening rule, usually one which excludes certain circumstances as being beyond the actor's control. Some of the clearest examples contain the exceptive particle *illā*, but it is not always present. Nor does the presence of *illā* always signal an exception. As I demonstrate in Chapter 8, the very common negative construction "There is no *x* except it is *y*" masks a categorical proposition: "All *x*s are *y*s".

Distinction

> The good that reaches you is from God, while the evil that reaches you is from yourself ...
>
> (Q 4:79)

> [Satan] has no power over those who believe and rely completely upon their Lord. His power is only over those who take him as a patron and those who ascribe partners to God.
>
> (Q 16:99–100)

> Those who extort usury ... say "Selling is like usury" whereas God has permitted selling and forbidden usury ...
>
> (Q 2:275)

Perhaps the most fundamental legal distinction is that which identifies the source of an action, result, or judgment: does it come from God, from oneself, or from Satan? Some distinctions are generic: good is from God, evil from the self (Q 4:79, cf. Q 16:33, 17:7, 17:15). Satan has no power of his own, only that given him by humans (Q 16:98–100, cf. Q 15:52,14:22). It was God who put mercy in the hearts of the Christians, but they invented monkery on their own (Q 57:27). Sometimes the agent of a particular result, such as a victory in battle, is distinguished from other possible agents. At the battle of Badr, "You did not kill them but God killed them" (Q 8:17).

Motive is the second criterion by which an action is classified. Evil (*junāḥ, sūʾ*) that is done out of ignorance and repented of will be forgiven (Q 33:5, 16:119). Fighting is sometimes necessary and hence justified, but Muslims are not to be the aggressors (Q 2:190). Those who try to justify usury on the grounds of its similarity to trade are answered with the distinction that God has permitted trade but forbidden usury, although he will forgive that which was perpetrated before receiving divine guidance and not repeated afterwards (Q 2:275). God rewards believers according to the best of their deeds, and not all of these rewards are the promised *quid pro quo*: some are added from God's "uncovenanted grace" (*faḍl* – Q 24:38).

We have already seen a good example of distinction by category, namely, the Covenant made with Abraham that God stipulates does not extend to wrongdoers (Q 2:124). Distinctions between covenantal obligations and their corollaries may also be a matter of degree, such as the distinctions between the position of the husband in the family and that of the wife (Q 2:228) and between the requirements of modesty for the man and those for the woman (Q 24:30–31).[13] The Prophet is to counsel fervent believers who "swear their strongest oaths" to leave their homes if he so commands that they should not swear – reasonable obedience (*ṭāʿa maʿrūfa*) is more appropriate (Q 24:53).

Certain distinctions among non-Muslims have legal implications for Muslims as well. Not all of the People of the Book are sinners who reject the prophets; some believe in God, command good and forbid evil, and hasten to do good works (Q 3:112–114). Those non-Muslims who do not fight the Muslims or drive them from their homes are to be dealt with kindly and justly, but God's strictures apply to the rest (Q 60:8–9). And categories change: the believing refugee woman of *Sūrat al-Mumtaḥana* may be a foreigner but she is first of all a believer, hence a legal wife for a Muslim but not for an unbeliever (Q 60:10). Those whom the Muslims have been fighting become their brothers by accepting Islam, but not if they then violate their oaths (Q 9:7–12).

God stipulates certain distinctions in matters of *ʿibādāt*. In times of danger, prayers may be shortened without blame, and the believers may pray in shifts (Q 4:101–102); illness and travel may also affect prayer (Q 73:20). The rationale for these is clear, while the stipulation that hunting during the *ḥajj* is forbidden but fishing is not (Q 5:95–6) is more obscure and must be explained by extra-Qurʾānic references. Finally, divine stipulations expressly re-establish legal distinctions that humans have obscured, as when they call "sons" those who are adopted (Q 33:4–5) or divorce their wives by comparing them to their mothers (Q 33:45, 58:2).

Exception (*Istithnāʾ*)

The first Qurʾānic instance of the particle *illā* ("except") comes in the latter part of Q 2:26: *wa-mā yuḍillu bi-hi illā al-fāsiqīn* ("and by it He does not lead astray any except the sinners"). In his commentary on the verse, al-Qurṭubī gives the grammatical rule that enables the reader to distinguish a true exception (*istithnāʾ*) from a categorical statement of the form "There is no x except it is *y.*" To prove that the word *fāsiqīn* is made accusative not by the exceptive particle *illā* but by the transitive verb *yuḍillu*, Qurṭubī points out that exception can occur only after a grammatically complete statement (*ba'd tamām al-kalām*).[14]

> I bear witness that there is no deity except God ...

The *shahāda* and its closest Qur'ānic analogue are in the form of categorical denials followed by exceptions: "Know that there is no deity except God" (Q 47:19).[15] The word *ilāh*, "deity," signifies a genus, but the point of the declaration is that this is a genus with only one real member: all others are excluded as false or non-existent. A similar locution is slightly less emphatic: *Mā min ilāh illā Allāh* – "There is no deity except God" (Q 3:62).

Qur'ānic categories and their exceptions range from the broadest to the most exclusive:

> By the Age (or "the sun in the afternoon"), humanity is in a state of loss, except those who believe, and do good works, and counsel each other to be truthful, and counsel each other to be patient.
>
> (Q 103)

> O Prophet! We have made lawful ... [marriage with] a believing woman who dedicates herself to the Prophet, if the Prophet wishes to marry her – this is only for you and not the [rest of] the believers (*khāliṣa laka min dūn al-mu'minīn*) ...
>
> (Q 33:50)

As the Law creates categories, it creates exceptions to those categories. In another example having to do with marital law, certain classes of women are absolutely prohibited as legal wives: mothers and stepmothers, daughters and stepdaughters, sisters and foster-sisters, aunts and nieces, daughters-in-law and women who are each other's sisters.[16] Then comes the exception: existing marriages are excluded from the prohibition (*illā mā qad salaf* – Q 4:22–23).

The Qur'ān occasionally makes exceptions even for actions that ordinarily would be very serious sins. For example, those who make war against God and his Apostle but repent freely before being conquered are exempt from the normally very heavy punishments (Q 5:33–34). Muslims are commanded not to kill, but an exception is made for just cause (Q 17:33). Disobedience to parents is generally among the most serious of the sins after unbelief,[17] but there is an exception even to that rule, if the parents attempt to force *shirk* on the children (Q 29:8); Abraham himself suffered this painful experience (Q 6:74, 9:114, 19:41–50).

But what of cases in which the Qur'ān omits part of an argument? As Bernard Weiss notes, "... the total context must be taken into account, not just the immediate context."[18] Thus an important exception to the law against *kufr*, which allows verbal expressions in cases of compulsion under threat as long as the heart stays faithful, is expressed as a condition without a consequent:[19]

> Whoever declares unbelief in God after believing [in Him], except one who is compelled to do so, while his heart remains certain in faith – but whoever opens his breast to unbelief, the wrath of God is upon them and they shall have a painful punishment.
>
> (Q 16:106)

Ṭabarsī describes the syntax in terms of "implication" (*taqdīr*) and "abridgement" (*talkhīṣ*), pointing out that the next applicable passage comes four verses later:[20]

> But your Lord – to those who left their homes after being persecuted (*futinū*), then struggled (*jāhadū*) and persevered – your Lord, after these things, is forgiving and merciful.
>
> (Q 16:110)

Most juridical opinion on this passage concerns the legal status of the believer's forced renunciation. Jaṣṣāṣ, for example, emphasizes the necessity for the mental reservation mentioned in the Qur'ān; without it, the person forced to renounce Islam in fact becomes a *kāfir*. Similarly, one who is forced to curse the Prophet Muḥammad must mentally direct his curse at someone else named Muḥammad, otherwise he will in fact have cursed the Prophet. On the lenient side, Jaṣṣāṣ cites a *hadīth* to the effect that error (*khaṭa'*) and forgetfulness (*nisyān*) have the same effect as force in nullifying the penalty for behavior that would otherwise be sinful.[21] Ultimately, however, he spurns these mental games. "Our colleagues have said that the best thing is not to use dissimulation and not to exhibit *kufr*, even to be killed, even if something else is permissible for him."[22]

There are numerous examples in which the consequences of an action – legal or illegal – are distinguished from the action itself and are judged separately. A parallel to the forced *kufr* in Q 16:106 exists in verse 115 of the same sura (though without an exceptive particle): one who is forced by necessity to eat forbidden foods – "not wanting to do so and not doing it again" – will be shown mercy. The giver of charity must do so in God's name, yet it appears that some early worshippers tried to hedge their bets by assigning a "share" (sc. of tithes or sacrifices) to their idols and another share to God. But God is not mocked: all such "shares" are tainted by the process of division and God will have none of them (Q 6:136). By contrast, it is not obvious that spurning a strange god should be discouraged; yet too-zealous Muslims who curse the idols of others may cause the others to curse God, not an improvement of the situation (Q 6:108). Prey partly eaten by animals is unlawful unless slaughtered properly (Q 5:3); however, the quarry of animals "which you train to hunt as God has taught you" is lawful, provided that God's name is pronounced over it (Q 5:4).

War always requires especially stringent measures. Retreat in battle will bring eternal punishment, except that which is carried out for tactical reasons (Q 8:16). Without exception all are required to fight who have the means and the physical ability; but no blame will attach to the weak or the sick or those for whom no mounts can be found (Q 9:91–2), only (*innamā*) to those who have the means but make excuses to stay behind (Q 9:93–6). Treaties are to be observed, however disadvantageous, even with the polytheists (Q 9:7–10); but violators are to be fought and God will help the believers (Q 9:12–16).

ARISTOTLE'S FIVE "NON-ARTISTIC" PROOFS

In Chapter 15 of Book I of the *Rhetoric*, Aristotle discusses five "non-artistic" or "non-technical" proofs (*atechnoi pisteis*): laws, witnesses, contracts, evidence [of slaves] taken under torture, and oaths. A modern translator describes them as "documentary evidence that could be read out and used as a basis of argument in a trial."[23] They were "non-artistic" because the orator did not have to invent them; he needed only to *use* them, because they already existed.[24] The fact that Aristotle restricted them to forensic rhetoric need not limit their usefulness to us as a well-established, independent set of techniques with which to compare our list of "legal" arguments. There is one exception: nowhere does the Qur'ān mention, let alone validate, the use of torture.[25]

Laws

Much of Aristotle's discussion of laws as proofs turns on the difference between written laws, which change, and "common law," which he sees as the unchanging repository of fairness and justice. He instructs the orator in the argument appropriate to each so that he may argue on the basis of whichever one is in his favor.[26]

The Qur'ān, of course, also recognizes an unchanging Law, identifying both the realm of justice and the laws of nature with divine order. We have seen how, beginning with the earliest revelations, the Law embodied in the Covenant was used as a rule to validate arguments. The signs of God in creation and the Book that explains their significance once and for all constitute a message beyond which there is no guide and no salvation:

> Will they not look at the kingdom of the heavens and the earth and all the things that God has created? It may be that their time on earth is coming to an end. In what Message (*ḥadīth*) after this will they believe?
>
> (Q 7:185, cf. Q 45:6, 77:50)

As for contrasting the law of God with the laws of men, human beings outside the Covenant are rarely credited with anything like laws: the usual references are to "opinion" (*ẓann*, e.g. Q 6:116) or "desires" (*ahwā'*), with an occasional hint of something more:

> Judge between them by what God has sent down and do not follow their desires (*ahwā'ahum*); and beware lest they charm you away from part of what God has sent down . . . Is it the *ḥukm* (judgment, rule) of the Jāhilīya that they want? But who is better than God with respect to judgment for a people whose faith is certain?
>
> (Q 5:49–50)

Witnesses

As Aristotle understood the term, "witnesses" are, first, poetry, proverbs, and other repositories of knowledge and wisdom; and second, the judgments of "well-known persons ... for their judgments are also useful in controversies about similar things."[27] Only in the third instance are witnesses people with knowledge of the event in question or of the character of the litigants; and Aristotle holds their factual knowledge to be of less importance than that of persons who can judge whether the act or a similar one was just or unjust, even if they have no other knowledge of the incident under adjudication. One who has no witnesses should call for a judgment on the basis of probabilities.[28]

The notion of "witness" in the Qur'ān is more complex.[29] It has already been discussed at length as one of the fundamental components of the Covenant, and numerous examples have been cited.[30] God himself is sufficient witness (e.g. Q 6:19, 46:8, 48:28), though it is not always clear when the word *shahīd* has its covenantal sense and when it is used as one of the names of God indicating omniscience (e.g. Q 41:53). A prophet is called *shahīd*, sometimes in the context of the Abrahamic Covenant (Q 22:78), and sometimes as a witness against his own people's transgressions (e.g. Q 16:89). Poetry and proverbs as evidence in the Qur'ān are out of the question, of course, nor is the Qur'ān itself called *shāhid* or *shahīd*, though sometimes context seems to imply it. "The unbelievers say, 'You are not an apostle (*mursal*).' Say: 'God is sufficient witness (*shahīd*) between you and me and whoever has knowledge of the Book'" (Q 13:43).[31]

In matters of law among human beings, the Aristotelian and the Qur'ānic concepts of witness are slightly more congruent. A "witness" (*shāhid* and *shahīd* are both used) is sometimes one with first-hand knowledge of disputed facts (e.g. Q 12:26, 46:10), sometimes a party's character witness (Q 5:107), sometimes a witness (or judge) because of his own good character (Q 5:95, 5:106, 65:2), sometimes a reliable supporter of one of the interested parties (Q 2:282), and sometimes just anyone handy (Q 2:282).[32] Finally, the word may simply indicate one who is present at a given time and place (Q 28:44). If killed there in a good cause, he is a martyr (Q 3:140).

Contracts

Aristotle's "Topics For and Against Contracts" are a mini-course in the tactics of negotiation: it is tempting to quote them in full. First, it must be established whether a contract exists; the same criteria are to be applied as those for witnesses. If there is a contract, the speaker supporting it can say

> ... a contract is a law that applies to individuals and particulars; and contracts do not make law authoritative, but laws give authority to contracts made in accordance with law, and in general the law itself is a certain kind of contract, so that whoever disobeys or abolishes a contract abolishes the laws[33]

Crime + Punishment

If opposing the contract, the speaker must determine whether it conflicts with laws or with existing contracts, "for later contracts take precedence, or else the earlier ones are authoritative and the later ones fraudulent (whichever argument is useful)."[34]

It has been amply demonstrated that in the Qur'ān the Covenant is the basis of all laws and the prototype for all contracts. Arguing against the existence of the Covenant is by definition impossible for Muslims, but much Qur'ānic argument serves to amplify its details for sincere questioners and hammer home its implications for quibbling hypocrites. The most vivid argument over the content of a "contract" is surely that ascribed to the Children of Israel in their attempt to evade their covenantal duty to sacrifice a cow (Q 2:67–71). Which cow? What color? "All cows look alike to us ... Then they sacrificed her, but they nearly did not" (Q 2:70–71). Many of the legal arguments already cited have contractual aspects as well, particularly those dealing with marriages, peaceful intercommunal relations, treaties, alliances, and commercial contracts. It would be superfluous to repeat them.

Coincidentally, the Qur'ān contains its own mini-course on contracts in the form of a very long verse which instructs the believers in proper procedure regarding debts, record-keeping, and contracts. It uses an arsenal of techniques – commands, exceptions, rationales – all of which we have discussed previously; thus it is a suitable subject for extended analysis according to the techniques that we have so far introduced.

My English rendering is provisional, reflecting some interpretation of terms on which differences of opinion have been recorded; the most important of these variants has been given in square brackets:

> O you who believe, when you contract a debt for a designated period of time, write it down. Let a scribe write

> it fairly, and let no scribe refuse to write – let him write as God has taught him to do. Let the debtor dictate, fearing God his Lord and not subtracting anything. If the debtor is mentally deficient, or infirm, or unable to dictate, let his guardian [or "the creditor"[35] – *walīyuhu*] dictate fairly. Call two witnesses from among your men, but if there are not two men, then a man and two women from among the acceptable witnesses, so that if one goes wrong the other can remind her. The witnesses are not to refuse when they are called. Do not be averse to writing it down, whether small or great, along with its term: that is fairer in the sight of God, more suitable as evidence, and more convenient to avoid doubt among yourselves; however, if it is a transaction carried out on the spot among you, then there is no harm in not writing it down. But take witnesses whenever you buy and sell to each other, and let neither scribe nor witness suffer harm: if you do, that would be a transgression on your part. So fear God, for God teaches you; and God knows all things.
>
> (Q 2:282)

Though the first phrase addresses all believers, the first verb limits the target audience to debtors. Then "debt" is defined, limited here to debt that is incurred for a fixed term. Finally a command is uttered: "write it down."

The first imperative is followed immediately by another set aimed at ensuring that the debt is properly recorded and attested.

First, the manner of recording is defined: it is to be done by an impartial scribe, who may not refuse to do so. The mood of the verb is not the imperative (*'amr*) but the jussive (*majzūm*). This reminds us that the root of the Latin term "jussive" is *jussum*, "command," that the Arabic positive imperative is derived from the jussive, and that the negative imperative *is* the jussive. Thus the jussive in Arabic is not primarily a surrogate perfect but an imperative. The debtor is commanded to dictate the terms accurately. If conditions obtain under which he cannot do so, his guardian is directed to act for him. The identity of this guardian is not specified, so presumably the word refers to the debtor's nearest male relative, but clearly cases would arise requiring a more precise definition of the concept of guardianship. As pointed out in Chapter 4,[36] another interpretation construes the possessive pronoun *-hu* as referring not to the debtor but to the debt itself, meaning that it is the creditor who is to do the recording. In any case, the debt is to be recorded.

Second, attestation is to be carried out by a specified number of male witnesses, or the legal equivalent. The witnesses, like the scribe, may not refuse, another third-person imperative.

Third, believers are given the reasons why these commands must be carried out, not divine fiat but earthly practicality: it is more equitable and certain, less open to doubt arising from differing recollections of the event.

Fourth, an exception to the rule is stipulated: on-the-spot transactions need not be recorded.

Fifth, the command to witness transactions is reiterated, assuming that the verb *tabāyaʿtum* is a synonym of the initial verb in the verse (i.e. *tadāyantum*)[37] and not a distinct type of transaction.

Sixth, the command is given that both scribe and witnesses are to be held harmless when fulfilling their duty to their fellow Muslims. Refusal to perform the function is not an option, but no penalty is specified.[38]

Finally comes the command to fear God who teaches and who knows all. The effect is to elevate the preceding stipulations above mere practical imperatives by the reminder that they have come from God.

Clearly, the legal concepts that occur in the verse – sale, debt, record, witness, legal competency, guardianship, immunity – are vast topics requiring much juridical expertise to refine. Later commentators added a note of textual complexity to this existing legal complexity. Certain authorities advanced the notion that the command to keep records had been abrogated by the subsequent verse (Q 2:283), which they interpreted to permit waiving the requirement for records in circumstances in which there was trust between the parties; while others construed the "trust" clause as rendering the whole matter of keeping records a recommendation rather than a requirement.[39] But the textual sequence of imperatives, provisions for their modification, and reasons for their existence is not affected by these extraneous considerations. The verse remains a prime example of how the Qur'ān combines multiple techniques to form a complex reasoned argument.

Oaths

Oaths as Aristotle describes them overlap very little with oaths described in the Qur'ān. Aristotle does not even reproduce an example of the oaths used in Greek courts of law. It is not the oaths themselves that are evidence to Aristotle but the parties' relative willingness or unwillingness to swear; because, although the judges were sworn, oaths were evidently not required of the litigants. False oaths were a problem, of course, but those reluctant to swear were not necessarily guilty. Aristotle quotes the poet Xenophanes (fl. ca. 500 BCE) to the effect that an oath is less serious to an irreligious man than to a religious man[40]

Oaths are prominent in the Qur'ān.[41] First of all, they are elements of the Covenant between God and humanity, as we have demonstrated at length in Chapter 1. Any serious oath between humans echoes the Covenant in that it is, in Mendenhall and Herion's incisive phrase, "a conditional self-cursing: i.e. an appeal to [God] to bring certain penalties upon the oath-taker if he violates the promise that he is swearing to keep."[42] God commands people to keep their oaths (Q 5:89, 16:91), but those unable to keep oaths made in good faith may compensate for them in prescribed ways (Q 5:89). Sometimes God mandates the dissolution of oaths (Q 66:2), but the word used, *taḥilla*, indicates that that is to be done for a higher purpose.[43] The strongest language is reserved for those who swear falsely to the Prophet (e.g. Q 9:95–96, 58:14–19) or break their oaths to him (Q 9:74, 48:10) or to God (Q 3:77). Those who broke the treaties made at the Sacred Mosque (Q 9:7) and attacked the religion were to be fought (Q 9:12), the more so as they intended to expel the Apostle and were the aggressors (Q 9:13).

Clearly, false or frivolous oaths were a problem in Arabia as well as in Greece. Oaths that are not meant seriously (Q 2:225, 5:89) will not bring punishment, but one who uses oaths constantly or indiscriminately is called "despicable" (*ḥallāf mahīn* – Q 68:10). God *will* call to account those who swear oaths to collude in wrongdoing (Q 2:224–25, 16:92, 16:94) and the waverers (Q 5:53) and hypocrites (Q 63:1–2) who screen their machinations with false oaths.

The Qur'ānic role of witnesses is related to that of oaths, as we have seen, though establishing the precise relationship made work for lawyers.[44] Greek litigants had the option of not swearing oaths in court, but it does not appear that the Qur'ān allows refusal. We have seen that Muslims may not refuse when called upon to be witnesses to a contract (Q 2:282). Oaths may be part of that function, as they clearly are in the case of the two witnesses to a will made by one who is dying: they are to be taken aside after prayer to swear that they wish to gain nothing thereby (Q 5:106). If it becomes known that they have sworn falsely, oaths against them are to be sworn by those whose inheritance was affected (Q 5:107); but there apparently the matter is to end, lest it result in an infinite series of oaths (Q 5:108).

AN EXCURSUS ON PERFORMATIVE UTTERANCES

Which characters in the Qur'ān meet the criteria of "believers"? Of "Muslims"? Is there a difference?

> The desert Arabs say, "We believe (*āmannā*)." Say: "You have not believed; rather say 'We have submitted (*aslamnā*),' for faith has not yet entered your hearts ..."
> (Q 49:14)

This passage introduces a sequence of verses (Q 49:14–18) that explains the difference between "belief" (*īmān*) and "submission" (*islām*), and between the verbs *āmana* and *aslama*, the latter being the appropriate designation for "outward and physical"actions as yet unaccompanied by the proper "inward and spiritual" state. It is intriguing to note that although the noun *mu'min* occurs far more often than *muslim*, no one truthfully states that he is a *mu'min* except the Prophet (Q 10:104), Moses (Q 7:143), the followers of Ṣāliḥ (Q 7:75), and Pharaoh's repentant magicians (Q 26:52). By contrast, people declare themselves *muslimūn* or *min al-muslimīn* some sixteen times, in five of which they are instructed to make such a declaration; in three more instances, the verb is used to the same effect.[45] None, of these declarations is called invalid, not even that of Pharaoh, who makes his act of faith after seeing the Children of Israel saved from drowning (Q 10:90). The passages look at first like definitions, but I believe that they are better understood as examples of those curious speech acts known as "performatives."

A performative utterance is one that does not describe an action but itself constitutes that action, when said under the proper circumstances by one with authority to do so.[46] Very often these have legal import: "You're under arrest!" "I declare this court adjourned." "I accept your offer." "I now pronounce you husband and wife." The last example bridges law and religion, perhaps the origin of such utterances. For example, many of the Christian sacraments are or are accompanied by performatives: "I baptize you in the Name of the Father, the Son, and the Holy Spirit." In the Qur'ān, human beings' acceptance of the Covenant is a speech act (Q 7:172), as are God's curse upon Iblīs until the Day of Judgment (*inna 'alayka al-la'na* – Q 15:35) and his grant of a stay of punishment until the Day of Resurrection (*fa-innaka min al-munẓarīn* – Q 15:37). In actual practice, uttering the *shahāda* with intent, in the presence of Muslims, is considered to make one irrevocably a Muslim: "I witness that there is no deity but God; I witness that Muḥammad is the Messenger of God."

Speech acts seem to be the appropriate models for such verses as Q 2:133:

> Were you witnesses when Death appeared to Jacob, when he said to his sons, "What will you worship after me?" They said, "We shall worship your God and the God of your fathers Abraham and Ishmael and Isaac: One God, and we [hereby] submit to Him."
>
> (Q 2:133)

The concluding phrase *wa-naḥnu lahu muslimūn* may be a simple statement of adherence; but given the occasion, I consider that this deathbed promise is more appropriately viewed as a speech act, a formula that once spoken creates an irrevocable commitment. Two other verses contain even longer lists of undertakings and conclude with a similar phrase (Q 3:64) or the same one (Q 3:84). People ask or are advised to die as Muslims (Q 2:132, 3:102, 7:126, 12:101). In such cases, an unverifiable inner state would lack the legal force of a formal verbal undertaking.

> Religion in God is Islam. And those who were brought the Book did not differ among themselves until after knowledge had come to them, out of mutual envy ... So if they argue with you, say: "I have committed myself (*aslamtu wajhī*)[47] to God, as have those who follow me." And say to those who were brought the Book, and the *ummīyīn*: "Have you committed (*a-aslamtum*)?" And if they commit, then they are rightly guided. If they turn their backs – well, you have only to give them the message. God sees His servants perfectly.
>
> (Q 3:19–20)

The verb phrase *aslamtu wajhī* (Q 3:20) and its analogues (e.g.

Q 2:112, 4:125) may at some point in history have signified an actual prostration; but if the utterance is understood as a speech act, physical prostration has become superfluous because the words *are* the act. It is also significant that when a verb occurs in the formula, it is most often in the perfect aspect, as in wishes, curses, and other magical utterances. That which is desired is spoken of as already having taken place.

It is worth noting that Jaṣṣāṣ, in his interpretation of the phrase "There is no compulsion in religion" (*lā ikrāha fī al-dīn* – Q 2:256), holds that the Islam of one who has been compelled to accept it is valid under law, as are forced manumission of slaves and forced divorce.[48] This is to be contrasted with his position that forced *kufr* is invalid.[49] While he admits that Mālik and al-Shāfiʿī did not validate forced divorce, manumission, or marriage, his own Ḥanafī colleagues accept it on the grounds that the relevant verses (Q 2:230, 16:91, 5:89), like Q 2:256, do not contain the crucial element of mental reservation present in Q 16:106. This lends strength to the idea that the verbal formula is legally effective and irreversible regardless of the circumstances under which it was uttered.

Not every word can be a speech act. Even though apostasy can occur after *islām* (Q 9:74) as it can after *īmān* (Q 2:109, 3:106, 9:66, 16:106), we have seen that no act of *islām* is said to be invalid. Contrast this with the verb *āmana*: of the thirty-two times that people say "We believe," eighteen of them are true statements, one is true for some and false for others, and fully twelve of them are lies. Those who call themselves *mu'minūn* are not necessarily such (Q 2:8, 5:41–43, 24:47), but none who call themselves *muslimūn* are said to be liars, hypocrites, or unbelievers *at the same time*, though in the end they may disbelieve. This appears to support the theory that a *muslim* is one who has performed a particular audible, visible act, while a *mu'min* is such by virtue of an interior state verifiable only by God.

A performative that does not fulfill the necessary conditions is not called "false" but "unhappy," "infelicitous," or – in Austin's vivid term – a "misfire."[50] When, after dying and being faced with punishment, unbelievers say, "We believe!", it is too late (Q 40:84–5, cf. Q 34:52, 32:29, 15:2). Their profession of faith is ineffective, because the time and place necessary for the validity of the act have vanished.

The verb *kafara* on certain occasions also shows characteristics of a speech act. The people of Noah and the nations of ʿĀd and

Thamūd reject their prophets by saying, "We deny (*kafarnā*) that with which you have been sent" (Q 14:9, cf. Q 7:76, 41:14). Abraham and those with him use the same formula to reject the false gods of their tribe (Q 60:4). The sinners use the word on the Day of Judgment to repudiate the false gods they used to associate with God: "*Kafarnā bi-mā kunnā bi-hi mushrikīn*" (Q 40:84). And in a supremely ironic usage, Satan utters the word to declare his rejection of that to which he himself has seduced the doomed sinners:

> God gave you a true promise. I gave you a promise and I broke it ... I hereby repudiate (*kafartu*) your previous acts of associating me [with God]. Certainly the wrongdoers will have a painful penalty!
>
> (Q 14:22)

Other passages (e.g. Q 4:150–151, 34:31) show "those who disbeliev(ed)" (*alladhīna kafarū*) making declarations of unbelief, but it is not clear whether it is those or prior declarations that have earned them the designation. Sometimes participles are used instead of conjugated verbs, but with the same effect: those of the "arrogant party" who reject the prophet Ṣāliḥ declare, "We reject what you believe in (*innā bi-lladhī āmantum bihi kāfirūn*)" (Q 7:76); others say, "We reject that with which you have been sent (*innā bi-mā ursiltum bi-hi kāfirūn*)" (Q 34:34; cf. Q 41:14, 43:24 and 30).

One apparently does not become a *mushrik* by simply declaring oneself to be, but a declared rejection of *shirk* is an effective speech act. Three times a formula occurs in which the speaker formally dissociates himself from the polytheistic practices of others. The Prophet (or any hearer) is told in Q 6:19 to declare *innī barī' mimmā tushrikūn*: "I am innocent of whatever you associate with [God]." Abraham uses the same formula to his people after concluding that the heavenly bodies are not divine (Q 6:78); he follows that with another very significant speech act: "I turn my face (*wajjahtu wajhī*, cf. *aslamtu wajhī*) to the Creator of heavens and earth as a monotheist (*ḥanīf*^{an}), and I am not among the *mushrikīn*" (Q 6:79). Finally, Hūd calls his people to witness that "I am innocent of whatever you associate with [God] that is not He (*min dūnihi*)" (Q 11:54–55).

The fields of Qur'ānic exegesis and Islamic law are still largely separate, despite the existence in both of books on *aḥkām al-*

Qur'ān. Al-Qurṭubī's *al-Jāmi' li-Aḥkām al-Qur'ān*, "well organized and extremely usable,"[51] appears to be the one most widely consulted, and I have used it with great profit. Books of this genre are keys to the analysis of Qur'ānic argument in general but have a practical importance in that they also help to define real-world acts as within or without the Law, as exempt from or subject to real punishment. God knows what is in the heart; humans must reason correctly about their own and others' actions.

6

COMPARISON

Comparison is an activity of the intellect fundamental to humans' understanding and evaluation of the world; and it is one of the principal means used in the Qur'ān to teach moral and spiritual discernment. Most Qur'ānic arguments contain elements of comparison or contrast,[1] especially the legal arguments,[2] which by definition prefer the better over the worse and the just over the unjust. The four categories of comparison treated in this chapter are similarity, analogy, parable, and degree, the first and last of which contain subcategories as well. Both Classical Arabic and Classical Western rhetoric have developed topics and figures of speech for multiple aspects of comparison, demonstrating that though fundamental, the mental exercise is hardly simple. Some of the topoi and tropes from both traditions are appropriate to the present discussion, but others are not, for example, those whose effects depend upon Arabic etymology and rhetoric and thus can only with difficulty translated or schematized as complete arguments.

SIMILARITY

"Similarity," says rhetorician Edward P.J. Corbett,

> is the basic principle behind all inductive argument and all analogy ... The rhetorical form of induction ... is the example – drawing a probable conclusion from a single instance of similarity. Perhaps the simplest way to differentiate analogy from induction by example is to say that whereas analogy argues from the similarities of dissimilar things, example argues from the similarities of similar things.[3]

The Qur'ānic similarities examined here are mainly those signaled by the word *mithl* (and occasionally *mathal*). They fall naturally into three groups: similarity of genus, similarity of action, and similarity of consequence. We shall first consider examples of each class individually, then see how they are combined in stories of the prophets to form something very like a logical analogy.

Similarity of genus

The Qur'ān shows great concern to distinguish the genus of all created beings from that of the Divine. Thus we have seen that an important element of the definition of prophets is that, like the people to whom they are sent, they are *human* beings. An apparently simple example of this is Qur'ān 3:59: "Jesus with God is like Adam: He created him from dust, then said to him 'Be!' and he was." This is in fact the culmination of a preceding sequence of verses demonstrating that the relation of Christ Jesus son of Mary (Q 3:45) to God is that of Apostle (Q 3:49–58). This point has double implication: (1) if Jesus is an apostle, he is not the son of God; (2) if he is an apostle, then he is human. Humans also confuse God with man-made idols. One way in which the Qur'ān addresses this confusion is to show that humans and idols alike are of the genus of created beings. "Those whom they invoke besides God create nothing and are themselves created – dead things, not living, nor do they know when they will be raised up" (Q 16:20–21; cf. 17:57, 22:73).

The generic similarity between earthly rewards or punishments and their counterparts in the hereafter is only linguistic, but hypocrites and unbelievers may ignore the difference until it is too late:

> Know that your wealth and your children are only a temptation (*fitna*), and that it is God Who has with Himself the supreme reward.
>
> (Q 8:28)
>
> Among the people are those who say "We believe in God", but when they are persecuted for God's sake, they treat this human trial as though it were the punishment of God ...
>
> (Q 29:10)

The Qur'ān often defines God's omnipotence and omniscience by showing that they extend similarly to opposites, such as the completed and the future act, the believer and the sinner, the secret and the open. "Your Lord knows best who strays from His Path, and He knows best who is truly guided" (Q 68:7). "I know what you hide and what you reveal ..." (Q 60:1).

Similarity of action

In discussing the two legal arguments labeled "reciprocity" and "equivalence,"[4] we have seen that the Qur'ān assesses certain acts as legally similar whether they are similar in fact or are only legally equivalent. Rhetorical similarities exist outside the legal context as well, whenever the Qur'ān repeats a word or uses one that is related or similar. The exegete's initial task is to determine whether the word in the second instance means the same thing as in the first or is being used in a different sense.[5] For example, believers are told: "Whoever commits aggression against you, commit aggression against him to the same extent that he committed it against you ..." (Q 2:194). Exegetes have pointed out that retaliating for or repelling aggression is not the same as committing it in the first place, despite the use of the same word (*iʿtadā*) for both.[6]

Similar actions toward a common end will produce similar rewards or punishments. Christians and Jews who believe as the Muslims believe are on the right path (Q 2:137). Unbelievers, however, want to persuade the believers to reject belief, thereby putting them on the same level as themselves (Q 4:89). Similarity is also the basis of arguments based on *sunna* and other sorts of precedent in sacred history, including the negative precedent exemplified in the vanished nations' uniform rejection and persecution of the prophets sent to them, and their resulting destruction.[7]

The Qur'ānic covenantal obligations, positive and negative, which bind both parties express the legal principle of reciprocity in terms of similarity of action. "Whoever [of the thieves] repents (*tāba*) after his crime and behaves virtuously (*aṣlaḥa*), God will turn (*yatūbu*) to him ..." (Q 5:39). Earthly actions produce similar ones in the hereafter. "O you who believe, when you are directed to make room in your councils, then make room, and God will make room for you ..." (Q 58:11). The reciprocity expressed in verses like these is not that of equivalent legal obligation between humans but that of mutual commitment between parties to the Covenant, who are unequal but whose obligations to each other can be expressed in identical terms because they are equally binding. A rhetorical variant compares divine and human actions using understatement, even irony: "They plot and God plots, and God is the best of plotters" (Q 8:30, cf. 10:21, 13:42, 86:15–16).

If time, place, and circumstance are wrong, however, similar actions will not produce similar results. We have seen that spending one's wealth and fighting in the path of God bring more reward when done earlier than when done later (Q 57:10); and that the action of believing before death will result in salvation, while the same action done after death will not.[8]

The only thing truly similar to an act of God is another act of God. A *topos* that often accompanies divine commands, arguments from precedent, and justification by signs is the assertion of God's power to repeat or equal his previous creation: as God has created a thing in the past, he can perform a similar action in the present or future. "Is not the One Who created the heavens and the earth capable of creating something like them?" (Q 36:81, cf. 17:99). "Say: 'Who will bring us back [to life]?' Say: 'He who created you the first time!'" (Q 17:51). "As We began the first creation We shall repeat it: a promise (*wa'd*) binding upon Us ..." (Q 21:104).

Similarity of consequence

The Qur'ān demonstrates that similar consequences may result from similar actions, such as God's creation and analogous resurrection of human beings; or they may result from legally equivalent but dissimilar actions, such as accepting an indemnity rather than insisting upon the execution of a killer. A similar consequence may result when humans imitate desirable or undesirable behavior, as discussed in connection with the notion of *sunna*: they will face the same consequences as those whom they follow. "If you hear the Signs of God defied and ridiculed, do not sit with them until they change the subject, otherwise you are like them" (Q 4:140). Sometimes it comes in a warning. "If they turn away, say: 'I warn you of a thunderbolt like the thunderbolt of 'Ād and Thamūd!'" (Q 41:13).

When two contradictory actions are shown to produce an identical result, the locution is a demonstration of ineffectiveness or futility.[9] "It is the same to them whether you warn them or do not warn them: they will not believe" (Q 36:10, cf. 7:193, 26:136, 71:5–10). "He calls upon [deities] other than God who neither hurt nor help him" (Q 22:13). A variant of the formula is directed at those of the Prophet's interlocutors who misunderstand his role. "Say: 'I only call you to my Lord . . . I have no capacity to harm you or to guide you'" (Q 72:20–21). "Say: 'Do you see? Whether God destroys me and mine or has mercy on us, who can protect the unbelievers from a painful punishment?'" (Q 67:28).

Demonstrations of futility are occasionally amusing. One who ignores God's Signs is like a dog: "If you attack him he hangs his tongue out, and if you leave him alone he hangs his tongue out"(Q 7:176). When they predict doom, however, few Qur'ānic constructions are more ominous. "Ask for forgiveness for them or don't ask: if you ask seventy times that they be forgiven, God will never forgive them . . ." (Q 9:80, cf. 63:6).

> They will all stand before God; and the weak will say to those who thought themselves important: "We were your followers: can you help us avoid any of God's punishment?" They will answer: "If God had guided us, we would have guided you. Now it is all the same to us whether we are despondent or stoic: there is no way out!"
> (Q 14:21, cf. 52:16)

Stories of the prophets

Some of the most easily recognized arguments from similarity are those that draw upon the precedent of previous prophets and their reception by the people to whom they were sent. These stories combine the three types of similarity we have examined in this section and sometimes add an interesting twist to the Qur'ān's depiction of argument by detailing the *ad hominem* arguments used against particular prophets.

As we have seen, a major component of the definition of a prophet is that he is a human being (Q 14:11, 18:110, 41:6), that is, not an angel (Q 6:50) but of the same genus as his audience. As humans, the prophets were raised from among their own people (Q 12:109), spoke their language (Q 14:4), had wives and children (Q 13:38), ate food (Q 21:8), and walked in the markets (Q 25:7). Their opponents, however, seized upon this similarity and used it to argue against them. With such people, the prophets' very humanity discredited them, let alone their similarities to and associations with the physically or politically disadvantaged, such as Moses's (putative) speech defect (Q 43:52), his and Aaron's membership in an oppressed minority (Q 23:47), Lot's sexual morality as contrasted with the prevailing standard (Q 7:80–82) and Noah's following among the lower classes (Q 11:27). Prophets should have *some* kind of sign (Q 21:5, 17:90–93). Real messengers from God, thought Pharaoh, should be angels with showers of gold bracelets (Q 43:53, cf. 23:24); that is, prophets should be less like humans and more like gods.

ANALOGY

Analogy in logic is a form of induction that, on the basis of certain similarities observed between a known individual on the one hand and an unknown individual on the other, predicts the occurrence in the unknown of further similarities to the known. It is considered a "weak form of reasoning"[10] that produces probability but not certainty. Examples of analogy in this technical sense do not stand out in the Qur'ān, but two applications of the principle contribute a great deal to the sum of Qur'ānic argument.

It was hinted above that an analogy could be constructed from the stories of the prophets. Certainly the structural and thematic similarities of these stories are easy to trace, and their purpose is clear to any hearer or reader. There are passages in the Qur'ān, such as the first half (verses 1–47) of Sura 21 *al-Anbiyā'*, that speak of the missions of the prophets as a single phenomenon having generalized characteristics, and then there are the sequential stories such as those found in Suras 7 *al-A'rāf*, 11 *Hūd*, 19 *Maryam*, and 26 *al-Shu'arā'*. It is not a great leap of logic, then, to conclude that the function of a highly schematized sequence of prophet-tales is to set up the basis for an inductive analogy that will prove the validity of Muḥammad's mission.

This sounds familiar enough, but a caveat is in order: here we are applying "analogy" as a technical term in logic, not as the equivalent of the Arabic word *qiyās*, which is only a partial synonym. The favorite hadīth of those opposed to the use of *qiyās* in Islamic law is quoted by Ibn Ḥazm, among others: "'Analogy' (*al-qiyās*) is a menace (*shu'm*): the first one to use analogy was the Devil."[11] The reference, of course, is to Q 7:12 and 38:75–76:

> [God] said [to Iblīs]: "What has prevented you from bowing down at My command?" He answered: "I am better than he: You created me from fire, and you created him from clay."
>
> (Q 7:12)

This analogy is perhaps the briefest and clearest in the entire Qur'ān: fire is a nobler element than earth, hence Satan concludes that a being created from it is superior to a being – Adam – who was created from earth.

People of the Book argue about things of which they have some knowledge, and they also argue about things they know nothing about – in other words, they analogize on the act of arguing, not on the knowledge that is the prerequisite for argument.

> You are the ones who argued over that which you knew something about. Why do you argue about something you know nothing about? God knows and you do not.
>
> (Q 3:66, cf. 45:24)

They are also guilty of anachronism in their analogical reasoning, arguing about Abraham as though the Book had been in existence during his lifetime.

> O People of the Book! Why do you argue about Abraham when the Torah and the Gospel were not sent down until after him? Will you not reason (*a-fa-lā taʿqilūn*)?
>
> (Q 3:65, but cf. 89:19)

As possessors of scriptures, the People of the Book are to be blamed for failing to detect similarities between past cases of prophethood and the present case that should have led them to a correct conclusion.

> O People of the Book! Our Apostle has come to you, clarifying [matters] for you after a break in [the sequence of] Apostles, so that you will not say, "No bearer of good news came to us, no warner." Now a bearer of good news, a warner, *has* come to you. And God has power over all things.
>
> (Q 5:19)

In other words, they will be blamed for their failure to draw a valid analogy. A single inconsistency is not necessarily the result of a false analogy, but a consistent pattern of error goes beyond simple ignorance and pursuit of pleasure. In Q 3:65 cited above, the error is specifically the failure to use one's power of reason.

The pagans have their own lapses of analogy. The Qur'ān takes them severely to task for ascribing daughters to God, not only because God is One without consort or offspring (Q 6:100-01), but because daughters are so undesirable that the pagans themselves despair when they are born, or they contemplate infanticide (Q 16:57–59, 17:40, 43:17). "A male child for you and a female for Him? That would be an unfair allotment!" (Q 53:21–22, cf. 37:153–154, 43:16, 52:39). People who have – for a while – been given "wealth and sons" analogize on that basis that all else will be given in proportion (e.g. Q 23:54–56). But the pagans are most often condemned for their failure to recognize the uniform extent of God's power. They hold certain correct notions about the deity known as *Allāh* but they fail to draw the correct conclusions from his status as creator and preserver, returning to their idols when they have received from God what they want.

> When they get into a boat, they pray to God, devoting all their faith to Him; but when He has brought them safely to land, they are suddenly polytheists again!
> (Q 29:65, cf. 10:22–23, 11:9–10, 16:51–56, 23:84–91)

Analogy in its nontechnical sense "argues from the similarities of dissimilar things."[12] The Qur'ān is rich in these, some quite well-known, some obscure in both wording and significance. We shall mention only a few. Obstinate unbelievers are "like cattle, only farther astray" (Q 7:179). The Jews who bear the law and then throw it off "are like an ass carrying books" (Q 62:5). Those who reject God's signs "will not enter the Garden until a camel passes through the eye of a needle" (Q 7:40, cf. Matthew 19:24, Mark 10:25, Luke 18:25); and we have already seen the dog whose tongue hangs out no matter what happens (Q 7:176).

One of the best known and most beautiful analogies comes in the Verse of Light: "The example of His Light (*mathalu nūrihi*) is like a niche in which there is a lamp; the lamp is in a glass; the glass is as though it were a shining star ..." (Q 24:35).

PARABLE

"Analogy" shades into "parable" when it begins to exhibit a bit of plot, though the Arabic word *mathal* can cover both, as well as "example" in general. A parable is a sort of allegory that "is very short and simple and narrates or describes a familiar occurrence in nature or life that by analogy conveys a spiritual truth."[13] The

Qur'ān uses parables and other *amthāl* on two levels: (1) it tells the stories themselves, and (2) it comments upon the fact that it is doing so.

The Qur'ān takes examples and parables from every level of creation. In the human realm, we see the hypocrites compared to benighted travelers who lose their fire (Q 2:17–18) and to those caught in a storm (Q 2:19–20). Oath-breakers are compared to a woman who unravels her own spinning (Q 16:92), polytheists to a man serving many masters who disagree with one another (Q 39:29), lost souls and believers to the blind and the sighted (Q 11:18–24). Animal species are analogues of human communities (Q 7:37). Besides the gnat, the dog, the ass, and the cow already encountered, there are parables of the spider's weak house (Q 29:41) and the bee's industry and productivity (Q 16:68–69).

The vegetable kingdom is also lavishly represented, and these parables tend to be longer: charity is like a seed (Q 2:261), good and evil words like good and evil trees (Q 14:23–26), the consequences of faithless self-regard like a blighted garden (Q 68:17–33). A parable from the mineral kingdom deserves to be better known:

> He sends down water from the sky which the valleys let flow according to their capacity. And the stream carries scum, which rises to the top, like the scum that rises from what they smelt to make jewelry and tools. Thus does God cast Truth and Falsehood: for the scum disappears as dross; and what benefits people remains on the earth. Thus does God shape parables.
>
> (Q 13:17)

The Qur'ān often calls its audience's attention to the fact that it is using parables and analogies: the word *mathal*, with its plural *amthāl*, occurs 88 times. "God is not ashamed to use an analogy – some tiny gnat or something larger" (Q 2:26). "We have in this Qur'ān directed every kind of parable to the people; and humans are the most disputatious of creatures" (Q 18:54, cf. 17:89, 30:58, 39:27). These *amthāl* are instructive demonstrations from God, but humans are not free to make up their own comparisons. "Do not coin *amthāl* for God: God knows and you do not" (Q 16:74). God's is "the loftiest *mathal* in the heavens and the earth" (Q 30:27). I have classed the Verse of Light (Q 24:35) as an analogy rather than a parable because no action is involved, but the opposite case could be made as well, on the basis of its length and the extent of its analogies. That verse too ends by commenting upon itself: "... God coins parables (or "analogies") for the people (*yaḍrib Allāh al-amthāl li-'l-nās*) and God knows all things" (Q 24:35).

DEGREE

Some of the most laconic and incisive comparisons in the Qur'ān use the elative (sc. comparative/superlative) forms of the adjective, namely, the *afʿal* pattern and the two anomalous forms *khayr* (better/best) and *sharr* (worse/worst). Others use verbs such as "increase" and "take away" to achieve the same effect. For our purposes, we shall divide these constructions into two classes. Those which express degrees of the same idea – e.g. "good" and "better" – will be treated in this section as a subset of "Comparison," as will those which imply a similar relationship but use only a single elative or a verb. Locutions in which elatives contrast two opposite ideas – e.g. "better" and "worse" – are in the next chapter, "Contrast." That is also where the reader will find most constructions that use a single elative to set up a pair of contraries: "Do you know better, or does God?" (Q 2:140). As before, however, there are passages that fit logically into both.

Good, better, best, and other terms of praise

Part of God's self-definition in the Qur'ān is found in the virtues expressed by the Divine Names (*al-asmā' al-ḥusnā* – Q 59:24, 7:180, 17:110, 20:8). While such verses as the Verse of Light (Q 24:35) and the Verse of the Throne (Q 2:255) dramatize in positive, non-comparative terms God's absolute transcendence and incomparability, other verses achieve the same end by implicitly denying the superiority of any other entity, using rhetorical questions that contain elatives. "Whose word is truer than God's?" (Q 4:122). "Who is more faithful to his Covenant than God?" (Q 9:111). "Who is better than God in judging a people whose faith is certain?" (Q 5:50) The comparison may take the form of a disjunction: "Is God better, or whatever it is that they associate [with Him]?" (Q 27:59), a verse which is then followed by a recital of signs in nature that prove divine authority (Q 27:60–65), using a method analyzed in Chapter 2. Some of the Divine Names and other epithets are also elative in form: the Most Merciful of those who have mercy (*arḥam al-rāḥimīn* – Q 7:151, 12:64, 21:83, cf. 23:109, 23:118), the Best of creators (Q 23:14), the Best of judges (Q 7:87, 10:109), the Most Generous (*akram* – Q 96:3), and the Omniscient (*a'lam*).[14]

God is occasionally compared to human beings, not always without irony: "[The unbelievers] plot, and God plots, and God is the best plotter (*khayr al-mākirīn*)!" (Q 8:30, cf. 10:21, 13:42). "Are you asking them for some reward? But the reward of your Lord is greater, and He is the best provider" (Q 23:72). The latter verse points to a more common *topos* than direct comparison of God to humans, namely, comparison of heavenly rewards to the rewards of this world. Sometimes such comparisons refer to the world in a negative manner: "The life of this world is nothing but a game and a pastime, and the Hereafter is better . . ." (Q 6:32). But more common are comparisons of what is good with what is better. "To those who do good, there is good in this world, and the Hereafter is better. How excellent is the abode of the pious!" (Q 16:30, cf. 16:41, 16:95, 18:45–46, 20:131, 28:60, 62:11, 87:17). Also common is the assertion that one thing is "better" (*khayr*) than another without characterizing the second as either good or bad. "The Last (sc. Hereafter) is better than the First" (Q 93:4). It is not always clear whether *khayr* is being used as an elative or as a noun:

> O you who believe, when you consult with the Apostle in private, bring a freewill offering (*ṣadaqa*) first: that is better (or "a benefit" – *khayr*) for you, and more pure (*aṭhar*). And if you do not find the means to do so, God is Forgiving, Merciful.
>
> (Q 58:12)

Comparisons between human beings are most commonly made on the basis of faith and unbelief; when that is the case, they are contrasts and will be treated in the next chapter. More subtle are comparisons between members of a single class. For example, God has raised some prophets over others (Q 2:253, 17:55), even though humans are not allowed to act on this distinction (e.g. Q 2:136). In the chapter on legal arguments, we noted that the process of comparison is used in family law to determine that one's own relatives are to be given priority over other believers (Q 33:6), as it is used to prefer some Muslims over others on the basis of works or gender.

> Those who believe and emigrate and struggle in the path of God ... are of a higher rank with God. (*aʿẓamu darajat^an ʿind Allāh*) ...
>
> (Q 9:20, cf. 57:10, 4:95)

> Women have rights such as those held over them according to the accepted practice (*bil-maʿrūf*), and men have a degree (*daraja*) over them.
>
> (Q 2:228)

The plural *darajāt* is used both with additional elatives (Q 9:20, 17:21) and without (Q 4:96, 6:83) to describe believers ranked according to their deeds (Q 6:132, 20:75, 46:19, 58:11) or by God's will (Q 6:83, 6:165, 8:4, 12:76, 43:32). This is the case on earth and more so in heaven:

> See how We have preferred some of them over others; and certainly the Hereafter is greater in ranks (*darajāt*) and greater in preference (*tafḍīl*).
>
> (Q 17:21)[15]

Muslims are required to exercise their own powers of comparison as well. Thus they are to rank their relationships according to the criterion of belief, not that of desire or other human weakness. We have seen the legal requirement to prefer believers over unbelievers as friends or allies (e.g. Q 3:28). The same is true of marriage:

> Do not marry polytheist women until they believe: a believing slave woman is better than a [free] polytheist woman, even though she pleases you. And do not marry [your daughters] to polytheist men until they believe: a believing slave is better than a [free] polytheist, even though he pleases you ...
>
> (Q 2:221)

The Qur'ān uses comparison to point out the differences that exist within the ranks of unbelievers. Christians are declared to have the best will toward the Believers, Jews and pagans the worst (Q 5:82); it is the Christian men of learning and monks who are most strongly affected emotionally when hearing the Qur'ān and who will be rewarded accordingly (Q 5:82–85). Some of the People of the Book, if entrusted with a large sum of money, will return it immediately, while others will not return a single dinar left in trust unless they are pressed to do so (Q 3:75).

Even actions that are not the subject of command, prohibition, or punishment are often compared in the Qur'ān on the basis of their relative moral content. These actions generally fall into the intermediate legal categories that *'ulamā'* later ranked as recommended (*mandūb*), indifferent or permissible (*mubāḥ*), and repugnant (*makrūh*). Here is one example of each.

> If you give your extra alms (*ṣadaqāt*) openly it is good; and if you hide them and make sure they reach the poor it is better (*khayr*) for you: it will absolve you of some of your evil deeds. And God is well aware of what you do.
>
> (Q 2:271)

One's children and servants are to ask permission to enter a room at the times when one is likely to be undressed.

> After those times [i.e. sleep and siesta], there is nothing wrong (*la … junāḥ*) if you or they move about among each other … but when the children among you come of age, they should ask permission, as those who were before them asked permission …
>
> (Q 24:58–59)

There are certain mitigations for the repugnance of divorce:

> When you divorce women and they have reached the end of their waiting-period, do not prevent them from marrying their former husbands, if they agree mutually in the proper manner. Those of you who believe in God and the Last Day are exhorted to do that: it is more honorable and pure for you (*azkā lakum wa-aṭhar*). God knows and you do not.
>
> (Q 2:232)

Another sort of argument by comparison aids believers in their moral judgments by assigning an action to a position on the scale that has ideal piety or justice at one end and sin and injustice at the other. Most such constructions measure from the positive end of the scale. "Be just: that is closer to piety (*al-taqwā*). And fear God: God certainly knows what you do" (Q 5:8). Creditors who have become Muslims must renounce the usurious interest they were charging but may recover their capital (Q 2:278–279):

> And if the debtor is in difficult circumstances, then defer it until he can repay it easily; and if you forgive it as charity (*taṣaddaqū*), it is better for you, if you only knew.
>
> (Q 2:180)

The full range of this scale, however, is contained in a negative example (which actually belongs in the next section) that combines elements of comparison and contrast: when the hypocrites were told to fight or at least defend the city but did not do so, they replied:

> "If we had known how to fight we would have followed you." On that day they were closer (*aqrab*) to unbelief than they were to belief.
>
> (Q 3:166)

Other virtues or positive qualities appear as elatives that express superior strength, complexity, or virtue. "Are you harder to create (*ashaddu khalq^{an}*) or the heaven that He built?" (Q 79:27).[16] "Creation of the heavens and the earth is certainly greater (*akbar*) than the creation of human beings, but most people do not understand" (Q 40:57). "O you who believe! Do not allow some men to laugh at others who may be better (*khayr*) than they, or women [to laugh at] women who may be better than they . . ." (Q 49:11). And we have seen Satan's argument that he was superior (*khayr*) to Adam based upon the substance from which each was made (Q 7:12, 38:76).

Finally, comparisons between good things may be expressed not as explicit comparisons but as increase. "It is He Who sent tranquility (*al-sakīna*) down into the hearts of the believers, to add faith to their faith . . ." (Q 48:4).

> God increases in guidance those who are rightly guided; and with God enduring deeds of virtue have the best reward and the best return (*khayr^{un} . . . thawāb^{an} wa-khayr^{un} maradd^{an}*).
>
> (Q 19:76)

Bad, worse, worst

The Qur'ān compares evils by measuring from the negative end of the scale. "God does not forgive that anything should be associated with Him, but He forgives whom He will for what is less than that ..." (Q 4:48). "The worst beasts in God's sight are those who disbelieved and will not believe" (Q 8:55, cf. 8:22). "Those People of the Book and polytheists who disbelieve are in the fire of Hell eternally: they are the worst of creatures" (Q 98:6).

As is the case with ultimate good, ultimate evil is frequently defined in the Qur'ān by a comparison in the form of a rhetorical question: "Who is worse than x?"

> Who is more evil (*aẓlam*) than one who forges the Lie against God even as he is being called to Islam? God does not guide an evil nation.
>
> (Q 61:7, cf. 6:21, 6:157, 10:17, 11:18)

> Who is in greater error (*aḍall*) than one who worships something other than God, which will never answer him [from now] until the Day of Judgment?
>
> (Q 46:5)

> Who is in greater wrong (*aẓlam*) than one who is reminded of the Signs of his Lord and turns his back on them? We shall certainly be avenged upon the sinners!
>
> (Q 32:22)

These two elatives, *aẓlam* and *aḍall*, are virtually the only ones used in such implicit superlatives.

The Qur'ān uses elatives to set most legal priorities.[17] A number of these mandate the choice of what is bad over what is worse, such as the verses which stipulate that *fitna* is even more serious (*ashadd*) than killing (Q 2:191, 2:217), and that blocking access to the Sacred Mosque is more serious (*akbar*) than fighting in the Sacred Month (Q 2:217). "Those who were left behind ... hated to fight ... They said, 'Do not go out in the heat!' Say, 'The fire of Hell is hotter!'" (Q 9:81). Preferring something bad to something worse can work to the sinners' benefit when it causes them to consider their own salvation. "We shall make them taste the punishment here below before that greater punishment, so that perhaps they will turn around" (Q 32:21). But that Meccan verse holds out more hope than does a Medinan one: "There is a punishment for them in this life, and the punishment of the Hereafter is harsher (*ashaqq*), where they have no one to protect them against God" (Q 13:34).

Arguments that warn believers against mistaken priorities are sometimes couched in positive rather than negative terms. "They swear to you by God in order to please you, but God and His Apostle are more worthy that they should please *them*, if they are believers" (Q 9:62). "Do not buy a small gain at the price of God's Covenant: what is with God is better for you, if you only knew it" (Q 16:95). "In the hearts of [the hypocrites] you are more terrifying than God. That is because they are a people without understanding" (Q 59:13).

The horror of Hell is demonstrated by adding the bad to the worse. "Whoever was blind (*aʿmā*)[18] in this world will be [more] blind (*aʿmā*) in the next, and further astray from the Path" (Q 17:72). But of all the descriptions of Hell where horror is piled upon horror, none is more devastating than that in the first of the *Hāʾ-mīm* suras: "A call will go out to those who disbelieved: 'God's hatred of you is stronger than your hatred of yourselves … '" (Q 40:10).

Proportion

Another sort of argument from comparison resembles the legal argument from equivalence, but it adds the principle of proportion. What is involved is not a single predetermined quantity but a constant relation between two or more quantities: though the quantities vary, the proportion does not. The clearest examples are legal ones: (1) the division of an estate that assigns constant proportions according to gender and degrees of relationship (Q 4:11–12); (2) the principle that assigns slaves half the penalties of free persons (e.g. Q 4:25); and (3) the stipulation that in the case of divorce before consummation of the marriage, the men are to compensate their divorced wives monetarily, the rich according to his means, the poor according to his (Q 2:236). I have discussed the first two of these in Chapter 5.

When God calls upon the Prophet to exhort his followers to fight, his argument is based upon proportion in the form of odds. He promises that twenty steadfast believers (*ṣābirūn*) will conquer 200, and 100 will prevail over 1000 (Q 8:65). But for the present, given a certain weakness, "if there are a hundred steadfast among you, they will conquer 200; and if there are 1000, they will conquer

2000, by the permission of God. And God is with the steadfast" (Q 8:66). While the passage is more hortatory than legal in the strict sense, it forms the basis for the legal doctrine that Muslims are not obliged to fight when the odds are more than 2 to 1.[19]

Pharaoh rejected Moses for failing to produce angels and showers of gold (Q 43:53) and for belonging to a subject people (Q 23:47). In an echo of the latter argument, Muḥammad's opponents use proportion to strike an unmistakably bourgeois note. "Why has this Qur'ān not been sent down to some important man from one of the two cities?" (Q 43:31). "Those who disbelieve say about those who believe, 'If [the Book] were any good, *they* would not have got it before we did!'" (Q 46:11).

Arguments *a fortiori*[20]

A special kind of comparison is the relational argument that is called in Latin a fortiori and in Arabic *al-jadal bi-'l-awlā* or *bi-'l-aḥrā*. As its Latin name indicates ("from the stronger"), it argues on the basis of relational inequality – greater likelihood, greater power, greater knowledge – and is so called even though one form argues "from the weaker," as will be seen below.

The conventional logical scheme of this sort of argument is:

A is greater than B.
B is greater than C.
Therefore A is greater than C.[21]

Although at first glance such an argument resembles a syllogism (and indeed great efforts have been expended to convert it to one), most logicians agree that such a conversion is invalid.[22] A syllogism has three terms, while the argument *a fortiori* has four: A, greater-than-B, B, and greater-than-C; and the two premises have no common term. Moreover, the relations between them are not equivalent but asymmetrical – that is, directional and non-reversible. "A is greater than B" cannot be converted to "B is greater than A" without changing the meaning. By contrast, taking a Qur'ānic equational definition as an example of symmetry, the proposition "God is the Lord" is symmetrical: it can be converted to "The Lord is God" with no change of meaning.

Many arguments of which the terms are signs of divine power are arguments *a fortiori*. "Are you harder to create (*ashaddu khalq*^{an}) or the heaven that He built?" (Q 79:27). "Creation of the heavens and the earth is certainly greater (*akbar*) than the creation of human beings, but most people do not understand" (Q 40:57).

What must be done to convert the logical schema to the Qur'ānic style is to identify the greatest term with God. God (A) has power over ("is greater than") B, which is greater than C, hence God has power over C as well.

The argument in Q 40:57 may then be recast as follows:

> God has the power to create the heavens and the earth.
> Creation of the heavens and the earth is greater than the creation of human beings.
> Therefore God has the power to create human beings.

If God can create humans, he can revive them after death. Arguments *a fortiori* are used at least a dozen times to prove God's power to resurrect the dead.

> Do they not see that God, Who created the heavens and the earth and was not fatigued by their creation, is capable of bringing the dead to life? Indeed, He has power over everything.
>
> (Q 46:33, cf. 17:49–51)

The theme is restated in Q 22:5, which expands at much greater length upon the miracle of the creation of human beings – a litany of the Ages of Man and of rain sent to revive the barren earth.

While the birth and existence of living beings are demonstrable facts, the same cannot be said for resurrection of the dead. The Qur'ānic answer to doubters of resurrection is an assertion of similarity between creation of the human from a drop of sperm (Q 86:6), or from nothing (Q 19:67), and the re-creation of "rotten bones" (Q 79:11) or "dust" (Q 50:3) as a living being, up to "the tips of his fingers" (Q 75:4). While the wording compares re-creation to creation, none of the passages says that it is greater. On the contrary, when one of these *topoi* is analyzed as an *a fortiori* argument, the initial creation must be emphasized as the greater miracle, resurrection only a repetition of it; and this the Qur'ān does, albeit without making it explicit by using the elative form. Otherwise the argument would say that whoever has power over the less difficult (creation) has power over the more difficult (resurrection), a clear fallacy.

Arguments *a fortiori* impress upon hearers of the Qur'ān the power that God has over them by comparing it to his demonstrated power over more powerful but now vanished nations; and they show his mercy to sinners by comparing it to the mercy shown to those who had been even worse sinners.

> How many generations (*qarn*) before them have We destroyed, who were stronger than they in power, so that they passed on through the land – and did they find a refuge? In that there is most certainly a reminder for anyone who has [an awakened] heart or who lends an ear, and is a capable witness.
>
> (Q 50:36–37, cf. 19:74, 30:9)

> The People of the Book ask you to have a Book sent down to them from heaven. And they asked Moses for something greater than that: they said, "Show us God openly!" ... And We forgave that ...
>
> (Q 4:153)

This is the form of *a fortiori* argument called *a maiore ad minus* – "from the greater to the lesser." If a thing is true (or untrue) of the greater of two things, it is all the more likely to be true (or untrue) of the lesser. An example of the negative mode can be found in Q 7:185: "Have they not examined the realm of the heavens and the earth and everything that God has created? ... In what message (*ḥadīth*) after that will they believe?" (cf. Q 45:6, 77:49–50). That is, if the deniers will not believe in the signs of divine power in the universe, they will not believe in anything else.

The other form is called *a minore ad maius* – "from the lesser to the greater". If a thing is untrue (or true) of the lesser of two things, it is all the more untrue (or true) of the greater. Among the most vivid examples of this type of argument is one of the challenges issued to the idolaters:

> O people! ... Those to whom you pray besides God will never be able to create a fly, even if they all worked together on it! And if the fly took something away from them, they could not get it back!
>
> (Q 22:73)

In other words, putative gods who cannot create even a fly certainly cannot create the heavens, the earth, and humanity.

An example in the positive mode was considered by al-Shāfiʿī to be the strongest form of *qiyās* – another argument, incidentally, against too readily translating that word as "analogy."

> The strongest [form] of *qiyās* is for God to forbid in His Book, or for the Prophet to forbid, a small amount of something; thus it is known that if a small amount is forbidden, a great deal of it is forbidden equally with the small amount, or more so, because of the preponderance of the much over the little... God said: "So whoever has performed an atom's weight of good shall see it; and whoever has performed an atom's weight of evil shall see it" [Q 99:7–8]. So whatever is greater than an atom's weight of good is even more praiseworthy; and whatever is greater than an atom's weight of evil is even more sinful.[23]

Many verses portray the full range of God's concerns, from "everything on land and sea" to "a grain in the depths of the earth" (Q 6:59). An interesting variant of the *a fortiori* argument can be generated by applying it not to the most visible and the greatest but to the invisible and the tiniest, which, we are told, God is not embarrassed to use as an example – "from a gnat upwards" (Q 2:26). Consider Q 20:7: "If you speak aloud [or not], God knows the secret and what is even more hidden." Although arranged rhetorically with the "greater" term, which is also the rhyme-word, at the end, it is an argument *a maiori ad minus*; the "greater" term is greater not in size but in subtlety and intangibility. If God knows what is more secret than the secret, he also knows the secret. Here the scale moves in the other direction. And lest anyone try to exclude one end of the scale from consideration, there is an answer for him as well:

> Those who disbelieved said, "The Hour will not come upon us!" Say: "O yes it will! By my Lord Who knows the Unseen, it will come upon you. There escapes Him not an atom's weight in the heavens or the earth; nor is there anything smaller than that or greater, but that it is in a clear Record."
>
> (Q 34:3, cf. 10:61)

7

CONTRAST

The Qur'ān is in many ways a single enormous contrast. Insofar as it shows God to be the Unique and Incomparable Reality, its chief method of demonstrating that proposition and its corollaries must be not comparison but contrast. Many Qur'ānic passages phrased as comparisons prove on analysis to be contrasts, just as we have seen that many expressions that appear to be grammatical comparatives are in fact superlatives. The arguments here grouped under the rubric of "Contrast" are difference, inequality, opposition, contrariety, contradiction, reversal, and antithesis. All work in the same way in that they all turn ultimately on the ontological difference between good and evil, faith and disbelief, virtue and sin, the natures of which are stipulated by Revelation in the form of premises usable by reason. Contrast in the Qur'ān is thus the fundamental organizing principle, and "comparison" is one of its subsets; this reverses the arrangement of topics in classical rhetoric, where contrast is a subset of comparison.

The outcome of the cosmic struggle does not depend upon skill in argument. However useful rhetorical analysis may be in this study, our categories are after all ultimately theological.[1] By the divine fiat that both creates and defines reality, the two sides cannot be equal and the victory is never in doubt. Where the scale of behavior seems to have intermediate degrees, as we saw in the preceding chapter, they are measured by their relationship to the extremes and may, in fact, be assimilable to one or the other end of the scale. "Be just: it is closer to piety" (Q 5:8). That is, to be pious, one must be just. "[The Hypocrites] said: 'If we had known how to fight, we would have followed you.' On that day they were closer to unbelief than to belief" (Q 3:167). In other words, one who does not aid the Prophet cannot truly be called a believer.

By now it is clear that a single complex Qur'ānic argument is usually expressed many times, in different ways and from different points of departure. A contrast may appear as an antithesis or as a formal disjunction; as a set of contradictories, contraries, or inequalities; or in a list of generic differences. I shall discuss them in reverse order of specificity, with the most general first.

DIFFERENCE

As the essential definition of God is that he is One, the Qur'ān engages the audience's attention by arguing the primordial contrast between God and everything else: "There is nothing like Him (*laysa ka-mithlihi shay'*)" (Q 42:11). "No one is equal to Him (*lam yakun lahu kufūw*^{an} *aḥad*)" (Q 112:4). Divine unicity, however, does not entail any limitations on the variety of God's creation or the extent of his knowledge and power. On the contrary, the Qur'ān cites difference and variety of creation as signs of God's power operating in the world. "Among His Signs is the creation of the heavens and the earth, and the difference of your languages and your colors ..." (Q 30:22) "If God had willed, He would have made you a single nation, but [He did not], in order to test you ..." (Q 5:48). A seldom-cited verse affirms human individuality as well: "Everyone acts in his own way (*kull*^{un} *ya'mal 'ala shākilatihi*), but your Lord knows best who is best-guided on the Path" (Q 17:84).

These verses begin to illustrate the rhetorical topic known as "difference" in the way that we use it here: to cover the broadest denial of similarity, expressed in diverse and sometimes amorphous ways. There are few adjectives, verbs, or particles that consistently signal the sort of relationship we are calling "difference." Each argument must be examined in relative isolation, taking care not to overlook rhetorical differences between passages with similar content. Corbett's distinction is helpful:

> Difference involves unlike or dissimilar things, things which differ in *kind*; contraries, on the other hand, involve opposite or incompatible things of the same kind. Differences become apparent when we compare things: contraries become apparent when we relate things. *Liberty* and *license* would be an example of difference; *liberty* and *slavery* would be an example of contraries.[2]

Here we shall treat three broad areas of difference: genus, motive, and action.

Difference of genus

> You will find others who want to be safe with you as well as with their own people: whenever they are sent back into temptation's way, they fall in.
>
> (Q 4:91)

The notion of "opposite" is popularly used to express the lack of harmony between, say, a virtuous word and a treacherous deed – "He says one thing and does the opposite." Technically, however, there is no "opposition" here but rather a double difference, in content and in genus: the "opposite" of a word is not a deed but another word. Thus it is more appropriate to class passages that draw such distinctions as examples of "difference" rather than of "opposition." This characterizes the many descriptions of how the Hypocrites behave: their deeds by definition belie their words. "They have taken their oaths as a cover and blocked the path of God. How evil are their deeds!" (Q 63:3).[3] "If we had known how to fight, we would certainly have followed you" (Q 3:167, cf. 4:73). Even more notorious are some of the poets: "Do you not see ... that they say what they do not do? Except those who believe, and do good works, and remember God often ..." (Q 26:226–228). Nor do believers escape the charge: "O you who believe! Why do you say that which you do not do? ..." (Q 61:2).

Many examples of difference can be found in the Qur'ānic definitions of "prophet," particularly the relational, exclusionary definitions – those which say what a prophet is *not*. Unable to grasp the idea that a prophet is an ordinary mortal man who says extraordinary things, the prophets' audiences argue against them by assigning prophethood to a different class of beings. A prophet, in their view, *should* be an angel (e.g. Q 25:7) or at least a person of importance (Q 43:31). If not, his claims cannot be taken seriously, and he must be either abnormal in some way or a liar. He is no prophet but a soothsayer, a madman, a poet, or a forger (Q 52:29–33); a lying sorcerer (Q 38:4); or the mouthpiece of a foreigner (Q 16:103, cf. 41:44).

When "appearance and reality" differ, they too are commonly called "opposites" when they should more accurately be described as "different." For example, the criterion for terming a deity false is that it be proven to have no power. But what of the *apparent* power of Satan? As Abraham's adversaries admit (Q 21:58–67), an idol just sits there silently, no matter how much power its worshippers credit to it. Satan is different: though not a deity, he is not ineffective. He is a creation of God and alive, not a stick or a stone; presumably he has the sort of abilities associated with the other *jinn*, such as flying through the air. In addition, unlike the idols, he has effective power over the fates of human beings, albeit only what they grant him. "You shall have no power over My servants, except those who have gone astray and followed you. And Hell is the promise for them all!" (Q 15:42–43, cf. 14:22, 4:118–121). The Qur'ān thus makes clear that Satan's "power" is not real power but is of a different genus altogether.

> Fighting may be prescribed for you when it is hateful to you. It may be that you hate a thing when it is good for you; and it may be that you love a thing when it is bad for you. God knows and you do not.
>
> (Q 2:216)

At first glance, Q 2:216 seems to be a simple contrast, like the phrase "command the good and forbid the evil." But the contrary verbs "love" and "hate" are not aligned with the contrary nouns "good" and "bad." The genera are crossed: one may hate what is good and love what is bad. This is not the usual Qur'ānic antithesis, because both alternatives are admitted to be in one way or the other unpleasant to the audience. The final sentence adds a contradiction, using the verb *ʿ-l-m* to express knowledge and its contradictory – that is, the same verb negated[4] – to express ignorance (cf. Q 16:74). To appreciate the complexity of the verse, one need only compare it with its partial but far simpler analogue at the end of Q 4:19: "It may be that you hate something and God puts a lot of good into it."

Another sort of argument from generic difference contrasts non-parallel aspects of what would otherwise be classed as simple opposites. For example, in Sura 87 the Qur'ān describes the virtuous person by what he does, the sinner mainly by what will happen to him:

> So remind! in case the reminder does some good. He who fears [God] will remember, but the most wretched will evade it – he who will come to the Great Fire, and in it will neither die nor live; while he will thrive who has

> purified himself, who utters the name of his Lord, and who prays.
>
> (Q 87:9–15)

In a variant of the above, an object may be contrasted with an action. Abraham has no reason to fear his people's idols, but his people have reason to fear God's wrath for having worshipped those idols.

> How can I fear what you have associated with God, when you are not afraid for having associated with God something for which He sent down no authority? Which of the two parties has the greater right to security? If you only knew!
>
> (Q 6:81)

Difference of motive

Because the earthly, physical outcomes of identical actions may be beyond the actors' control, their relative motives are the locus of moral difference.

The well-known *ḥadīth* "Actions are [judged] only by motives" (*innamā al-aʿmāl bi-al-niyyāt*)[5] sums up in four words a point amply illustrated in the Qur'ān. For example, the vital key to understanding the difference between the motives of two parties both of whom build and maintain mosques is to know whether or not their members are Muslims.

> It is not for polytheists to build mosques to God while witnessing unbelief against their own souls ... Only one who believes in God and the Last Day and who prays and gives charity is to build mosques to God. Do you consider giving water to pilgrims and maintaining the Sacred Mosque to be like one who believes in God and the Last Day, and fights in the Way of God? They are not equal in God's sight ...
>
> (Q 9:17–19)

Later, the same sura scrutinizes the motives of those who founded a rival "mosque" for purposes of "damage and unbelief and to divide the believers" (*ḍirār^{an} wa-kufr^{an} wa-tafrīq^{an} bayn al-mu'minīn*):

> They will swear, "We intended only good!" But God bears witness that they are liars. Do not stand in it, ever! A mosque founded in piety from the first day is more worthy that you should stand in it . . .
>
> (Q 9:107–108)

We see thus that, although in the end the argument resolves into the dichotomy between faith and unbelief, it must begin by discovering the difference between two apparently identical actions. Evil done in ignorance, then repented of and amended, can be forgiven (e.g. Q 16:119). Those who worship other deities on the understanding that they will bring them closer to God will be judged "on that in which they differ:" those whose motives in fact are falsehood and *kufr* will find no guidance (Q 39:3).

It is easy to recognize those who witness to their own *kufr*. It is far more difficult to know which individuals among professed Muslims are in fact hypocrites. Arguments fail if evidence is lacking. Perhaps the only certain way is to wait until the Day of Judgment, when the hypocrites will be outside the wall and will call through the gate to the believers:

> "Weren't we with you?" They will answer: "Yes, you were, but you were tempting yourselves, and waiting [for something to happen to us], and you had doubts, and your [false] hopes blinded you, until God's Command came to pass. And the deceiver deceived you about God."
>
> (Q 57:13–14)

Difference of action

The function of prophethood and the relation of a prophet to God may be defined by means of commands paired with prohibitions. This is a very common way of conveying difference. God is to do *x*, Muḥammad is to do *y*; and Muḥammad is to do *y*, he is not to do *z*.

> Do not move your tongue over [the Qur'ān] to make it come quickly. Our task is to collect it and read it out; so when We have read it, you are then to follow its reading . . .
>
> (Q 75:16–18)

> Those who have no hope of meeting Us say: "Bring us a Qur'ān other than this one, or change it!" Say: "It is not

> for me to change it on my own. I only follow what has been revealed to me. I fear the punishment of a Momentous Day, if I were to disobey my Lord."
>
> (Q 10:15)

> So remind [the world]! For certainly you are one who is to remind them; you are not to control them. Except that whoever turns away and rejects belief, God will inflict upon him the greatest punishment.
>
> (Q 88:21–24)

Corbett's definition of "difference"[6] helps us to classify a great many such pairs of positive and negative verbs. The fact that they are combined adds a range of meaning that they would not have individually; and while a given pair are sometimes simple contraries or contradictories,[7] often the purpose of combining them is to demonstrate to the audience that the second is another *kind* of action more appropriate to the circumstances than what is actually being done or contemplated. We have already seen this pattern in some of the legal arguments cited as examples of "distinction," as when believers who swear that they will leave their homes if the Prophet commands it are told that reasonable obedience (*ṭāʿa maʿrūfa*) is more appropriate than an oath (Q 24:53).[8] We also encounter "difference" where words are defined in terms of those actions they do not entail as well as those they do. *Birr* (piety), for example, is not the turning of one's face toward a particular direction but is other *kinds* of acts: belief, charity, prayer, fulfillment of oaths, and patience in adversity (Q 2:177).

Actions that differ in kind from those mandated by God or a prophet may be actively sinful, as when the Children of Israel in Moses's absence make and worship a golden calf (Q 7:148–154) despite the futility of such a practice and Moses's prior refusal to accept it (Q 7:138–140); or they may be self-imposed and pointless, as in the description of Jewish dietary restrictions (e.g. Q 3:93) or the pagan beliefs regarding sacrificial animals, which become blasphemy if wrongly attributed to God (Q 5:103). Those who would be called believers must also beware of actions inconsistent with belief:

> You will not find a people who believe in God and the Last Day loving those who work against God and His Apostle,

> even if they were their fathers, or their sons, or their brothers, or their own tribe ...
>
> (Q 58:22)

Quite common is a sort of verbal doublet that cannot apparently be equated with any single rhetorical figure in either English or Arabic, though al-Bāqillānī (d. 403/1013) says that such constructions "have been called *tajnīs*."[9] Concisely and elegantly, and for purposes of contrast, it uses the same verb but with a different actor and sometimes a form of negation. "God knows and you do not know" (e.g. Q 16:74). "Human vision does not encompass Him: He encompasses human vision" (Q 6:103). "He is not to be asked about what He does, but *they* will be asked" (Q 21:23). "Say to those who do not believe: 'Do what you can! We, too, are doing. And wait! We, too, are waiting'" (Q 11:121). Sometimes the verbal change is from active to passive. "He protects but cannot be protected against" (Q 23:88). "They have adopted ... deities who do not create a thing but are themselves created ..." (Q 25:3, cf. 7:191, 10:18, etc.).[10] Some of these can also be classed as examples of "antithesis," which we shall discuss at the end of this chapter.

The Qur'ān's choice of vocabulary makes it clear that the mental state of a responsible human being results from his own thinking, over which he has complete control. It is not a "given," protests to the contrary notwithstanding. As we have dealt at length elsewhere with belief and disbelief not as psychological states but as actions performed,[11] here we shall choose another set of mental operations to illustrate the notion of "difference:" knowledge, doubt, conjecture, and ignorance. The Qur'ān almost invariably uses the active verb *irtāba* or some derivative of the root *m-r-y* to describe those who doubt revelation, whereas the doubters describe their own state in passive terms: "We are in doubt." They never use *irtāba, imtarā,* or *shakka* even when using other active verbs such as *kafara.*

> "We deny (*kafarnā*) the [the Message] with which you have been sent, and we are in serious doubt (*innā la-fi shakk ... murīb*) about that to which you call us." Their apostles asked: "Is there any doubt about God, Maker of the heavens and the earth?"
>
> (Q 14:9–10, cf. 11:62, 11:110, 41:45)

"Doubt" in this verse is virtually synonymous with *kufr*; indeed, "doubt" is contrasted elsewhere with the verb "believe" (*yu'min* –

Q 34:21). Other contrasts exhibit difference, not contrariety, when doubt is set against both "truth" (*ḥaqq* – Q 10:94) and "knowledge" (*ʿilm* – Q 4:157, 42:14). Doubt is a different kind of mental operation: it may be well- or ill-founded, but as long as the doubter does not act to remove his doubt, he cannot *know* one way or the other. In the Qur'ān, of course, this is precisely the point of the argument: what constitutes the doubters' *kufr* is their refusal to correct their doubt by referring to the only source of truth, which is the message brought by the Prophet. It is curious that "certainty" is not presented as the opposite of "doubt." Only once do the words *shakk* and *yaqīn* even appear in the same context, the verse that denies that Christ Jesus was crucified; but even there the two words are not opposites:

> Those who differ on the matter are in doubt (*shakk*) about it: they have no knowledge (*ʿilm*) of it except pursuit of a conjecture (*illā ittibāʿ al-ẓann*); but certainly they did not kill him (*wa-mā qatalūhu yaqīn^{an}*)
>
> (Q 4:157)

The verb of knowing (*ʿ-l-m*) is virtually never contrasted with the usual verb of not knowing or being ignorant (*j-h-l*).[12] Izutsu has demonstrated that it is more pertinent to contrast *ʿilm* with another mental operation altogether. In a diagram perhaps inspired by the logical "square of opposition," he has set the Qur'ānic use of *ʿilm* over against *ẓann* – "mere conjecture."[13] To put it in my own terms, the act of *ẓann* is not to be found on the continuum that extends from absolute knowledge through partial knowledge to absolute ignorance. Rather, it is of a different category: like dreams and "tales of the ancients," it is a fabrication, the contrary of reality. The word *ẓann* can be variously translated as "guess," "conjecture," "speculate," or "think," as in "wishful thinking." Against those who deny the afterlife, the Qur'ān argues, "They have no knowledge of that; they are only guessing" (Q 45:24). It describes those who boast that they have crucified Christ as only pursuing conjecture (*ẓann*) (Q 4:157).

> You thought (*ẓanantum*) that God did not know (*lā yaʿlam*) much about what you were doing. That wishful thinking of yours about your Lord has destroyed you. Now you are one of the lost.
>
> (Q 41:22–23)

INEQUALITY

A distinctive kind of Qur'ānic contrast is that which argues that two things are not equal, using some variant of the root *s-w-y*. It may appear, in translation, that this topic should be grouped with "arguments from degree" in the previous chapter; but in fact most of the passages are not comparisons but contrasts, often in the form of parables ending in rhetorical questions. "Is the blind equal to the sighted, or is the darkness equal to the light?" (Q 13:16, cf. 6:50, 35:19). "Are they equal – those who know and those who do not?" (Q 39:9). "A man obligated to a number of partners who quarrel among themselves and a man obligated to a single man – are they equal?" (Q 39:29, cf. 16:75).

The formula may in fact be a matter of degree where it is used in a legal argument:

> They are not equal – those believers who sit at home when there is nothing wrong with them and those who devote their wealth and their persons to struggle in the path of God. God has granted those who devote wealth and self to the struggle a degree of preference over those who sit it out. To each God has promised good; but God has preferred with a great reward those who fight over those who just sit.
>
> (Q 4:95)

We have seen such passages among the legal arguments in Chapter 5, while other legal arguments use "inequality" to indicate absolute exclusion, as in the passage previously cited in this chapter which flatly declares that maintenance of the Sacred Mosque is not equal to belief in God and struggle in the path of God (Q 9:19).

Finally, "inequality" is used without parable or figurative language to indicate the ultimate dichotomy. "The bad and the good are not equal, even if the abundance of the bad is pleasing to you . . ." (Q 5:100). "Is the one who believes like the one who sins? They are not equal" (Q 32:18).

"Inequality" seems an ironic understatement when used to describe the final sorting-out:

> Inhabitants of the Fire and inhabitants of the Garden are not equal. It is the inhabitants of the Garden who are the winners.
>
> (Q 59:20)

> Do those who commit evil acts think that We shall make them like those who believe – equal their lives and equal their deaths? How badly they judge!
>
> (Q 45:21)

OPPOSITION

The array of Qur'ānic arguments from opposition bewilders the one who tries to classify them. Opposites may exclude, include, compare, or contrast, depending upon whether they are applied to Creator or creation. As noted above, the theological concept of "opposition" is more broadly appropriate to Qur'ānic reasoning than is the logical-rhetorical concept of "contrariety," which can allow intermediate positions. Therefore we shall call "opposites" most of what a logician would call "contraries." Nevertheless, there are some legitimate examples of the latter; in those cases, we class "contrariety" as a subset of "opposition" and discuss it at the end of the next section. Still more restrictive is the logical concept of "contradiction," depending as it does on the existence of identical propositions that differ only by the presence in one of the negative. "Reversal" describes the process by which one of a pair of opposites becomes the other. "Antithesis" is an extended contrast, the opposite of "analogy."

The reader who wishes an exhaustive catalogue of definitions, synonyms, and antonyms for the basic Qur'ānic terms indicating belief and disbelief must consult the superb works of Toshihiko Izutsu.[14] In *Ethico-Religious Concepts in the Koran*, he mines the text to construct the "semantic field" of a particular concept, notably that of *kufr*, using multiple verses to establish contextual definitions, which include synonymous expressions as well as descriptions of the actions and attitudes of those who exemplify the concept. The use of opposites and contraries (e.g. the opposition of *kufr* to *shukr* and *īmān,* and its equation with *shirk* and *iftirā'*)[15] is integral to his method; my own overlaps his in this area more than any other. His purpose, however, is to define the concepts whether the passages in which the words occur are intended as definitions or not; mine is to analyze the structure of Qur'ānic argument, of which opposites and contraries are only two among many constituents.

Opposites and contraries

The Qur'ān uses extremes inclusively, enclosing a category, to demonstrate to human beings that that category is entirely within God's power and that what they might consider the "negative" half of it is not to be excluded. "It is He who brings laughter and tears, death and life" (Q 53:43–44). "From a sperm-drop He creates [the human being] and shapes him, then smoothes his path, then causes him to die and entombs him, then resurrects him when He wishes" (Q 80:19–22). Many of the passages that point to the Signs of God in nature do so in a similar manner, by asserting God's control over pairs of opposites: day and night (e.g. Q 17:12), heaven and earth (e.g. Q 2:164), East and West (Q 2:115, 73:9), land and sea (Q 6:59, 10:22).

God himself has many "opposites," things wrongly worshipped which lead the worshipper astray. Idols are obvious: I cite Qur'ānic demonstrations of their ineffectiveness throughout this text. Others are Iblīs (Q 18:50) and one's own desires:

> Have you then seen the one who takes his own passion as his deity? Knowing this, God has led him astray and sealed his ear and his heart, and covered over his sight. And then who after God will guide him? Should you not bear this in mind?
>
> (Q 45:23, cf. 25:43)

Some of the Divine Names have opposites that indicate "not-God":

> That is because God is the Truth (*al-Ḥaqq*); and everything you call upon besides Him is falsehood (*al-bāṭil*). And God is the Exalted, the Great.
>
> (Q 31:30, cf. 22:62)

Some of the Divine Names *are* opposites:

> He is the First and the Last, the Evident and the Hidden (*al-Ẓāhir wa-al-Bāṭin*) . . .
>
> (Q 57:3)

The text often depicts the relation between God and humanity as one between opposites. "God is rich (sc. self-sufficient) and you are poor (sc. in need of something beyond yourselves)" (Q 47:38). "Do you know better or does God?" (Q 2:140). "They see [the Day of Judgment] far away: We see it near" (Q 70:6–7). "O people! You are in need of God, while God is He Who needs nothing and Who is to be praised" (Q 35:15). "Then God turned to them (in mercy), and then many of them again turned blind and deaf; but God sees very well (*baṣīr*) what they are doing" (Q 5:71).

Here we also class those passages that speak of God as guiding some human beings and leading others astray: "God leads astray (*yuḍill*) whom He will and guides (*yahdī*) whom He will. And He is the Powerful, the Wise" (Q 14:4, cf. 16:93, 74:31, 13:27). Some of the passages show that "leading astray" is a punishment for sin: "He leads none astray except the sinners, who break God's Covenant after it has been confirmed ..." (Q 2:26–27, cf. 9:37, 14:27). At least one (Q 13:27) shows guidance as subsequent to – and a reward for – repentance. Unquestionably the verbs are to be understood as they are translated here: parallel, transitive and in the active voice. The theological difficulties caused by such passages are well known and have been dealt with exhaustively in works on Islamic theology. Suffice it to say here that, in the rhetoric of Qur'ānic argument, it is a false dichotomy to view such pairs of opposites as mutually exclusive, when *in these contexts* it is more productive to view them as coordinated, inclusive, and indicative of God's total power over humanity. Similar pairings contrast those whom God has blessed and those with whom he is angry (Q 1:7), those to whom he turns and those whom he punishes (Q 3:128, 9:106), those whom he saves and those whom he leaves on their knees (Q 19:72).

Some of the clearest pairs of opposites reinforce the contrast between the fates of the saved and those of the damned. Some pairs are directional: the saved receive their Books of Deeds in their right hands, the damned in their left (Q 69:19, 25, cf. 84:7, 10); they hold positions either on the auspicious right (*aṣḥāb al-maymana*) or on the quite literally sinister left (*aṣḥāb al-mash'ama* – Q 90:18–19). The hypocrites are outside the wall, the believers inside (Q 57:13); the arrangement is such that the saved and the damned are able to speak to each other and compare notes (Q 7:44, 50).[16] Contrasts are drawn on virtually every other basis as well. The saved have balances weighted on the side of good, while those of the damned are light (Q 7:8–9). On the Day of Judgment, faces of the former will be bright and beaming, those of the latter covered with dust (Q 80:38–41). The food and drink of Paradise will be pure and delicious (e.g. Q 80:25–28), those of Hell harmful and revolting (e.g. Q 88:5–7).

It seems superfluous to add that opposite fates are the result of opposite actions, namely, belief and the refusal to believe, though it is worth restating the argument that accepting or rejecting belief equals keeping or breaking the Covenant. In Izutsu's phrase, it is "the grand moral dichotomy."[17] As we have already discussed *islām, īmān,* and *kufr* at length in Chapter 5 as performative utterances, we shall mention only a representative sample here. Believers (*mu'minūn*) are contrasted with those who knowingly refuse to believe (*kāfirūn* – Q 74:31, cf. 64:2), with "sinners" (*fāsiqūn* – Q 3:110, cf. 32:18), with "evildoers" (*ẓālimūn* – Q 17:82), with the sick at heart (Q 74:31), with those who turn their backs (Q 24:47), and with followers of Satan (Q 34:20). In what is possibly the earliest use of the word *muslim*, Muslims are contrasted with "criminals" (*mujrimīn* – Q 68:35). They are also contrasted with those who disbelieve (*alladhīna kafarū* – Q 15:2; cf. 3:80), with those who block the Path of God (*wa-ṣaddū ʿan sabīl Allāh* – Q 16:88–89); and with those who are unjust (*al- qāsiṭūn* – Q 72:14–15).

> Those who reject belief among the People of the Book and the polytheists are in the fire of Hell – in it forever. They are the worst of humanity. Those who believe and do good works – they are the best of humanity.
>
> (Q 98:6–7)

Contrariety exists within a single individual and within any natural group. By way of balancing the impression that the believers are capable only of good, the Qur'ān notes that they, too, perform both good and evil deeds (*sayyi'āt*) and are in need of forgiveness for the latter. "Those [who do good deeds and turn to God] are the ones from whom We accept the best of what they have done and pass over their evil deeds" (Q 46:16, cf. 39:35). Nor are other groups entirely good or evil. Among the People of the Book are those who are capable of belief as well as *kāfirūn* and those "in whose hearts is a disease" (Q 74:31, 35:32); and there are good and evil *jinn*:

> Among us are Muslims and among us are the unjust (*al-qāsiṭūn*). Those who submit (*aslama*) are the ones who have chosen guidance (*rashad^{an}*); as for the unjust, they are the fuel of Hell.
>
> (Q 72:14–15)

Other phenomena of daily life harbor contrary aspects. A single substance – wine – and a single class of action – gambling – have both beneficial and sinful effects, but wine and gambling are ultimately harmful because their sinful aspects are greater than their benefits (Q 2:219). Although the sort of conjecture (*ẓann*) that substitutes for knowledge of scripture is a sin, it appears that not all *ẓann* is sin: "O you who believe! Avoid speculating [sc. about your neighbors' lives] to any great extent, because some speculation is sinful (*baʿḍ al-ẓann ithm*)" (Q 49:12).

One characteristic of contraries is that in some categories they admit intermediate positions between the two extremes, but humans are not free to argue that any given category admits intermediate positions, let alone that they themselves may decide where those positions lie. Thus it is not permitted to obey the Prophet in some things but not others (Q 47:26), or to believe in part of the Book and reject the rest (Q 2:85, 13:36), or to believe in some of the apostles and reject others (Q 4:150). God does not exempt even the Prophet from the possibility that, under pressure from the scoffers, "perhaps you would leave aside part of what We revealed to you" (Q 11:12).

A few passages seem to indicate a position between belief and unbelief. The Beduin include those who have "submitted" but not yet believed.[18] The passage has already been noted in which the hypocrites say, "If we had known how to fight we would have followed you," and God remarks, "On that day they were closer to unbelief than to belief" (Q 3:167).[19] He knows what is in their hearts but threatens no explicit punishment. Compare that with the following passage:

> Among human beings are those who worship God on the edge: if good befalls them, they are content; but if temptation strikes them, they fall on their faces. They lose both this world and the next: *that* is loss made manifest! They pray to things besides God that will neither harm nor benefit them: *that* is going far astray! They call upon something whose harm is closer than its benefit: what an evil patron and what an evil associate!
>
> (Q 22:11–13)

The end of the passage explains the beginning: such people are believers but, as Izutsu says, "very imperfect" ones, who fall all too easily into sin.[20] The last verse seems to imply that the false gods can provide some benefits along with the harm they do; but given that this is a Medinan or late Meccan sura, we must interpret this implication as ironic understatement. The idols will certainly bring harm – that is, punishment – to their worshippers, while the benefits are "far away" because in fact they do not exist at all.

Finally, a word must be said about logical contraries and theological ones. Sura 56 *al-Wāqiʿa* describes a long series of Divine Signs in creation, asking human beings whether it is they or God who creates the sperm, causes the seed to grow in the ground, brings down drinking water from the clouds, and grows the tree that feeds the fire (Q 56:58–72). Only two possible agents are stipulated – God and human beings. A logician would argue that perhaps it is a third force that creates these phenomena, or that a separate force creates each phenomenon, or that "creation" is not how they come into existence at all – in other words, that the choice between divine and human agency does not exhaust the possible alternatives.

The Qur'ān itself uses that technique to get around the false dichotomy posed by People of the Book.

> They say: "Be Jews or Christians and you will be guided!" Say: "Rather, the religion (*milla*) of Abraham – a monotheist (*ḥanīf*), not one of the polytheists!"
>
> (Q 2:135)

A passage in Sura 23 *al-Mu'minūn* considers possible explanations for the Meccans' refusal to heed the Prophet. Is the message something new and unheard-of (Q 23:68)? Do they not recognize the Apostle (Q 23:69)? Do they think that he is possessed by *jinn* (Q 23:70)? Is he asking them for money (Q 23:72)? All of these possibilities are dismissed in favor of the only one left: "You are calling them to the Straight Path, and those who do not believe in the Hereafter have turned away from that Path" (Q 23:73–74, cf. 24:50).

This brings us within the realm of the disjunctive syllogism, which we shall take up in Chapter 9.

Contradictories

Because they allow intermediate positions, contraries may not both be true but may both be false, as we demonstrated in the previous section. The genus of "contradictories", however, brings us back to the second of the so-called Three Laws of Thought: a thing cannot be both true and false (or *A* and *not-A*) at the same time. We have seen that most of the important Qur'ānic terms have a number of "opposites," each of which negates a single aspect of the meaning, but there are few full antonyms. Rather than impose a false symmetry by attempting to stipulate a single one of many "opposites" as the contradictory of the term in question, here I shall confine the category of "contradictories" to those pairs which use the identical words, distinguished only by the absence or presence of the negative: *A* and *not-A*. The same is true, *mutatis mutandis*, for propositions: *X* is *A* and *X* is *not-A*.

As I noted in the "Excursus on Performative Utterances" in Chapter 5, most people in the Qur'ān who call themselves *mu'minūn* are contradicted. "Among the people are those who say: 'We believe in God and the Last Day!' but they are not really believers" (Q 2:8). "They say: 'We believe in God and in the Apostle, and we obey!' Then a group of them turn their backs thereafter: they are not believers'" (Q 24:47). Their false assertions are also contradicted. "Those who refuse to believe say: 'We will never be resurrected!' Say: 'O yes, by my Lord, you will indeed be resurrected!'" (Q 64:7, cf. 23:35–37).

> Among [People of the Book] is a group who twist their tongues around the Book so that you will think [what they say] from the Book when it is not from the Book. And they say: 'It is from God!' when it is not from God, knowingly uttering lies against God.
>
> (Q 3:78)

Contradictories, like opposites, are sometimes used to indicate the extent of God's power.

> I swear by what you see and what you do not see that this is the word of a noble (*karīm*) Apostle; it is not the word of a poet.
>
> (Q 69:38–41)
>
> [On that] Day . . . you will see the people as drunk when they are not drunk: rather the punishment of God is extreme.
>
> (Q 22:2)

> Any to whom God does not give light has no light.
>
> (Q 24:40)

Reversal

Despite the emphatic distinctions made by the Qur'ān, its opposites, contraries, and contradictories are not necessarily ossified dualities: under certain circumstances, one of such a pair may be transformed into its opposite, a process which I term "reversal." It is above all the process by which an unbeliever repents and becomes a believer. Ṭabarsī says, "The origin of *tawba* (repentance) is turning back from what went on before (*al-rujūʿ ʿammā salaf*)."[21]

> [The polytheist, murderer, and fornicator] will have his penalty doubled on Resurrection Day and be abased in it forever, except whoever repents and believes and does good works. For them God will exchange their evil deeds for [or "transform them into"] good ones: God is Forgiving, Merciful.
>
> (Q 25:69–70)

Whatever the transformation, it is a sign of God. It may be an effect of one human's virtuous actions toward another.

> Good and evil are not equal. Pay back [evil] with what is better and see! He between whom and you was enmity will be like your warm friend!
>
> (Q 41:34)

If former enemies "repent, pray, and pay alms, then they are your brothers in Faith" (Q 9:11).

The most dramatic reversals are Signs of the Day of Judgment – "the Day when the earth will be changed into something that is not the earth, as will the heavens . . ." (Q 14:48). Natural processes will be reversed: "When the stars disappear, and heaven is split open, and the mountains are scattered like dust in the wind . . ." (Q 77:8–10). Some suras, such as 81 *al-Takwīr* ("The Folding Up"), 82 *al-Infiṭār* ("The Cleaving Asunder"), and 84 *al-Inshiqāq* ("The Crack-up"), are named for the long sequences of terrifying *bouleversements* with which they begin. Still more distressing is the reversal of feelings for one's friends and family. "On that Day, friends will be enemies, except for the righteous" (Q 43:67). A man will run away from his brother, his parents, his wife, and his children, each one preoccupied with his or her own fate (Q 80:34–37).

And the righteous, at long last, will get back at the sinners:

> Those who sinned used to laugh at those who believed, and wink at each other as they passed by ... But on this Day those who believe will laugh at those who refused to believe, looking out from their seats of honor.
>
> (Q 83:29–30, 34–35)

Antithesis

The definition of "antithesis" which best suits our purpose is that of James William Johnson, who calls it "the reverse of the analogy."[22] If an analogy is an "extended comparison" which establishes "a point-by-point correspondence between two situations or objects,"[23] an antithesis is an extended point-by-point contrast. Johnson sees antithesis as the basis of the disjunctive argument,[24] whereas I have given that role to contrariety and contradiction. Perhaps it is a matter of relative length. The elegant brevity prized by some rhetoricians[25] seems inconsistent with Johnson's stipulation that analogy and antithesis be of a certain length; and while I found numerous brief comparisons offered as examples of antithesis, Johnson's is the only one that views length as a meaningful structural characteristic.

We saw that the best examples of analogy in the Qur'ān are the extended parallel accounts of the prophets prior to the Prophet Muḥammad, which show how his experiences replicated those of his predecessors.[26] The best examples of antithesis are the "extended point-by-point" contrasts of the people in heaven with those in hell – the "Companions of the Garden" and the "Companions of the Fire." Such passages are so often repeated that their broad outlines can be sketched with little reference to particular verses. In Heaven are gardens, shade, rivers, and fruit trees; in Hell, fire, smoke, boiling liquids, and the foul tree of Zaqqūm. In Heaven, beautiful garments of silk and delicious foods and drinks; in Hell, bare skins burnt off and renewed to be burnt again (Q 4:56), bitter food (Q 83:14–16), and drinks either boiling hot or freezing cold (Q 78:24–25). In Heaven, peace, exaltation, joy, and freedom from "any lurking sense of injury" (Q 15:47);[27] in

Hell, pain, humiliation, despair, and mutual recrimination. In Heaven, eternal life; in Hell, neither life nor death.

Here is a comparatively brief example:

> God has promised the Hypocrites, male and female, and the Unbelievers the fire of Hell, to remain in it forever: that is sufficient for them. And God has cursed them, and they will have a punishment of long duration. (Q 9:68) . . . God has promised the Believers, male and female, gardens below which rivers flow, to remain in them forever, and fine dwellings in gardens of Paradise. And acceptance from God is supreme: that is the great victory.
>
> (Q 9:72)

Let us examine a longer example (Q 38:49–64) using Table 7.1 to chart the points of the antithesis.

The parallelism is very tight at first, then takes a more subtle turn in verses 52 and 58, the fourth verse of each sequence, where the pairing off with companions in Paradise (52) is set over against the pairing of punishments in the Pit (58). The security of God's promise (53) is contrasted with the confusion and mutual blame of

Table 7.1 Points of Antithesis

49: The righteous have a beautiful place to return to,	55: The wrongdoers have an evil place to return to:
50: gardens of Paradise whose doors are open to them.	56: Hell! they will fry in it – what an evil resting-place!
51: They shall recline and call for much fruit and drink,	57: So it is; and they will taste boiling drinks and bitterly cold and stinking ones,
52: and with them will be companions whose eyes do not wander.	58: and other things like them – linked in pairs.
53: This is what you were promised on the Day of Accounting.	59–63: No greeting for them . . . "Lord! Whoever got us into this – give him a double punishment in the Fire! . . . Why don't we see people whom we used to laugh at? . . ." (They quarrel over whose fault it all is)
54: This is Our bounty, which can never be exhausted	64: That is a fact: argument among the people of the Fire

those who used to ridicule the virtuous (59–63). The last pair, while not parallel in construction, show antithesis of a sort: the saved have God's bounty pouring upon them continuously (54), while the damned have only each other in an atmosphere of mutual hostility (64).

Occasionally we discern a reversal of the order of individual elements in a kind of mirrored symmetry:

> Those who reject belief among the People of the Book and the polytheists are in the fire of Hell, remaining in it forever. They are the worst of humanity. Those who believe and do good works – they are the best of humanity. Their reward with God is gardens of Paradise below which rivers flow, remaining in them forever . . .
>
> (Q 98:6–8)

Rhetoricians call this sort of arrangement *antimetabole*. The punishment of the damned is described first, followed by their description as "the worst of humanity:" while the saved are first described as "the best of humanity," and then their reward is described.

Further antitheses of Heaven and Hell can be found in Suras 11:106–108, 69:21–37, 75:5–22, 79:35–41, and 88:2–16, among many others. Sura 56, in particular, is more than one-third antithesis (verses 8–9, 27–56, and 88–94), and it is rich in opposites, contraries, and comparisons as well (verses 3, 57–73, and 81–87). Some of the longer antitheses in these suras include subsections which use antimetabole, but space does not permit a full analysis.

Finally, we shall offer an antithesis that does not deal with Heaven and Hell. The beginning of Sura 80, where Muḥammad "frowns and turns away" from the blind man, proves to be unexpectedly complex – an antithesis containing an antimetabole, upon which yet another antithesis is constructed.

The antimetabole comes where verses 5 and 6 reverse the order of topics in verses 1 and 2. Verses 1 and 2 describe first the Prophet and then the one who seeks him; verses 5 and 6 first describe the one whom the Prophet seeks, then the Prophet himself. Verses 3–4 and 7 describe Muḥammad's proper role: each verse follows its initial sequence in the same relative order. The order observed in verses 5 and 6 is also observed in a second reference to the blind man in verses 8–10; thus verses 5–6 and 8–10 form the second

Table 7.2 Antithesis

1: He frowned and turned away	5: As for the haughty man who needs no one,	8–9: As for the one who came to you making a true effort,
2: when the blind man came to him	6: you pay attention to *him*!	10: you allowed yourself to be distracted from him!
3–4: How do you know? He might become [a] pure [Muslim]! Or he might remember [his relation to God], and that memory would benefit him!	7: It is not your fault if he does not become [a] pure [Muslim]	

antithesis. Verses 5 and 8–9 describe, respectively, the haughty and the earnest interlocutors, verses 6 and 10 the Prophet's inappropriate reactions to both.

The content of Qur'ānic contrast may seem familiar, but, as I have demonstrated, the language used to convey it is full of subtle variations. A small difference in syntax or vocabulary may put virtually identical figures into quite different categories, unnoticed by the hearer or reader who concentrates only on the ethical, legal, or eschatological conclusions of the argument. In the same way, it is possible to miss those arguments in the Qur'ān that must be analyzed using syllogistic logic because they are worded in rhetorically effective ways that may omit one premise or the conclusion. Chapter 8 will analyze Qur'ānic arguments that can be assimilated to the Aristotelian categorical syllogisms. Chapter 9 will revisit the topic of contrast as the basis for the disjunctive syllogisms developed by the Stoics; the chapter will conclude with conditional syllogisms, also Stoic in origin. For purposes of analysis, I shall reword the arguments according to the classical models developed by the Peripatetics and Stoics.

8

CATEGORICAL ARGUMENTS

The work that first piqued my interest in Qur'ānic reasoning was *al-Qisṭās al-Mustaqīm* by al-Ghazālī[1] when, while researching Ghazālī's role in combating the spread of esoteric (*Bāṭinī*) Shiʿism, I found *Qisṭās* mentioned along with his major anti-Bāṭinī book, *al-Kitāb al-Mustaẓhirī fī Faḍā'iḥ al-Bāṭinīya*.[2] In *Qisṭās*, Ghazālī combines anti-Bāṭinī argument with logic, another of his perennial fields of interest; but while *al-Kitāb al-Mustaẓhirī* is a work of dialectical theology (*kalām*) with strong psychological and political elements,[3] *al-Qisṭās al-Mustaqīm* is presented as a handbook designed to help the individual believer assess the validity of any argument, including the contention that only the Shiʿi Imām holds the secret of Qur'ānic interpretation. Ghazālī says that, by using nothing more than the "just balance" (*al-qisṭās al-mustaqīm* – Q 17:35, 26:182), which he identifies with the patterns of argument found in the Qur'ān itself, a believer will be able to win debates (*jidāl, mujādala*) with any who would challenge his faith. The "just balance" consists of five "scales" (*mawāzīn;* sing. *mīzān*), which are none other than the first, second, and third figures of the Aristotelian syllogism, and the Stoic conditional and disjunctive syllogisms.

The second author whom I cite in the Introduction,[4] the Ḥanbalī jurist Najm al-Dīn al-Ṭūfī, begins his *ʿAlam al-Jadhal fī ʿIlm al-Jadal* with a digest of logic, dialectic, and debating techniques, then seeks their application in the Qur'ān, sura by sura and verse by verse. Though his book is much longer than Ghazālī's, it is in one way less inclusive, as Ṭūfī omits disjunction (*taqsīm*) from the section on inference.[5] He regards disjunction as a dialectical tool, a form of counter-argument (*iʿtirāḍ*) that forces one's opponent to accept either-or constructions, which can then be demolished. True inference is either categorical or conditional:

> We say, and in God is our success, that inference (*al-istidlāl*) absolutely and in every case (*muṭlaq^an wa-fī ayy ḥukm kān*) does not extend beyond the categorical and conditional (*istithnāʾī*) form, the rules of which are established in logic. Let us use in our examples the first type (*ḍarb*) of the first figure of the categorical syllogism, because it is easier and clearer. As for the conditional syllogism, it has one figure and no more.[6]

He then explains how to use these arguments and how to refute them. Ṭūfī refers twice to Ghazālī, the second time to *Iḥyāʾ ʿUlūm al-Dīn*,[7] but never to *Qisṭās* even though his language and examples are often reminiscent of it, as in his reduction of the two figures of the conditional syllogism to a single one.[8] In this and the next chapter I shall use Ghazālī as my primary source, in part because, unlike Ṭūfī, he classifies his Qurʾānic arguments by type and not by sura. I shall add references to Ṭūfī and my own Qurʾānic examples as needed.

During his first period of teaching, Ghazālī composed at least two books on logic, *Miḥakk al-Naẓar fi al-Manṭiq* and the exhaustive *Miʿyār al-ʿIlm*, usually subtitled *Mantiq Tahāfut al-Falāsifa* (*The Logic of "The Incoherence of the Philosophers"*), which he wrote, in part, to explain the terminology used in *Tahāfut*.[9] *Al-Qisṭās al-Mustaqīm*[10] was composed much later, probably before the end of his eleven-year spiritual retreat (1095/488–1105-06/499) and his return to Nishapur.[11] R.J. McCarthy calls *Qisṭās* "a somewhat curious attempt to Islamicize, or 'Quranize,' some of the Aristotelian, and Stoic, logic which he expounded more 'scientifically' in others of his works."[12] One of Ghazālī's techniques for "Islamicizing" logic is to keep the use of technical terms to a minimum, particularly those which might carry negative connotations. Thus for "syllogism" he uses the word *mīzān* where in his earlier works he used *qiyās*, and for "enthymeme" he speaks of a figure with "an understood premise" (*iḍmār aṣl*)[13] rather than of an "incomplete" or "defective syllogism" (*qiyās nāqiṣ*).[14] When he uses the more technical term *muqaddama* for "premise," he puts it into the mouth of his interlocutor;[15] Ghazālī in his own voice uses *aṣl*. While it is true, as Chelhot points out, that he does not even use the word "logic" (*mantiq*),[16] he twice advises the hearer (and, of course, the reader) who wants more detail on the subject to consult his longer books, *Miḥakk al-Naẓar* and *Miʿyār al-ʿIlm*[17]. And when he launches into his analysis of syllogisms, his terminology is quite technical enough for the subject, as will be seen below.

Qisṭās is cast as a dialogue between the author and an unnamed *Bāṭinī*, who asks Ghazālī by what scales he weighs the truth of knowledge. Is it the scale of opinion and "analogy" (*mīzān al-ra'y wa-al-qiyās*) or the scale of authoritative teaching (*al-ta'līm*)? "But in that case you need to follow the infallible Imam, the authoritative teacher, and I don't see that you are trying to find him!"[18] Ghazālī replies:

> As for the scale of ra'y and qiyās, God forbid that I should resort to it, because it is the scale of Satan. And whoever of my colleagues claims that it is the scale of knowledge, I ask Almighty God to protect me from the evil he does to the religion, because he is an ignorant friend of the religion, and that is worse than an intelligent enemy. If God had blessed the doctrine of the esotericists with success, the first thing they would have learned would have been the art of debate (*al-jidāl*) from the Holy Qur'ān, For God Almighty says, "Summon to the way of your Lord with wisdom and good preaching; and argue with them according to what is best" [Q 16:125]. And note that one group is summoned to God by wisdom, another by preaching, and another by argument ...[19]

By what means, the Bāṭinī repeats, does Ghazālī weigh his knowledge? Ghazālī replies that he weighs it by the Just Balance, following God and being taught by the Qur'ān, which says, "Weigh by the Just Balance (*al-qisṭās al-mustaqīm*)" (Q 17:35). What is this "Just Balance?" Ghazālī replies that it is the five scales that God sent down in his Book and instructed his prophets in their use. "And where are these five scales in the Qur'ān? Is this anything more than a lie and a false allegation (*ifk wa-buhtān*)?"[20]

Ghazālī answers the second question first:

> Haven't you heard Almighty God's words in Sura *al-Raḥmān*: "The Merciful taught the Qur'ān, created the human being, taught him intelligent speech. The sun and the moon follow calculated courses, and the stars and the trees bow down. And the heaven – He raised it and set up the Scale (*al-mīzān*), so that you may not go beyond the scale. So establish the weight (*al-wazn*) with justice

> (*al-qisṭ*), and do not cause the scale to give short weight (*wa-lā tukhsirū al-mīzān*) . . ." [Q 55:1–9]. And have you not heard His words in Sura *al-Ḥadīd*: "We have sent our Messengers with clear proofs (*al-bayyināt*) and sent down with them the Book and the Scale (*al-mīzān*), so that people may behave justly (*li-yaqūm al-nās bi-l-qisṭ*) . . ."
> [Q 57:25][21]

His Bāṭinī companion shows "certain signs of analytical ability" by explaining to Ghazālī how he would determine whether a scale in the public market was giving true weight, thus demonstrating that necessary knowledge results from premises whose truth is determined by experience and sense data (*al-tajriba wa-l-ḥiss*).[22] Thereupon Ghazālī – hoping to alert him to the true nature of his sect and its secret teaching – agrees to explain to him the five scales revealed in the Qur'ān. Ghazālī distinguishes this divine Scale from the material (*jismānī*) scales that weigh wheat and barley and gold and silver; yet the operations of market scales supply terminology for the extended analogy that shapes the epistle.

Ghazālī does not claim explicitly that the proofs which he extracts from the Qur'ān are evidence of its divine inimitability (*i'jāz*), but they are unquestionably of divine origin.

> Know with certainty that this scale (*mīzān*) is the scale of the knowledge of Almighty God, and the knowledge of His Angels, and His Books, and His Apostles, and His Worlds of the Seen and the Unseen (*mulkihi wa-malakūtihi*), so that you may learn from His Prophets how to weigh by it, as they learned from His Angels. For the First Teacher is God (swt), and the second is Gabriel, and the third is the Prophet (s). And all people learn from the Prophets that which they have no way of knowing except through them.[23]

Ghazālī begins the main body of *al-Qisṭās al-Mustaqīm* with a discussion of categorical syllogisms. Although they are the logical figures most immediately recognizable as such, categorical syllogisms arranged in schematic order are not found in the Qur'ān any more than they are found in ordinary human speech or in non-technical prose. Rather, the purpose of schematizing any argument is to restate common thought-processes in order to clarify whether or not a judgment is warranted by the evidence upon which it is based. Most non-technical language omits one or more premises in reasoning to a conclusion, usually because the premises are self-evident or universally accepted.

The categorical syllogism is Ghazālī's first scale, which he calls "the scale of equilibrium" (*mīzān al-taʿādul*). It has three forms, the greater (*al-akbar*), the middle (*al-awsaṭ*) and the lesser (*al-aṣghar*), corresponding to the first, second, and third figures. His method is first to give examples from the Qur'ān, then – at his interlocutor's request – examples from everyday life. He defines each *mīzān* and explains the basis of its validity. When his interlocutor asks why the scales are called "greater," "middle," and "lesser," Ghazālī explains:

> The first scale is the widest of the scales, since knowledge can be derived from it by universal (*ʿāmm*) affirmation, particular affirmation, universal negation, and particular negation: thus four types of intelligibles (*al-maʿārif*) can be weighed by it. As for the second, only negatives can be weighed by it, but both the universal and the particular negative may be so measured. As for the third, only the particular may be weighed by it ... Indeed, weighing a universal case by it is one of the scales of Satan.[24]

Toward the end, he sums up the ways in which one ascertains the truth of all the scales: by sense-data, experience, continuous authority (*al-tawātur al-kāmil*), intuition (*bi-awwal al-ʿaql*), or by deduction (*al-istintāj*) from all of these.[25]

In classical formal logic, the four types of proposition enumerated by Ghazālī are abbreviated and arranged as follows:

A (universal affirmative)
E (universal negative)
I (particular affirmative)
O (particular negative)

They are the building-blocks of all syllogisms. The signifying vowels are incorporated into nineteen Latin mnemonic terms, which serve as names for the valid moods. For easy reference, I shall explain and use a number of these as the chapter progresses.

The first figure

Ghazālī begins his explication with the passage in which Abraham argues with Nimrod over the nature of divine power (Q 2:258):

> Know that the greater scale is the scale of Abraham (a.s.) which he used with Nimrod. From him we learned this scale, but through the medium of the Qur'ān. Now Nimrod had claimed to be divine . . .[26]

Abraham's exercise in reasoning with the "mighty hunter" did not begin well. When Abraham said, "My Lord is the one who gives life and death," Nimrod replied, "*I* give life and death." "He meant," says Ghazālī, "that he gave life to the sperm by sexual intercourse, and he gave death by execution."[27] Then Abraham realized that his example was too difficult for Nimrod to understand, so he turned to something clearer:

> Abraham said: "God causes the sun to rise from the East; so *you* make it rise from the West!" Thus he who rejected faith was confounded. God does not guide a people who do wrong.
>
> (Q 2:258)

That this constitutes a proof Ghazālī knows from another verse: "That was Our proof (*ḥujjatunā*) which We brought to Abraham against his people" (Q 6:78).[28] Now he analyzes how the figure works, as the Bāṭinī analyzed the workings of the scale for weighing gold and silver, and he discovers that it is the result of two premises which combine to produce a result: knowledge. Because the style of the Qur'ān is characterized by "ellipsis and concision" (*al-ḥadhf wa-l-ījāz*), Ghazālī proceeds to set out the proof in conventional form:

> [Whoever has power over the sunrise is God].[29] (A)
> My god is the one who has power over the sunrise. (A)
> Therefore, my god is God ("and not you, Nimrod!")[30] (A)

He concludes by explaining that he knows the truth of the major premise (i.e. that which involves the predicate of the conclusion) by universal stipulation, and that of the minor premise (i.e. that which involves the subject of the conclusion) by sense-data. The Bāṭinī understands the reasoning, but only in this context: "How am I to weigh by it the rest of the intelligibles (*al-maʿārif*) which are difficult for me?"[31] Ghazālī explains:

> This is inferred from the fact that a judgment about a predicate is necessarily a judgment about that of which it is predicated (*al-ḥukm ʿalā al-ṣifa ḥukm ʿalā al-mawṣūf bi-l-ḍarūra*) . . . Thus "the one who makes the sun rise" is the predicate of the Lord (*al-Rabb*), and we have already stated that whoever is characterized as "the one who makes the sun rise" is [characterized] by divinity.[32]

After two everyday examples in which he proves that a mule with a distended stomach is not pregnant and that a worm is a sentient being, Ghazālī adds a condition to his definition: the predicate must be co-extensive with the thing described (*musāwiya li-l-mawṣūf*) or more general than it (*aʿamm minhu*), so that the statement about it will necessarily include that of which it is predicated.[33] Now he cites a well-known example of the same figure from the field of Islamic jurisprudence (*fiqh*):

> All wine (*nabīdh*) is intoxicating. (A)
> All intoxicants are forbidden. (A)
> Therefore all wine is forbidden. (A)[34]

Aristotle considered the first figure to be "the 'perfect' syllogism," the model for all other forms of argument.[35] Ghazālī's examples are of the first mood of the first figure, which is the basic form of the categorical syllogism in all presentations of logic. Medieval logicians gave this first mood the mnemonic name "Barbara," in which the arrangement of the vowels indicates that it is constructed entirely of universal affirmative or "A" propositions. Validity of the figure depends upon a double rule: "The minor premise must be affirmative; the major premise must be universal."[36] Its characteristic arrangement is that the middle term (i.e. the one that does not appear in the conclusion) is the subject of the major premise and the predicate of the minor premise.[37] Ghazālī's restatement of his Qur'ānic example follows this pattern, but his legal example reverses the arrangement and puts the minor premise first.[38] Most syllogistic proofs in the Qur'ān appear reducible to the first figure, for the same reason that most of its rhetorical proofs are based on contrast: when the aim is to alert the hearer to One Truth and One Reality, the most fitting method is by this *Dictum de omni et nullo* – the Law of All or None.[39]

Here are two examples used by the Ḥanbalī jurist and theologian Najm al-Dīn al-Ṭūfī, schematized and with the intervening supporting verses removed. Of the first he concludes, "It is a syllogism (*qiyās*) of the first form, clear in and of itself (*bayyin bi-dhātihi*):"

> Those who disbelieved will be driven to Hell in a crowd until, when they arrive, its gates will be opened and its keepers will say, "Did not Apostles come to you from among yourselves, reciting the signs of God and warning you about meeting this Day of yours?" They will reply, "Oh yes, but the sentence of punishment against the unbelievers has now proven to be true!" To them will be said, "Enter the gates of Hell, to remain there eternally!"
>
> (Q 39:71–72)
>
> You were warned and continued to disbelieve. (A)
> All who were warned and continued to disbelieve will go to Hell. (A)
> Therefore, you will go to Hell. (A)[40]
>
> "When we die and have turned to dust [shall we return to life?] That would be a long way back!" We know what the earth takes away from them, and We have a Book that records all. But they deny the truth [even] when it comes to them, and they are in a state of confusion.
>
> (Q 50:3–5)
>
> Resurrection of bodies is a possibility announced by one who tells the truth. (A)
> Every possibility announced [as a fact] by one who tells the truth is a fact (*wāqiʿ*). (A)
> [Therefore resurrection of bodies is a fact.] (A)[41]

In the latter example, Ṭūfī equates the statement of the unbelievers with a denial of resurrection and God's reply with its affirmation, and he words the premises accordingly. In both cases, he has put the minor premise first, presumably because he considers that arrangement to be rhetorically more effective.

To Ghazālī's and Ṭūfī's four Qur'ānic syllogisms in Barbara I shall add two more simple ones. Note that the minor premises of both and the conclusion of the second apply to single individuals; but because an individual constitutes a logical class, the premises and conclusions are still considered A propositions.

> Spendthrifts are brothers of the satans (*al-shayāṭīn*), and Satan is ungrateful to his Lord.
>
> (Q 17:27)

> Spendthrifts are the brothers of the satans. (A)
> Satan is ungrateful to the Lord. (A)
> [Therefore, spendthrifts are ungrateful to the Lord.] (A)

> We never sent an apostle or a prophet before you but that, when he was reciting,[42] Satan threw [something false] into his recitation. So God abrogates what Satan throws in; then God confirms his Signs. And God is All-Knowing, All-Wise.
>
> (Q 22:52)

> All prophets have been interfered with by Satan. (A)
> You [, Muḥammad,] are a prophet. (A)
> [Therefore, you have been interfered with by Satan.] (A)

The second pattern is also found in Qur'ān 35:4 and other passages in which God consoles Muḥammad, whose own people have rejected him, by recounting similar episodes from the lives of previous prophets.

Although Ghazālī confines himself to the first mood of the first figure, he need not have done so, as all four moods can be found in the Qur'ān. The second mood of the first figure is called "Darii," signaling that it consists of one universal (A) and one particular (I) affirmative, with a conclusion that is also a particular affirmative (I). This mood is used to demonstrate the possibility that not all of the People of the Book are bound for Hell.

> But those among [the Jews] who are well-grounded in knowledge and the believers believe in what was sent down to you and what was sent down before you. And (especially) those who pray, and those who give alms and believe in God and the Last Day – We shall grant them a great reward.
>
> (Q 4:162)

> All who believe in Revelation, pray, give alms, and believe in God and the Last Day, will have a heavenly reward. (A)
> Some Jews believe in Revelation, pray, give alms, and believe in God and the Last Day. (I)
> Therefore, some Jews will have a heavenly reward. (I)

> And when [some Christians] hear what has been sent down to the Apostle, you see their eyes overflowing with tears, for the Truth which they recognize. They say, "Our Lord, we have believed, so record us among the witnesses.[43] Why should we not believe in God and the Truth that has come to us, when we long for our Lord to admit us to the company of the righteous?" For what they have said God has rewarded them with Gardens beneath which rivers flow, dwelling eternally therein. That is the reward for those who do good (*al-muḥsinīn*).
>
> (Q 5:83–85)

> All who believe in the truth of Muḥammad's message will go to heaven. (A)
> Some Christians believe in the truth of Muḥammad's message. (I)
> Therefore, some Christians will go to heaven. (I)

More common than syllogisms in Darii are those in the third mood, "Celarent", which produce a universal negative (E) conclusion on the basis of a universal negative (E) major and a universal affirmative (A) minor premise. The legal and theological uses of universal negative conclusions are clear:

> Those who believe in God and the Last Day do not ask you to exempt them from fighting with their goods and their persons; and God knows well those who fear Him. Only those who do not believe in God and the Last Day, and whose hearts are in doubt, will ask you for exemption. Thus in their doubt they waver.
>
> (Q 9:44–45)

> Those who ask to be exempted from fighting do not believe in God. (E)
> [X, Y, and Z have asked to be exempted from fighting.] (A)
> Therefore, X, Y, and Z do not believe in God. (E)

> They attribute to some of His servants a share with Him [in His godhead]. Humanity is clearly ungrateful [to the point of blasphemy]. What! Has He taken for Himself daughters from out of His creation and bestowed sons upon *you*? When one of them is informed of [the birth of] one of those he has set up as a likeness to the All-Merciful,

> his face darkens and he is filled with silent rage. Is one decked out in ornaments and inarticulate in debate [fit to be associated with God?]
>
> (Q 43:15–18)

> One decked out in ornaments and inarticulate is not a fit partner for God (even among the polytheists). (E)
> Women are decked out in ornaments and are inarticulate. (A)
> [Therefore women are not fit partners for God.] (E)

To complete the four moods of the first-figure syllogism, let us consider the eponymous passage from Sura 26 *al-Shuʿarāʾ*, which can be rendered as a syllogism in "Ferio," which consists of one universal negative (E) and one particular affirmative (I) premise yielding a particular negative (O) conclusion. The combination of negative and particular propositions restricts the form's usefulness, yet the complexities of Qur'ānic diction undoubtedly hide many more.

> And the poets – it is those gone astray who follow them. Have you not seen that they wander through every valley, and that they say things that they do not do? Except those who believe, and do good works, and remember God often, and triumph after having been wronged. Those who have wronged them will learn what a disastrous turn they will take!
>
> (Q 26:224–227)

> [No believers say things they do not do.] (E)
> Some poets are believers. (I)
> Therefore some poets do not say things they do not do. (O)

The second figure

As his primary example of the second-figure syllogism, Ghazālī uses another episode from the life of Abraham:

> When the night grew dark around him, he saw a star. He said: "That is my Lord." And when it set he said: "I do not love things that set!" And when he saw the moon rising, he said: "That is my Lord." And when it set, he said: "If my Lord does not guide me, I shall certainly be one of those

> who go astray!" And when he saw the sun rising, he said: "That is my Lord: that is the greatest one." And when it set, he said: "O my people! I declare myself free[44] of what you associate with God! I turn my face as a monotheist (*ḥanīf^an^*) to the One Who created the heavens and the earth, nor am I one of those who associate other deities with God!"
>
> (Q 6:76–79)

The rule of the second-figure syllogism is: "One premise must be negative; the major premise must be universal."[45] Ghazālī's first example is of the first mood of the second figure, which is called "Camestres" to show that its major premise is a universal affirmative (A), its minor premise a universal negative (E), and its conclusion also a universal negative (E). He begins with the bare phrase "I do not love things that set" (*lā uḥibb al-āfilīn*) and renders the syllogism as follows:

> The moon sets (*al-qamar āfil*). (A)
> The Deity does not "set." (E)
> Therefore the moon is not a deity. (E)[46]

Again the Bāṭinī asks that the reasoning be clarified, "For denying divinity to the moon is clear to me." Ghazālī explains:

> [For] every pair of which something that is predicated of one is denied of the other, those two things are unlike ... That of which something is denied that is affirmed of another thing is unlike that other. "Setting" is denied of God; "setting" is affirmed of the moon; and this makes the distinction between the two logically necessary ...[47]

He admits that Abraham's knowledge that God does not "set" is not *a priori* (*lam yakun dhālika al-ʿilm awwalīy^an^ lahu*) but is derived from two other premises that have produced his existing knowledge that God does not change: (1) everything that changes is contingent (*ḥādith*); (2) "setting" is a type of change.[48]

Ghazālī's next example comes from confrontations with the Christians and Jews:

> The Jews and Christians say, "We are the sons of God, and beloved of Him." Say: "Then why does He punish you for

your sins?" No, you are human beings from among those He has created. He forgives whom He will and punishes whom He will . . .

(Q 5:18)

Ghazālī's schema for this Qur'ānic rebuttal is in the third mood, "Cesare," of which the major premise and the conclusion are universal negatives (E) and the minor a universal affirmative (A):

[Sons are not punished.] (E)
You are punished. (A)
Therefore, you are not sons. (E)

His third example is in Camestres:

Say: "O you who are Jews, if you are the friends of God to the exclusion of other people, then hope for death, if you are sincere!" But they will never hope for it, because of what their hands have done before. And God knows all about those who do evil.

(Q 62:6–7, cf. 2:94–95)

[The friend (*al-walīy*) hopes to meet his Friend (*walīyahu*- sc. God).] (A)
The Jew does not hope to meet God. (E)
Therefore, the Jew is not the friend of God. (E)

Ghazālī's everyday example is in Camestres as well:

A stone is an inanimate object (*jamād*). (A)
A human is not an inanimate object. (E)
Therefore, a human being is not a stone. (E)[49]

"Say: 'Do I want anyone other than God as Lord, when He is Lord of all things?'" (Q 6:164). From this verse in Sura 6, to which he compares Q 6:14 and Q 6:114, Ṭūfī extracts the following syllogism:

Everything except God has a lord (*kull mā siwā Allāh marbūb*).
Nothing that has a lord *is* a lord (*lā shay' min al-marbūb bi-rabb*).[50]

> Therefore, nothing except God is a lord (*fa-lā shay' mimmā siwā Allāh bi-rabb*).

The syllogism appears at first glance to be made up not of simple but of "covertly multiple premises."[51] However, by taking into account the construction of the Arabic language upon roots and patterns, the terms can in fact be reduced to three, resulting in a syllogism in Camestres.

> All that is not-God has a lord. (A)
> Nothing that has a lord *is* a lord. (E)
> Therefore, nothing that is not-God is a lord. (E)

The conclusion is still not the one desired, however, but as it is a universal negative proposition, it can be converted:

> Therefore, there is no lord except God (*fa-idh^{an} lā rabb illā Allāh*).

Still attracted to cases that are more complex than his own analysis indicates, Ṭūfī tackles a long passage in which some of the prophet Ṣāliḥ's people reject his prophethood because he is unable to prevent them from defying divine commands, while others among his people attempt to defend him. "If you wish," says Ṭūfī, "you may arrange it using the categorical (*ḥamlī*) method:"[52]

> Every apostle tells the truth. (A)
> Everyone who tells the truth brings about what he promises. (A)
> You, Ṣāliḥ, cannot bring about what you have promised. (E)
> Therefore, you are not an apostle or a truth-teller. (E)
> (Q 7:73–77)

Ṭufī ignores the fact that there are too many terms here for a single syllogism; it is actually two, both in Camestres:

> Everyone who tells the truth brings about what he promises. (A)
> You, Ṣāliḥ, cannot bring about what you have promised. (E)
> Therefore, you are not a truth-teller. (E)

Every apostle tells the truth. (A)
You are not telling the truth. (E)
Therefore, you are not an apostle. (E)

But while the opponents' reasoning is valid, Ṭūfī points out that their premises are irrelevant (*mamnūʿatān*). First, the promised punishment will come not immediately but later, to allow the people time to repent, as was the case with Jonah. Thus the recalcitrant people of Thamūd will not be around to profit from arguments based upon their own demise. Second, it is in any case not a prophet who brings on the punishment, but God Himself.

Countless examples of Camestres can be found in the Qurʾān. I shall add only four schemata from well-known *topoi*:

> The Creator of the heavens and the earth – how can He have a son when He has no consort? . . .
>
> (Q 6:101)

[All who have sons have consorts.] (A)
God has no consort. (E)
Therefore, God has no son. (E)

> Those [false deities] whom they invoke besides God have not created anything but are themselves created.
>
> (Q 16:20)

God is a creator. (A)
No idols are creators. (E)
[Therefore no idols are God.] (E)

> We know well that they say: "It is a human being who dictates to him!" But the language of the one to whom they incline is foreign, obscure, while this is a clear Arabic tongue.
>
> (Q 16:103)

[Whoever dictates in a language must speak the language.] (A)
X does not speak the language. (E)
Therefore X does not dictate [the Qurʾān to Muḥammad]. (E)[53]

> Or [the unbelievers' state] is like the darkness of a bottomless ocean . . . And one to whom God gives no light *has* no light.
>
> (Q 24:40)

[All who have light have light from God.] (A)
No unbelievers have light from God. (E)
Therefore, no unbelievers have light. (E)

The second mood of the second-figure is called "Baroco," signaling that it consists of one universal affirmative (A) and one particular negative (O), with a conclusion that is also a particular negative (O). The fourth mood is called "Festino:" universal negative (E), particular affirmative (I), and particular negative (O). The passages exemplifying the first-figure syllogisms in Darii (see above) with which Ghazālī demonstrates the possibility that not all of the People of the Book are bound for Hell can, without violence to the text, also be expressed as second-figure syllogisms. We have converted the first to Baroco, the second to Festino.

All who believe in Revelation, pray, give alms, and believe in God and the Last Day, will have a heavenly reward. (A)
Some Jews do not believe in Revelation, pray, give alms, and believe in God and the Last Day. (O)
Therefore, some Jews will not have a heavenly reward. (O)
(Q 4:162)

None who believe in the truth of Muḥammad's message will go to hell. (E)
Some Christians believe in the truth of Muḥammad's message. (I)
Therefore, some Christians will not go to hell. (O)
(Q 5:83–85)

The third and fourth figures

Ghazālī's "lesser" scale is the third figure of the categorical syllogism, "which we have learned from God (swt) where He dictated it (*'allamahu*) to Muḥammad (s) in the Qur'ān."[54] This time it comes from the life of Moses:

They do not give God His due when they say: "God revealed nothing to any human." Say: "Who revealed the Book that Moses brought as a light and a guide to humanity? But you put it on pages which you show and many of which you hide ..."
(Q 6:91)

Or, in Ghazālī's rendering:

> [Moses was a human being.] (A)
> God sent a book to Moses. (A)

These premises necessarily produce a particular conclusion (*qaḍīya khāṣṣa*):

> Therefore, God sends books to some humans. (I)

Ghazālī notes that the first premise is known through sense-data, the second because it is accepted by the opponents, as proven by the fact that they hide some of what God revealed. This is a rhetorical proof, notes Ghazālī, "and for that it is enough that the two premises be accepted by the opponent ... even if someone else might have some doubt concerning the matter ... And most Qur'ānic proofs proceed in this manner."[55]

Ghazālī's first non-Qur'ānic example is:

> A snake is an animal. (A)
> A snake walks without legs. (A)
> Therefore, some animals walk without legs. (I)

All these are examples of the first mood of the third figure, called "Darapti" for its arrangements of universal and particular propositions. The rule for the third figure is: "The minor premise must be affirmative; the conclusion must be particular. To this should really be added: one of the premises must be universal."[56]

Ghazālī's definition is that:

> [For] every two predicates applied to a single thing, some instances of each of the predicates must necessarily apply to the other ... Do you not see that, if it is predicated of the human being both that he is living (*ḥayawān*) and that he is a body, it necessarily follows that some bodies are living; while it does not follow that every body is living; nor should you be misled by the possibility of describing every living thing as being a body. Since applying each predicate to the other is not necessary in every case, the knowledge obtained thereby is not necessary [either].[57]

In addition to four valid moods of the first-figure syllogism and four of the second, there are six valid moods of the third-figure syllogism (of which the first is Darapti) and five of the fourth figure, for a grand total of nineteen valid moods of the categorical syllogism. Omitting the fourth figure entirely, Ghazālī does not go beyond Darapti, nor shall we. The point is not to exhaust the resources of classical formal logic (or the reader!) but to show how Qur'ānic arguments work both rhetorically and logically. The reader trained in symbolic or mathematical logic may wish to bring these methods to bear as well. But one should remember that the Qur'ān was revealed in natural language, in words. Numbers and non-verbal symbols indeed have meaning, but calling them "language" is ultimately a metaphor. Misplaced concreteness is also a fallacy.

9

CONDITIONAL AND DISJUNCTIVE ARGUMENTS

Ghazālī's fourth and fifth scales were schematized not by the Peripatetics but by logicians of the Stoic school. They posited as axioms five "undemonstrated" arguments, two conditional and three disjunctive, from which they held that all other arguments could be derived.[1] They did not use Aristotelian terminology: where the Peripatetics used "A," "B," and "C" to represent terms (i.e. adjectives or nouns), the Stoics used "first," "second," and "third" to represent entire propositions. Ghazālī treats conditional arguments much less analytically than he does categorical ones; thus I have rearranged his examples considerably in order to illustrate the points at issue. Because he and Ṭūfī do not distinguish between the two types of conditional syllogism in a schematic way, and because Ṭūfī dismisses disjunctive syllogisms as merely a rhetorical device and omits them altogether, I begin with the Stoic schemata, providing Ghazālī's, Ṭūfī's, and my own examples as needed.

CONDITIONAL ARGUMENTS

The classic Stoic schema of the type 1 conditional is:

If the first, then the second.
The first.
Therefore the second.

It should be noted that the valid form of type 1 (*modus ponens*) is that which affirms the antecedent. The classical example of it is:

If it is day, then it is light.
It is day.
Therefore it is light.

The schema of the type 2 conditional is:

> If the first, then the second.
> Not the second.
> Therefore, not the first.

Thus the valid form of type 2 (*modus tollens*) denies the consequent:

> If it is day, then it is light.
> It is not light.
> Therefore, it is not day.[2]

The fallacious forms of conditional argument are so close to the valid ones, and the classical examples so forgettable,[3] that I have chosen other examples more likely to be remembered. The fallacy characteristic of type 1 is that of *affirming the consequent*. Logician Irving Copi's example is part of an old debate:

> If Bacon wrote *Hamlet*, then Bacon was a great writer.
> Bacon was a great writer.
> Therefore Bacon wrote *Hamlet*.[4] [Fallacious]

The fallacy of type 2 is that of *denying the antecedent*. Copi's example, again, is tailored for the academic audience:

> If Carl embezzled the college funds, then Carl is guilty of a felony.
> Carl did not embezzle the college funds.
> Therefore Carl is not guilty of a felony.[5] [Fallacious]

This is a clear fallacy. The felonies of academics are not limited to embezzlement.

The Arabic language is rich in constructions that express the nuances of condition, consequence, implication, and entailment. The three conditional particles *in, idhā*, and *law* are usually understood to indicate, respectively, pure hypothesis, time-related possibility ("if-and-when," "whenever"), and condition contrary to fact. Other conditionals are expressed by such words as "whoever" (*man*), "whatever" (*mahmā*), and "wherever" (*aynamā*). All are used in the Qur'ān, but we shall not pursue the lexical differences between them, only establish that the word in question actually signals the existence of a conditional relation. Not every conditional construction is introduced by a particle: often the relationship is expressed through syntax and grammar alone: "Keep your covenant and We will keep Ours" (Q 2:40). The converse is also true: not every "if"-word sets up a conditional proposition. It may actually mask a categorical statement: "Do not fear them but fear Me, if you are believers!" (Q 3:175).

The conditional syllogism is Ghazālī's fourth "scale," which he calls *mīzān al-talāzum*, the "scale of mutual implication."[6] He defines it very succinctly, not drawing a clear distinction between the two types of conditional inference and putting the second type first:

> Everything that is consequent to something (*lāzim li-al-shay'*) follows it (*tābiʿ lahu*) in every case; so that denying the consequent necessarily denies the antecedent (*al-malzūm*). The existence of the antecedent necessitates the existence of the consequent. As for negation of the antecedent and affirmation of the consequent, nothing results from these two; rather, they are of the scale of Satan.[7]

At the end of his short chapter, Ghazālī finally sets out consistent illustrations of the valid and the invalid conditionals. As in his definition, he describes both the valid forms and puts the type 2 argument first. I have separated and rearranged them to suit the present context.

The type 1 ("constructive") mode:

> If Zayd's prayer is valid, then he is ritually pure.
> It is known that his prayer is valid.
> Therefore, he is ritually pure.

If the antecedent is denied instead of affirmed, a fallacious form results.

> If Zayd's prayer is valid, then he is ritually pure.
> His prayer is not valid.
> Therefore, he is not ritually pure. [Fallacious]

" . . . because the invalidity of his prayer may be because of the failure of some condition other than ritual purity; because this is denial of the antecedent, and it does not indicate denial of the consequent."[8]

The type 2 ("destructive") mode:

> If Zayd's prayer is valid, then he is ritually pure.
> It is known that he is not ritually pure.
> Therefore, his prayer is not valid.

If the consequent is affirmed instead of denied, a fallacy is produced, "because his prayer may be invalid for another cause (*ʿilla*), because this is the existence of the consequent and does not indicate the existence of the antecedent." Ghazālī illustrates the fallacy as follows:

> If Zayd's prayer is valid, then he is ritually pure.
> Zayd is ritually pure.
> Therefore, his prayer is valid.[9] [Fallacious]

Type 1 conditionals ("constructive" mood) in the Qurʾān

One does not find in the Qurʾān a great many full conditional arguments of the first type, that is, those which produce a conclusion by affirming the antecedent. Here is one of the clearest examples:

> The Jews and the Christians will never be happy with you unless you follow their religion. Say: "The guidance of God *is* guidance!" And if you gave in to their desires after the knowledge that has come to you, you would find no protector against God, and no supporter.
>
> (Q 2:120)

Here is the argument:

> If you do not follow their religion, the Jews and Christians will never accept you.
> You do not follow their religion.
> Therefore, the Jews and Christians will never accept you.

Far more common are versions in which only the antecedent is stated, leaving the rest to be inferred by the audience. Sometimes in lieu of the consequent there is a rhetorical question:

> Say: Do you see that if [the Revelation] is from God and you reject it, who is in greater error than one who has split off far away?
>
> (Q 41:52, cf. 46:10)

The argument is, of course, meant to be completed as follows:

> If the Revelation is from God and you reject it, [then you are in error (*ḍalāl*).]
> [The Revelation is from God and you reject it.]
> [Therefore, you are in error.]

The bracketing reflects the fact that not even the whole conditional proposition is stated explicitly, only the antecedent. The listener or reader extrapolates the consequent from the rhetorical question that follows it, then uses it to complete the argument.

The type 1 conditional proceeds by affirmation; and this positive form or "constructive mood" of a conditional is far less effective rhetorically than is the negative or "destructive mood." There are no surprises, and the conclusion can be an anticlimax. It must be noted that the terms "constructive" and "destructive" indicate only that the antecedent is being affirmed or the consequent denied; they do not imply the respective absence or presence of negatives in the argument. The first example given here (Q 2:120 above) is in the constructive mood, even though it contains grammatical negatives; for that very reason it is rhetorically effective and comes to a resounding conclusion.[10] In some of the best-known Qur'ānic passages, conditionals in the constructive mood are strengthened by their twins in the destructive mood, as I shall illustrate below.

Both of Ghazālī's paraphrases of the Qur'ānic arguments and the first part of his definition are of the Stoic type 2, in which the consequent is denied. Obviously, he found type 2 to be more useful in argument than type 1; however, he evidently found type 1 easier to demonstrate, as three of his four everyday examples affirm the antecedent. I paraphrase only the first, because the second and fourth have the same form; the third is of type 2.

> If the sun is up, the stars are hidden.
> The sun is up.
> Therefore the stars are hidden.[11]

Type 2 conditionals ("destructive" mood) in the Qur'ān

Qur'ānic conditional arguments proceed far more often by denying the consequent (type 2) than by affirming the antecedent (type 1), and they often appear to reflect actual debates. Both the prophets and their opponents use them:

> Those who associate other deities with God will say: "If God had willed, we would not have associated them with Him, nor would our fathers; nor would He have forbidden us anything . . ." In this way those before them denied [the Truth], so that they tasted Our punishment. Say: "God's is the decisive argument (*fa-li-Llāh al-ḥujja al-bāligha*): if He had willed, He would indeed have guided you all." Say: "Bring your witnesses to testify that God has forbidden it;" and if they testify, do not testify with them . . .
>
> (Q 6:148–150; cf. 10:99–100, 16:35)

The polytheists argue as follows:

> If God had willed, we would not worship many Gods.
> [We do worship many gods.]
> [Therefore God did not will (otherwise).]

The Prophet's rebuttal:

> If God had willed, he would have guided you all.
> [God did not guide you.]
> [Therefore God did not will (otherwise)[12]

Though the Qur'ān can hardly be expected to acknowledge the point, the result of the debate is a logical deadlock, as both parties reason validly in the same conditional schema to prove opposite points. Perhaps for that reason, Muḥammad is instructed, in effect, to begin his efforts again by reciting what God has in fact prohibited: idolatry (*shirk*), disrespect for parents, infanticide, murder, and the like, all of them laws observed by the Abrahamic faiths equally. Not coincidentally, the passage ends with a reference to the Covenant: "Keep the Covenant of God: that is what He has charged you with so that perhaps you will remember" (Q 6:152).[13]

Ṭūfī grants a certain validity to the polytheists' statement by accepting it as "true in itself," since everything that happens indeed happens by the will of God, "but they expressed it in a tone of sin and obstinacy (*al-ʿanat wa-l-ʿinād*) . . . and they were reproved for it because their motive was corrupt."[14]

Ghazālī's example of the Qur'ānic conditional syllogism is a type 2 argument. He bases it upon three verses:

> If (*law*) there were gods besides God in them, then both [the heavens and the earth] would have come to ruin.
>
> (Q 21:22)
>
> Say: "If (*law*) there were other gods along with Him, as they say, they would have sought a way to get at the Lord of the Throne (*la-btaghaw ilā dhī al-ʿarsh sabil*)" [sc. to kill Him, then contend with each other for godhood][15]
>
> (Q 17:42)
>
> If (*law*) these were gods, they would not have gone to Hell; but all of them are there eternally!
>
> (Q 21:99)

From these three verses he constructs two arguments:

> If there were two gods in the world, it would be ruined.
> It has not been ruined.
> Therefore there are not two gods.[16]
>
> If there were other gods than the Lord of the Throne, they would have sought a way to get at the Lord of the Throne.
> It is known that they did not seek such a thing.
> Therefore, there are no gods except the Lord of the Throne.[17]

The second argument is based upon the last two verses, as Q 21:99 provides the grounds for denying the consequent: the evidence that the so-called deities found no way to approach God is that they are in Hell forever.

Ghazālī's everyday example comes from *fiqh*:

> If the sale of something absent (*ghāʾib*)[18] were legally valid (*ṣaḥīḥ*), [its legality] would be clearly implied (*fa-yulzamu bi-taṣrīḥ al-ilzām*).
> It is not clearly implied.
> Therefore, [the sale] is not legally valid.[19]

My first example in this section, Qur'ān 6:148–150, illustrated the practical application of the type 2 conditional in debate. A similar passage has an even more confrontational tone in that the consequent is not a proposition but a command:

> Say [to the Jews]: "If the Final Home in God is for you alone and no one else, then wish for death, if you are telling the truth!" But they will never wish for it, because of what they have already done; and God knows all about the wrongdoers.
>
> (Q 2:94–95, cf. 62:6–7)

> "If you (Jews) are assured of heaven, then wish for death."
> They will never wish for death.
> Therefore, they are not assured of heaven.

Conditionals in which the consequent is in the form of a command are classic forms of challenge. Ṭūfī calls Qur'ān 2:23–24 "a conditional inference in the form of an exposure of weakness and a challenge" (*sūrat al-taʿjīz wa-l-taḥaddī*).[20]

> If you are in doubt about what We revealed to Our servant, then produce a sura of the same sort, and call your witnesses – besides God! – if you are telling the truth. And if you do not – and you never will – then beware of the Fire whose fuel is humans and stones, made ready for those who refuse to believe.
>
> (Q 2:23–24)

The construction with a condition followed by an imperative is treated further below, and especially in Chapter 4. Forensic techniques are the subject of the last chapter of this book.

One of the verses used in the classic arguments for the Qur'ān's "miraculous inimitability" (*iʿjāz*) is a conditional:

> Do they not pay due attention to the Qur'ān? If it were from anyone other than God, they would have found much discrepancy in it.
>
> (Q 4:82)

The theologians completed the argument validly as follows:

> If the Qur'ān were not from God, they would have found much discrepancy in it.
> They found no discrepancy in it.
> Therefore, the Qur'ān is from God.

Heretics seized upon the verse as a challenge. Ibn al-Rīwandī's *Kitāb al-Dāmigh* was an attack upon the Qur'ān; two of his examples of alleged contradiction were between Qur'ān 6:59 and Qur'ān 2:143 and 47:31, and between Qur'ān 41:9 and Qur'ān 41:10.[21] But the proposition in Q 4:82 cannot validly be disproven by affirming the consequent:

> If the Qur'ān were not from God, they would have found much discrepancy in it.
> They did find discrepancy in it.
> Therefore, the Qur'ān is not from God. [Fallacious]

The major premise must be reworded if a type 2 syllogism is to be maintained:

> If the Qur'ān were from God, they would have found no discrepancy in it.
> They did find discrepancy.
> Therefore, it is not from God.

Thus the Qur'ānic wording as it stands cannot be used in a type 2 conditional to prove the opposite of what it asserts. A type 1 conditional *can* be built on the verse as it stands:

> If the Qur'ān were not from God, they would have found much discrepancy in it.
> The Qur'ān is not from God.
> Therefore there is discrepancy in it.

This is a formally valid argument, but it does not appear to reproduce Ibn al-Rīwandī's train of thought, since his point was to prove that the Qur'ān was not from God, and the existence of discrepancy was his minor premise, not his conclusion.

Ṭūfī's treatment is extended, analytic, and addresses all objections. The adversaries, he says, have argued against the Qur'ānic conclusion in two ways. The first is to deny the inseparability (*mulāzama*) of the two propositions. They do not concede that a human source would be inconsistent, because many humans are capable of avoiding self-contradiction (*tanāquḍ*), and it is possible that Muḥammad was like that. Their second argument is not to concede denial of the consequent: they claim that in fact the Qur'ān does contain discrepancies. On the first point, Ṭūfī allows that, although few humans could avoid inconsistency without help from God, some might, but not an illiterate person like the Prophet. On the second, he again allows that there are differences in the Qur'ān, but these are due to differences in time, place, and circumstance. No two cases in the Qur'ān are exactly alike, but when different verses address a single case, there are no discrepancies.[22]

Pure, mixed and ambiguous conditionals

All of Ghazālī's conditionals and most of the Qur'ānic ones are not "pure" conditionals but "mixed" ones; that is, the first premise is a conditional but the second premise and the conclusion are categorical statements. Pure conditionals (or "pure hypotheticals") are of the following form:

> If the first, then the second.
> If the second, then the third.
> Therefore, if the first, then the third.[23]

The Qur'ān contains very few "pure" conditionals immediately identifiable as such, though close analysis would undoubtedly uncover more. The most obvious come from Q 76:29–30 and its analogue Q 81:27–29 and have had vast implications for the development of Muslim theology.

> This is a reminder: so whoever wills will take a path to his Lord; and you do not will unless God wills.
> (Q 76:29–30, cf. 81:27–29)

Schematized, the argument is:

> If [and only if] God wills, you will.
> If you will, then you will take a path to your Lord
> Therefore, if God wills, you will take a path to your Lord.

Thus the type 1 and type 2 conditionals are not "pure" but "mixed" conditionals. Sometimes they are intertwined. Qur'ān 2:23–24, cited in the previous section[24] as an example of challenge, actually contains one argument of each kind. The first is a type 2:

> If you are in doubt about Revelation, then produce a sura like it.
> You cannot produce a sura like it.
> Therefore, fear the Fire prepared for the *kāfirīn*.

The second is a type 1:

> If you cannot produce a sura like it, then fear the Fire.
> You cannot produce a sura like it.
> Therefore, fear the Fire.

An oft-quoted example of Qur'ānic style comes in a consolation to the Muslims after the battle of Uḥud:

> If God supports you, then none can overcome you; and if He abandons you, who is there to help you after that? So upon God let the believers rely.
>
> (Q 3:160)

The first argument is type 2:

> If God supports you, then none can overcome you.
> People have overcome you [today].
> Therefore God was not supporting you [today].

The second is type 1:

> If God withdraws his support, then none can help you.
> God withdrew his support [today].
> Therefore no one could help you.

Sometimes a too-close adherence to the Qur'ānic wording will produce a fallacious argument. For example, let us look at God's answer to Moses when Moses asks God to show himself so that he may look at him:

> "You will never see Me. But look to the mountain: if it stays firm in its place, you will see Me." But when He appeared in glory to the mountain, He made it like a flat plain, and Moses fell down, thunderstruck. When he came to his senses, he said "Glory be to You! I turn to You in repentance (*tubtu ilayka*[25]), and I am the first of the believers."
>
> (Q 7:143)

If we take the wording of the major proposition directly from the text, we produce the following argument:

> If the mountain stays firm in its place, you will see me.
> The mountain does not stay in its place.
> Therefore, you will not see me. [Fallacious]

This argument is invalid because it denies the antecedent, yet its strong conclusion satisfies the hearer's faith. Reversing antecedent and consequent preserves the conclusion:

> If you are able to see me, the mountain will stay in its place.
> The mountain does not stay in its place.
> Therefore, you will not see me.

If we insist on keeping the Qur'ānic language of the major premise, we can construct a valid argument but cannot prove the point at issue, which is that God cannot be seen:

> If the mountain stays firm in its place, you will see me.
> You will not see me.
> Therefore, the mountain will not stay firm in its place.

The twin theological questions of whether God could be seen and whether he spoke to prophets attracted the exegetes' attention to this long verse. As Rāzī says, "In the verse are eminent, lofty questions from the divine sciences."[26] Because the verse "connects" (*ʿallaqa*) the impossibility of seeing God with the impossibility of the permanent stability of the mountain as evidenced by its collapse, that appears to have satisfied Muʿtazilī-leaning exegetes, who devote more attention to the grammar of the statement, "You will never see Me (*lan taranī*)."[27] Rāzī, however, after enumerating (but not schematizing) the permutations of existence, non-existence, and possible existence of both the Beatific Vision and the permanence of the mountain, concludes that both are possible (*mumkin al-wujūd jā'iz al-ḥuṣūl*) and that that is enough upon which to base the conclusion. "*Wa-Llāhu a'lam.*"[28]

Other "if" constructions

Irving Copi has described four different types of implication commonly expressed by "if-then" statements. The first three express three sorts of connection: logic, definition, and causation; but the fourth "reports a decision of the speaker to behave in a certain way under certain circumstances."[29] This exactly describes the sort of declaration found in Q 39:7:

> If you refuse to believe, God is independent of you, but He does not accept rejection from His servants. And if you give thanks, He is pleased to accept it from you ...
>
> (Q 39:7)

Such statements go beyond observing the letter of the Covenant to set for human beings the proper moral tone.

Most if-statements in the Qur'ān prove on analysis to be rules or laws. Logically enough, many of these begin with an if-clause and end with a command; but they do not become actual arguments with consequences until the anticipated situation actually happens and the rule must be applied. "If you find no one at home, do not enter [the house] until you are given permission" (Q 24:28). The requirement to treat wives fairly begins with a conditional and ends with a command:

> If you fear that you will not be fair [to more than one], then [marry] one, or what your right hands possess: that will make you less likely to commit injustice.
>
> (Q 4:3)

It is then up to the prospective husband to reason that if he marries one woman because of her beauty, another because of her wealth, a third because of her father's influence, and a fourth because she is actually the one best suited to be his wife, he is likely to be unfair to one or more of them and should change his plans accordingly.

If I fear injustice, then I should marry only one.
I fear injustice.
Therefore I shall marry only one.

Qur'ān 4:101 combines a rule with two conditions, but are they alternatives or do they apply simultaneously?

> When you are traveling in the earth, there is no blame on you if you shorten your prayers, if you are afraid that the unbelievers will attack you.
>
> (Q 4:101)

Is it the "traveler's" (shortened) prayer that is to be further shortened or the basic prayer, that is, the one required of those staying at home? What if one is in fear but is not traveling? Interpretation of the conditions – home, travel, fear – has enabled legal scholars to derive three possible alternatives: *ṣalāt al-iqāma, ṣalāt al-safar,* and *ṣalāt al-khawf.*[30]

The same conditional constructions found in these laws of limited scope are also found in the sweeping moral principles arising from the Covenant. Let us look at a conditional that does not use a word for "if:"

> Because of [the sin of Cain], We decreed for the children of Israel that whoever kills (*man qatala*) a person, except for murder or corruption in the earth – it is as though he had killed all people. And whoever saves a life – it is as though he had saved all humanity.
>
> (Q 5:32)

This is a general moral principle that requires no particular application to lend it force. Of course, a particular instance has just preceded the rule and in fact is the occasion for its enunciation:

Whoever kills another person without just cause, it is as though he killed all humanity.
Cain killed another man without just cause.
Therefore, it is as though Cain had killed all humanity.

Once the circumstances have been identified and the proper rule applied, many if-constructions prove to be hidden categorical statements or even syllogisms.[31] The burden of countless Qur'ānic verses is expressed by the following conditional: "If you believe in and pray to the One God, fast, pay alms, and are good to your parents, you will go to heaven." This means the same as "All who believe in and pray to the One God, fast, pay alms, and are good to their parents will go to heaven." It remains for the believer to complete the argument in the proper way: "I believe in and pray to the One God, fast, pay alms, and am good to my parents. Therefore, I shall go to heaven, if God wills."

DISJUNCTIVE ARGUMENTS

If the Qur'ān may be called in rhetorical terms a single enormous contrast between God and his creation, in logical terms it is a single enormous disjunction between true belief and error. This is not to deny that there are intermediate stages and compatible alternatives in certain subsets of thought and action; but in the end all paths will have one of two ends: the Garden or the Fire.

Disjunction characterizes the third, fourth, and fifth of the Stoic "indemonstrable" arguments, as schematized by the operative formulae "Not both A and B" and "Either A or B (or C or D)."

The Stoic type 3 indemonstrable simply denies that two things can co-exist:

> Not both: it is day and it is night.
> It is day.
> Therefore it is not night

Its form is:

> Not both the first and the second.
> The first.
> Therefore, not the second.[32]

Note that the nature of this disjunction is to deny that it can be both day and night at the same time; but to deny one is not to assert that it *must* be the other – it may be twilight, or early morning before sunrise, or a total eclipse of the sun.

The Qur'ān consistently denies the possibility of co-existence between incompatibles, particularly when exposing discrepancies between what people say and what they do, or between incompatible beliefs held simultaneously.

> Why did you kill God's prophets in the past if you are believers?
>
> (Q 2:91, cf. 3:183)[33]

This argument may be schematized as follows:

> Not both: you kill God's prophets and you believe in God.
> You kill God's prophets.
> Therefore you do not believe in God.

The allegation is not that all unbelievers are guilty of the murder of prophets, only that such behavior is incompatible with belief. It is true, however, that the Qur'ān in some places, as here, speaks to current members of religious groups as though they are guilty of the sins of their ancestors; while in other places it distinguishes between the actions of individual members of those groups (e.g. Q 2:62).

Another verse demonstrates the unicity of God according to the same pattern:

> How can He have a son when He has no consort (*ṣāḥiba*)?
>
> (Q 6:101)

> Not both: God has no consort and God has a son.
> God has no consort.
> Therefore, God has no son.

The other *logical* possibility is that God has one or more consorts but has no son. It appears that no one was making such a claim, however, as the Qur'ān does not list it as an alternative to be denied.

The Stoics' fourth and fifth types of undemonstrated argument are disjunctions in the either-or mode. The fourth reaches its conclusion by affirmation, the fifth by negation.

> Type 4:
> Either the first or the second.
> The first.
> Therefore, not the second.[34]

> Type 5:
> Either the first or the second.
> Not the first.
> Therefore, the second.[35]

Because, as Ghazālī says, Qur'ānic language is elliptical and concise,[36] a statement that is the first premise of an understood disjunction can often be validly completed either way:

> Say: "Do you know best or does God?"
> (Q 2:140, cf. 16:74)

This yields both a type 4 and a type 5:

> Type 4:
> Either you or God knows best.
> [God knows best.]
> [Therefore you do not know best.]
>
> Type 5:
> Either you or God knows best.
> [You do not know best.]
> [Therefore God knows best.]

It is clear when one compares the two that type 5 is more effective rhetorically than type 4, which is anticlimactic and redundant here. Having declared that disjunction is a dialectical tool and not true inference, Ṭūfī does not even bother to analyze Q 2:140 as a disjunction but does what so many have done when analyzing Qur'ānic argument – veers off from analysis into a defense of Muḥammad's prophethood against the Jews who deny it.[37]

Type 4 is rhetorically effective only if the conclusion is also a climax:

> Those are the ones whom God has cursed: He has made them deaf and blinded their sight. Do they then not ponder on the Qur'ān, or are there locks on their hearts?
> (Q 47:23–24)
>
> Either they ponder on the Qur'ān or there are locks on their hearts.
> There are locks on their hearts.
> Therefore they do not ponder on the Qur'ān.
>
> Some people say: "We believe in God," but if they are harmed for God's sake, they treat oppression by human beings as though it were punishment from God. And when victory comes from your Lord, they will say, "We were

> with you [all along]." Does God not know what is in people's hearts?
>
> (Q 29:10)

> Either they will avoid human oppression or they will avoid divine punishment.
> They will avoid human oppression.
> Therefore, they will not avoid divine punishment

Ghazālī calls disjunction *mīzān al-taʿānud*, the "scale of mutual opposition." His definition of *mīzān al-taʿānud* covers only figures 4 and 5. His formulation of the syllogism is as idiosyncratic as his nomenclature, in that he has assimilated figure 3 to the other two, and he has restricted the validity of Qur'ānic disjunctions to those having only two disjuncts. His reason for doing so comes not from logic but from dialectic. In fact the Qur'ān contains not only exclusive disjunctions but also inclusive ones, which offer multiple disjuncts of which more than one can be true. Its central topics, of course, are not served by such constructions: no Qur'ānic disjunction allows a conclusion that God is multiple, or that Muḥammad is not the Apostle of God, or that the Covenant may be discarded.

As his only Qur'ānic example Ghazālī takes Q 34:24: "And surely we or you are rightly guided (*ʿalā hudā*) or in clear error (*fī ḍalāl mubīn*)." The full schema of the argument is as follows:

> Either we or you are in clear error.
> [It is known that we are not in error.]
> [Therefore you are in error.]

Ghazālī has chosen a verse that produces only one schema, though not all Qur'ānic disjunctions are so easy to handle. As with all the arguments in *Qisṭās*, he gives an illustration from everyday life as well. He compares the argument to the situation of one who enters a two-room house after someone else has entered it: if he does not see the person in the first room, he knows deductively that he is in the other "as certainly as if he had seen him."[38] Ghazālī's schema is of the fifth type, in which one of the disjuncts is negated to yield the positive conclusion. To this we may add further examples:

> They say, "The Fire will touch us for only a limited number of days." Say: "Do you have a promise from God

> – for He never breaks His promises – or are you saying something about God that you do not know?"
>
> (Q 2:80)

> Either you have a promise from God of limited punishment or you do not know what you are talking about.
> [You have no such promise.]
> [Therefore, you do not know what you are talking about.][39]

The following verse contains a comparison, but it is the two disjunctions that make it an argument, or rather two arguments, a type 4 and a type 5:

> Say: "Among your multiple 'gods' is there one who guides to the Truth?" Say: "God guides to the Truth. So is one who guides to Truth more worthy of being followed, or one who cannot guide unless he himself is guided? What is the matter with you that you judge in that way?"
>
> (Q 10:35)

> Either God guides to Truth or your "gods" guide to truth.
> God guides to Truth.
> Therefore your "gods" do not guide to truth.

> Either your "gods" lead or they themselves are led.
> Your "gods" cannot lead.
> Therefore they themselves are led.

As with the other areas of formal logic, Ghazālī is perfectly familiar with all forms of the disjunctive syllogism, which he has detailed in *Miʿyār al-ʿIlm* but called by its more technical name: the "conditional disjunctive syllogism" (*al-qiyās al-sharṭī al-munfaṣil*).[40] In *Qisṭās* he omits most of the eight forms possible for types 4 and 5 as he has omitted type 3 altogether, but he alerts both interlocutor and reader to the danger of positing only two disjuncts when more than two are possible:

> As for the definition (*ḥadd*) of this scale, it is that in everything that is reducible to two disjuncts (*kull mā inḥaṣara fī qismayn*), affirmation of one of them entails negation of the other, and negation of one of them entails affirmation of the other; but on the condition that the

> disjunction (*al-qisma*) is exclusive (*munḥaṣira*) and not inclusive (*muntashira*),[41] as weighing by the inclusive disjunction is Satan's method.[42]

Many Qur'ānic examples are dense and complex, offering multiple possible disjuncts. Qur'ān 5:43 describes three courses of action, which in exclusive disjunction may be distinguished as logical alternatives or combined in inclusive disjunction as indices of human ambivalence:

> How can they ask you to judge between them when they have the Torah in which is the rule of God? Then they turn away after that, and those people are not believers.
>
> (Q 5:43)

> Either they ask you to judge between them, or they have the Torah by which to judge, or they turn away entirely.

Other unmentioned but logical possibilities are that they ask yet another party to judge, or that they do without a judge altogether and settle things by force of arms.

Where multiple disjuncts are offered, multiplicity is usually on the wrong side. In Chapter 7,[43] we cite from Qur'ān 23:68–74 a list of possible reasons for the Meccans' rejection of the Prophet: the message is unheard-of, or they do not recognize Muḥammad, or they think that he is possessed, or they think he will ask them for money. But the actual reasons are that they hate the truth (Q 23:70) and that, not believing in the Hereafter, they have turned away from the Path (Q 23:74). This is an example of what Ghazālī calls "inclusive disjunction" (*qisma muntashira*), because the truth of one of these disjuncts does not entail the falsity of the others: those who reject Muḥammad may think *both* that his message is unheard-of and that he is possessed. A single verse in Sura 24 *al-Nūr* considers why it is that people summoned to the Prophet for judgment between them come only if the right is on their side. It offers three disjuncts, all simultaneously possible, and all inadmissible as excuses:

> Is there a disease in their hearts? Or do they doubt? Or do they fear that God and His Apostle will treat them unfairly? But they are the ones who are doing wrong.
>
> (Q 24:50)

And there are disjunctions within disjunctions. To cite only one example, a long passage from Sura 40 *Ghāfir/al-Mu'min*) is devoted to the words of the secret believer from among Pharaoh's people who defends Moses (Q 40:28–44). It contains a number of arguments, of which the most interesting comes at the beginning:

> If [Moses] is a liar, his lie will be counted against him; and if he is telling the truth, then some of what he is warning you about will happen to you. God does not guide one who goes too far and lies.
>
> (Q 40:28)

Ṭūfī notes that this is a valid disjunction (*taqsīm ṣaḥīḥ*),[44] but his paraphrase of the argument adds nothing significant. We may go a bit farther:

> Either Moses is lying or he is telling the truth.
> If he is lying, either you will follow him or you will not.
> If you follow him, you will not be punished [sc. all blame will lie upon him].
> If you do not follow him, you will not be punished.
>
> If he is telling the truth, either you will follow him or you will not.
> If you follow him, you will not be punished.
> If you do not follow him, you will be punished.

In other words, following Moses – whether he is lying or not[45] – will bring the follower no harm, while ignoring him is as likely as not to bring punishment. Thus if the potential follower accepts the message, he has only a 25 per cent chance of being punished. This is reminiscent of Pascal's "wager."

The long list of divine signs in Qur'ān 56:57–74 is punctuated with such verses as "Is it you who created it, or are We the Creators?" (Q 56:59). Though rhetorically effective, it does not present every theoretically possible source of these signs to hearers whose powers of spiritual discernment are presumed to be at best rudimentary. Because Ghazālī sees the dangers of too broad a range of choices, he calls incomplete disjunction the "scale of Satan." He gives non-Qur'ānic examples of its misuse in the chapter of the same name, notable among them the Bāṭinī disjunction that limits the source of human knowledge to a choice between the unaided human intellect (*al-ra'y al-'aqlī al-mahḍ*) and the teaching of the Hidden Imam.[46]

Finally, Muslims must beware of those who present them with false disjunctions that omit the only true alternative:

> They say: "Be Jews or Christians and you will be guided!" Say: "Rather, the religion (*milla*) of Abraham – a monotheist (*ḥanīf*), not one of the polytheists!"
>
> (Q 2:135)

10

TECHNICAL TERMS AND DEBATING TECHNIQUE

We may gauge from the foregoing chapters the extent to which the Qur'ān treats human beings as endowed with the capacity to assess arguments, weigh proofs, consider implications, and reach proper conclusions. Ideally, humans will see this capacity in each other as well and conduct themselves accordingly.

> Call to the way of your Lord by means of wisdom and beautiful preaching; and argue with them (*jādilhum*) according to what is best. For your Lord knows best who has strayed from His path.
>
> (Q 16:125)

> Do not argue with the People of the Book except according to what is best, except for those of them who have done wrong. And say, "We believe in what was revealed to us and what was revealed to you: our God and your God is[1] One, and to him we submit ourselves."
>
> (Q 29:46)

Muslim scholars long attempted to maintain this high standard when debating each other. Najm al-Dīn al-Ṭūfī treats the etiquette of debate as second only to its legality. In the second chapter of *'Alam al-Jadhal fī 'Ilm al-Jadal* he says, "The first [requirement] of both parties is that each must aim at showing the truth in his argument, not showing off his own superiority, and he must not care whether the argument (*al-ḥujja*) goes for him or against him." He quotes al-Shāfiʿī as having said, "I never debated anyone and then worried about who won the argument. If he won, then I followed him."[2]

But the realities of human nature are only too clear. Ibn al-Ḥanbalī (554/1159–60 – 634/1236–7) notes that of the 29 occurrences of the word *jadal* and its derivatives in the Qur'ān, all but three (Q 16:125, 29:46, and 58:1) are condemnatory.[3] The best known of the negative references is Q 18:54: "A human being is the most disputatious of all things (*akthara shay' jadal[an]*)." Ṭūfī's treatment of Q 18:54 is rather brief but uses a stunning illustration: the first "disputatious creature" is none other than ʿAlī. The Prophet came to ʿAlī and Fāṭima one night while they were sleeping and asked, "Are the two of you not praying?"

> So ʿAlī said: "Our souls are in the hand of God: He holds them where He will and sends them where He will." The Prophet (S) turned away, striking his hand upon his thigh and saying: "A human being is the most disputatious of creatures!"[4]

Many of the words and roots that later became technical terms in logic, rhetoric, and debate first appear in the Qur'ān as parts of arguments.

> They say: "None will enter Heaven except those who are Jews or Christians." That is what they wish! Say: "Give [us] your proof (*burhānakum*), if you are telling the truth."
> (Q 2:111)

> When it is said to them: "Pay attention to what is in front of you and what is behind you, so that you may receive mercy!", no single sign (*āya*) of their Lord comes to them but they turn away from it. When it is said to them: "Spend of what God has given you!", those who refuse to believe say to those who believe: "Are we supposed to feed those whom God could have fed if He had wished to? You are nothing but wrong!" And they say: "When will this promise (*waʿd*) come true, if you are telling the truth?" They will not have to wait for anything except a single blast, which will take them away in the very act of arguing! (*wa-hum yakhiṣṣimū*[5])
> (Q 36:45–49)

> Those who argue (*yuḥājjūn*) about God after a positive response to Him – their argument is void (*ḥujjatuhum dāḥiḍa*) with their Lord. There will be anger against them and a painful punishment.
> (Q 42:16)

> They say: "There is only our life here below: we die and we live, and only Time destroys us." They have no knowledge of that – they only conjecture. When Our Clear Signs are read out to them, their only argument (*ḥujjatuhum*) is to say: "Bring back our fathers, if you are telling the truth!"
>
> (Q 45:24–25)

To the nouns already cited – *burhān, jadal,* and *ḥujja,* and the verbs *ḥājja, takhaṣṣama*, and *jādala* – we may add *taḥājja* (Q 40:47), *bayyana* (e.g. Q 43:63), *bayyina* (e.g. Q 11:53 and Sura 98 *al-Bayyina*), *khiṣām* (Q 43:18), *istanbaṭa* (Q 4:83), *māra* (Q 18:22), *tamāra* (Q 53:55), *istaftā* (Q 18:22, 37:149), *nāzaʿa* (Q 22:67), *tanāzaʿa* (Q 4:59), and *ikhtalafa* (Q 22:69). I do not maintain that all developments in the field are anticipated in the Qur'ān. For example, although the important root *d-l-l* exists, as well as the noun *dalīl* (Q 25:45), neither occurs as a term of argument; the same is true for the roots *l-z-m, n-t-j, w-ṣ-f, w-j-b,* and many others.[6] But despite the absence of some descriptive technical terms, the Qur'ān combines the techniques, tropes, and syllogisms analyzed in this book to form arguments simple and complex, informal and formal, short and long.

It is in the analysis of extended arguments that *ʿAlam al-Jadhal* proves itself an indispensable tool. With help from Ṭūfī, we shall examine two long passages from the lives of Abraham and Moses and a number of shorter examples based upon incidents in the life of the Prophet Muḥammad, noting the techniques used or recommended and whether the intended audience are pagans or People of the Book.

The first example comes from Sura 21 *al-Anbiyā'*, in which Abraham begins with a verbal argument and ends with a demonstration that his father's idols can neither speak nor act (Q 21:51–67). Ṭūfī scrutinizes the arguments on both sides with great honesty and carefully chosen vocabulary. He observes that the idolaters answer Abraham's unsympathetic (*istifhām nafy wa-inkār*) and disingenuous question "What are these statues to which you are so devoted?" (Q 21:52) with an appeal to the "specious argument of imitating tradition" (*shubhat al-taqlīd*), that is, they argue on the basis of *sunna* and its resulting consensus. We saw in Chapter 2 ("Signs and precedents") the powerful appeal of such arguments, and the care with which the Qur'ān and its exegetes absolve Abraham of any culpability in offending tradition by disobeying his father on the one hand, and praying that he – an idolater – be forgiven, on the other.[7]

Despite using a few loaded terms, Ṭūfī gives the same logical weight to the idolaters' appeal to consensus (*ittifāq al-jamm al-ghafīr min al-ʿuqalāʾ*) as is normally given to the consensus of Muslims: that agreement of large numbers of informed people over a long period of time on something false is usually impossible (*mumtaniʿ ʿādat^an^*).[8] Abraham answers, not by denying the validity of the procedure but by discrediting the conclusion reached: "You and your fathers have clearly been in error" (Q 21:54). Ṭūfī sums up the implications of this exchange:

> Imitating tradition does not conflict with decisive proofs of the unicity of God, and agreement of large numbers of informed people on something false is usually not impossible, but it is unlikely, assuming that it is based upon some proof (*bi-sharṭ istinādihi ilā ḥujja*). By itself, however, it is neither impossible nor unlikely, otherwise your forefathers would have maintained their rejection of polytheism, in imitation (*iqtidāʾ^an^*) of Adam and the great majority of monotheists.[9]

But, says Ṭūfī, by granting that they are theoretically correct (*fa-lammā ṣaddaqahum fī maqām al-naẓar*), Abraham has left them uncertain as to whether he has brought them the truth or is making fun of them (Q 21:55). He assures them of his sincerity and argues for the existence of God on the basis of signs, that is, the existence of the heavens and the earth as a basis for induction. As Ṭūfī expresses it,

> These deniers of the divine attributes (*muʿaṭṭila*) knew no deity except their idols, so he demonstrates to them the existence of the True Deity by the existence of the heavens and the earth, using the effect to reason to the cause (*istidlāl^an^ bi-l-athar ʿalā al-muʾaththir*).[10]

So ends that day's debate.

Now Abraham carries out his demonstration, breaking all the idols except the biggest one, which he blames for having destroyed the others (Q 21:57–63). "[And if you don't believe me, then] ask them, if they are able to speak" (Q 21:63). The people must then admit that the idols cannot speak (Q 21:65). Ṭūfī notes that

Abraham has forced his opponents to accept two premises (*wa-kāna lahu fī dhālika ʿalayhim ilzāmān*): (1) the idea that God, like this idol, refuses to allow any others to be worshipped along with him; (2) their practice – for which he has rebuked them – of worshipping something which cannot speak, or do harm or good, or even defend itself (Q 21:66–67). According to Ṭūfī's reading, the idolaters then hold a brief conference apart, during which some begin to see the error of their ways (Q 21:64), but in the end they return to their stubborn resistance and come out of their meeting blaming Abraham for forcing them to do what cannot be done (*alzamūhu taklīf mā lā yuṭāq*), making them look absurd for trying to get answers from an inanimate object (Q 21:65). Ṭūfī interprets Abraham's reply:

> "*I* did not force you into doing something absurd, rather, I forced you to accept the absurdity [of what you are doing], which is your worship of something impotent and powerless." And when they were cut off from debate, they resorted to force . . . Thus we have showed that God (may He be glorified) meets proof with proof and power with power (*al-ḥujja bi-l-ḥujja wa-l-quwwa bi-l-quwwa*) and that He is victorious in both.[11]

Our example from the life of Moses is the long passage from Sura 26 *al-Shuʿarāʾ* that follows the command of the Lord of the Worlds to Moses and Aaron to lead the Children of Israel out of Egypt. Structurally, the passage resembles the previous episode from the life of Abraham in that it progresses from exchanges of words to active demonstrations: it begins with a painful confrontation between Moses and his foster-father Pharaoh (Q 26:18–22), moves on to an embarrassing exchange in which prophecies from Moses are answered with spiteful threats from Pharaoh (Q 26:23–37), and ends with a contest between magicians' tricks and prophetic miracles (Q 26:38–52).

Ṭūfī notes that Pharaoh's attitude in the initial confrontation involves two things: (1) his contempt for Moses, as embodied in the saying: "No one will respect you as an adult who knew you as a child;"[12] (2) his charges that Moses is guilty of ingratitude (*kufr al-niʿma*) to the one who raised him, as evidenced by his killing an Egyptian in the past and now attempting to destroy the Egyptian religion. To the charge that killing the Egyptian put him among the "ungrateful" (*min al-kāfirīn*), Ṭūfī notes that Moses counters with an admission of error committed before wisdom had come to him from God: "I did it then, while I was among those gone astray (*min al-ḍāllīn*)" (Q 26:20); he has admitted as much, says Ṭūfī, in Qur'ān 28:16. Moses fled, but God granted him the capacity for wise judgment (*ḥukm*) and made him one of the apostles (Q 26:21). He answers Pharaoh's reminder of benefits granted with a comparison: the harm Pharaoh did by enslaving the children of Israel will never be offset by his good deed of raising Moses. "Now the debate on this topic ends (*inqaḍat al-munāẓara*) and returns to the debate on the subject of apostleship."[13]

Moses's words in this second part of the exchange are essentially a definition of God. Pharaoh asks, "And what (*mā*) is the 'Lord of the Worlds'?" (Q 26:23), probably, notes Ṭūfī, because he is asking about what he thinks is an insensible thing (*mā*) like an idol or a planet and not a person or sentient being (*man*).[14] Moses replies, "Lord of the heavens and the earth and all that is between them ..." (Q 26:24); "Your Lord and the Lord of your earliest forefathers" (Q 26:26); "Lord of the East and West ..." (Q 26:28). Pharaoh interjects incredulously: "Do you not hear [what he is saying]?" (Q 26:25). Ṭūfī sums up the meaning of this rhetorical question with what is essentially a syllogism:

> Moses is claiming that the Lord of the Worlds is your Lord and the Lord of your earliest forefathers, that is, because they are part of "the worlds," so that Moses's Lord is his Lord.[15]

Then Pharaoh attempts to deny it by calling Moses insane (Q 26:27) and by claiming himself to be a god (Q 26:29). But as Moses continues, "Pharaoh abandons argument and resorts to force" by threatening to put him in prison.[16] Moses counters the threat by offering a demonstration, which, as Ṭūfī says, Pharaoh accepts for two probable reasons: (1) he does not think Moses capable of producing a proof that will confirm the truth of what he says; (2) he is doing it in the spirit of impartiality (*'alā jihat al-inṣāf*):

> Because any rational person – especially if he is a ruler – concerned with justice, if called upon to consider a rational proof (*ḥujjat al-'aql*), will be compelled by reason[17] to respond to it and prevented by [reason] from refusing it. So when Moses called upon him to give a rational judgment

> (*ḥukm al-ʿaql*), reason [or "justice"] prevented him from turning away.[18]

Thereupon, "Moses threw down his staff, and behold! It was a serpent plain [to see]; and he drew out his hand and behold! It was white for all to see" (Q 26:32–33). But Ṭūfī does not extend his analysis to the rest of the passage – not Moses's repeat performance before Pharaoh's magicians, or their acceptance of the Lord of the Worlds, or the pursuit of the Children of Israel, who are saved from the waters while Pharaoh's army is drowned. Ṭūfī is interested in argument, not history, and is satisfied with summing up the results of the debate without quite explaining *how* a sign functions as a proof:

> Then there happened between them what was already mentioned in Sura 7 *al-Aʿrāf*, in short, that he advanced his staff as an argument (*iḥtajja bi-ʿaṣāh*), and they opposed him with magic, and he refuted their opposing argument. So his proof remained untouched by any opponent, and his claim was proven.[19]

The Prophet Muḥammad brought the Message both to the pagan Arabs and to People of the Book. The pagan Arabs who deny Muḥammad's message have only two techniques of argument: citation of precedent in support of their idolatry, and demands that the Prophet accomplish things that he has never claimed to be able to do, such as bringing back their fathers (Q 45:24–25).[20] They find his arguments ineffective because he is unable to support his verbal warnings with these sorts of miracles, that is, with signs. Ṭūfī notes the similarity of Qur'ān 45:24–25 to 44:34–36: when the pagans deny the Resurrection, God answers by denying the validity of their assertion of eternal non-existence after death (*ajāba ... bi-manʿ daʿwāhum al-istimrār baʿd al-mawt ʿalā al-ʿadam*).[21] Though Ṭūfī does not mention the fact, both passages also contain arguments *a fortiori*. In Q 44:37, a question is asked concerning those who challenge the Prophet to bring back their fathers: "Are they better than the people of Tubbaʿ and those before them? We destroyed *them* because they were sinners!" That is, if We destroyed the greater, We can destroy the less. In Q 45:26, the Prophet first points out that it is not he but God who brings back the dead, after having first given them life, then death. In other words, God who creates life to begin with [sc. the greater miracle] is certainly capable of re-creating it.[22]

The pagans are cynical and dishonest in debate. We have already seen their tendency to argue both ways concerning the identity of Allāh, and to change the subject when they are losing.[23] When Jesus son of Mary is cited as an example to them, they pretend to believe that he is being advanced as a deity, and they try to force Muḥammad into a false choice between Jesus and their own idols:

> They say: "Are our gods better, or is he?" They refer to him only [to start] an argument against you, for they are truly an argumentative lot.
>
> (Q 43:58)

They expose their own inconsistency when they ascribe to God not sons but daughters (Q 43:16), even though any one of them will himself react with anger and grief when a daughter is born to him and not a son (Q 43:17). Interestingly, one sign that a daughter is inferior is that she is alleged to be unable to argue clearly (*fī al-khiṣām ghayr mubīn* – Q 43:18). As Ṭūfī notes, if God took a child, it would have to be one who, "when he fights, fights with heart and, when he speaks, speaks with clarity" (*idhā qātala qātala bi-janān wa-idhā naṭaqa naṭaqa bi-bayān*).[24]

In a sequence of three very long verses, God instructs Muḥammad in another effective way to counter the pagans' inconsistency. First, he is to hold them to their acceptance of Allāh as the High God, the Lord of the heavens and the earth; then he is to use contrast and comparison to demonstrate to them that their acceptance of lesser deities is inconsistent (Q 13:16).

> Say: "Do you take other gods than Him, who cannot benefit or harm [even] themselves?" Say: "Are the blind and the sighted equal? Are the darkness and the light equal?"
>
> (Q 13:16)

The next verse reinforces the demonstration with a sign of divine power – the bringing of rain that fills the wadis – followed by the parable that likens truth to that precious water and to the metal of tools and jewelry, falsehood to the useless scum that is sloughed off of these pure substances (Q 13:17).[25] The final disjunction is inescapable: those who respond positively will have all good things, while those who do not will go to Hell and will be unable to buy their way out (Q 13:18).

One way of countering the pagans' arguments is to dare them to act, as Moses does Pharaoh's magicians. When they challenge Muḥammad to bring back their fathers, a sign of power such as he has never claimed, he challenges them to produce something on the order of the single Sign that he *has* brought:

> They may say: "He has forged [the Qur'ān]." Say: "Bring ten suras 'forged' like it; and call on anyone you can [to help you], other than God, if you are sincere! Then, if [your false gods] do not respond to you, know that it has only been sent down with God's knowledge, and that there is no deity but He. So are you now *Muslimūn*?"
>
> (Q 11:13–14)

A similar passage (Q 2:23–24) is set very near the beginning of the Qur'ān, a challenge that alerts the hearer to the fact that s/he is being presented with an evidentiary miracle. Other challenges to the pagans are to show just what it is that their deities have created (Q 46:4), or to bring a book previously revealed or some trace of knowledge to show that they are telling the truth (Q 46:4, cf. 31:20, 6:148–50).

Confrontations with People of the Book are of a different order of seriousness. Because all worship the same Deity, the only one whose power is real, a challenge offered and accepted may turn into a trial by ordeal. One such example appeared in the previous chapter,[26] where Muḥammad is to challenge the Jews to "Wish for death" if their claims of righteousness and divine reward are made in good faith (Q 2:94–95, cf. 62:6–7).

Another exchange involves Christians:

> Say to whoever disputes you on the matter [of Jesus] after the knowledge that has come to you: "Come! Let us call our sons and your sons, and our women and your women, and ourselves and yourselves; then let us pray humbly and call down the curse of God on those who are lying."
>
> (Q 3:61)

This may reflect an actual incident in the life of the Prophet. Al-Wahidi (d. 468/1076) gives two versions, one on the authority of the Prophet's grandson al-Ḥasan that involves two Christian monks of Najrān, the other from Jābir b. 'Abd Allāh that involves a two-man delegation (*wafd*) from the same area. When the

Prophet said to the two monks, "Accept Islam and you will be saved (*aslimā taslamā*)," they replied, "We accepted it before you (*qad aslamnā qablaka*)." He refuted their claim by pointing out that they bowed to the Cross, believed that God had taken a son, and drank wine; they countered by asking, "What do you say about Jesus?" and the Prophet was silent. Thereupon God revealed Qur'ān 3:58–61, part of which asserts that God created Jesus, like Adam, from dust, then brought him to life with the command "Be!" (*kun* – Q 3:59). Muḥammad called the Christians to a meeting in which both would invoke God's curse (*mulā'ana*) and from which only one party would emerge alive. After some deliberation, the monks chose instead to pay tribute.[27] The invocation of curses upon oneself has already been discussed in Chapter One, where it constitutes the final solemnization of the Covenant.[28]

The passage immediately following the challenge of Qur'ān 3:61 contains an invitation to the People of the Book to reconcile with the Muslims on the basis of their shared beliefs: the unicity of God (Q 3:64), the position of Abraham as a monotheist who lived before revelation of the Torah and the Gospel (Q 3:65–68), the Signs of God (Q 3:70), the necessity for honoring a trust (Q 3:75–77), faithfulness to Scripture (Q 3:78–79), the worship of God and not men or angels (Q 3:79–80), belief in the Covenant of the Prophets (Q 3:81–83), and belief in God's Books and Prophets, without making distinctions among the latter (Q 3:84).

This is, however, a Medinan sura, and the calls for agreement are interspersed with warnings to the People of the Book not to assume undue authority. "It is God Who knows, and you do not know!" (Q 3:66). The Qur'ān charges some with wanting to lead the believers astray (Q 3:69), denying the Signs of God which they themselves witness (Q 3:70), concealing the truth (Q 3:71), and distorting Scripture (Q 3:78). All however, will be returned to God (Q 3:83).

There is a striking contrast between the Qur'ān's emphasis on the individual's responsibility for sin (e.g. Q 6:164, 17:15) and its often-repeated charge against the Jews for having killed prophets (e.g. Q 3:183). The Qur'ān uses the second person plural ("Why did you kill them?" – Q 3:183) in effect to assign collective responsibility to the Jewish opponents of Muḥammad for what it accuses their co-religionists of doing centuries before.[29] Similarly, Q 3:183 is followed by a passage (Q 3:187) on the scriptuaries' breaking of the Covenant, also a communal and not an individual affair. Conversion to Islam, then, offered the individual a new beginning.

In the end, God's proof is the only one that counts (*li-Llāh al-ḥujja al-bāligha* – Q 6:149). We have already seen that it is the sight of Hell that finally convinces the most stubborn of unbelievers, and by then it is too late (e.g. Q 89:32–26). But those who believe and pray for salvation will be answered by their Lord:

> I will never allow the deed of any one of you, male or female, to be lost. You belong to each other. And those who have emigrated, and been expelled from their homes, and suffered in My Path, and fought and been killed – I shall remit their sins and bring them into gardens beneath which rivers flow, a reward from God. And with God is the best reward.
>
> (Q 3:195)

11

CONCLUSIONS

Reasoning and argument are so integral to the content of the Qur'ān and so inseparable from its structure that they in many ways shaped the very consciousness of Qur'ānic scholars. Exegetes internalized the idiom, and perhaps for that very reason it did not become a separate genre within the field of *'ulūm al-Qur'ān*. That helps to account for the wide range of approaches to Qur'ānic exegesis and for every exegete's conviction that his approach is justified, indeed dictated, by the sacred text, whether his focus is simple commandments and prohibitions or extended logical analysis of the arguments that underlie the entire text. Thus a figure as controversial as Fakhr al-Dīn al-Rāzī could be accused of compiling a *tafsīr* that contained everything except *tafsīr*,[1] while he himself wrote at the end of his life that, after experiencing all branches of *kalām* and philosophy, "I have not found in them either satisfaction or comfort to equal that which I have found in reading the Qur'ān."[2]

Muslims esteem not just every verse of the Qur'ān but every single word as irreplaceably significant. Amidst the wealth of analysis that countless scholars have devoted to its individual words, verses, suras, themes, structures, and tropes; and to its commands, prohibitions, literary and historical content, theology, and parallels with other scriptures, I have attempted to focus my attention and that of my readers upon what I see as the Qur'ān's most basic framework of meaning. After returning to *al-Qisṭās al-Mustaqīm* and reapplying Ghazālī's methods to the Qur'ān, I discerned in it a far broader range of arguments than Ghazālī's five, whereupon I set out to classify the reasoned procedures by which the Qur'ān situates its rhetorical, historical, legal, and theological elements on its own spectrum of significance. I have attempted in this book to analyze as many types of Qur'ānic argument as I was able to recognize, using English terminology common to the humanities, together with certain indispensable terms in Greek, Latin, and Arabic. I have done it this way for two reasons. First, it seemed beside the point, in a book written in English, to reproduce the Arabic techniques of rhetorical and logical analysis, translate the Arabic terms, and then explain how they work using the terminology that I would be using in the first place. Second, many of the traditional techniques of analysis were heavily influenced by Qur'ānic style to begin with; thus using them alone to analyze the text would often yield what were essentially circular arguments.

Herein lies the value of Ghazali's system (and I hope, by extension, of my own): it is largely independent of language structures yet takes full cognizance of meanings to assure that any given argument is appropriately schematized and that all possible schemata have been taken into consideration.

Al-Ghazali epitomizes the scope of Qur'ānic reasoning in the following words:

> Whoever has a scale determines by it the measure of countless substances. The same is true for whoever has *al-qisṭās al-mustaqīm*: he has the Wisdom which brings to whoever has received it a great and endless benefit. . . . All sciences are not present in the Glorious Qur'ān in an explicit form, but they are present potentially (*bi-l-quwwa*), because of the existence therein of the True Scales (*al-mawāzīn al-qisṭ*) by which are opened the gates of infinite Wisdom.[3]

Using more technical language, al-Suyūṭī says essentially the same thing:

> The 'ulamā' have said that the great Qur'ān contains all types of proofs (*barāhīn*) and evidence (*adilla*): there is no type of proof (*burhān*) or evidence (*dalāla*) or disjunction (*taqsīm*) or warning (*taḥdhīr*) constructed from the entire range of things known by reason or authority which God has not articulated. But He conveyed it according to the customs of the Arabs, without the fine points of the methods of the theologians.[4]

Here follows a summary of the techniques found to be relevant for analysis of Qur'ānic argument, with their methodological applications.

Chapter 1 established that in the Qur'ān all history is sacred history and began with the cosmic rule that is the Covenant. Arguments based on the Covenant in the first instance refer to the contract made when God created the world and endowed human beings with benefits that they undertook to hold in trust with gratitude and reverence, or mismanage at their peril. Ultimately, all Qur'ānic arguments are based, directly or at some remove, upon the Covenant.

Chapter 2 analyzed two categories of phenomena that provide premises and supporting evidence for arguments based upon the Covenant: (1) the signs (*āyāt, bayyināt*) by which God proves his existence and power; and (2) the precedents (*sunan*) that he has set throughout history by his practice of sending prophets and scriptures to re-establish the Covenant, validate its contractual terms, remind forgetful humans of their responsibilities, and punish violators.

Chapter 3 demonstrated how the Qur'ān assimilates the precedents set by sacred history to the particularly strong Arab social concept of precedent, *sunna*. The result produces arguments based upon precedent that is divine, *sunnat Allāh*, an especially powerful method of addressing the concerns of an audience consisting of both scriptuaries (*ahl al-kitāb*) and pagan Arabs.

Chapter 4 used rule-based reasoning, which is a branch of legal logic, and the logic of commands to analyze the uniformity, predictability, and justification of divine laws, examining how the Qur'ān distinguishes them from the arbitrary and capricious actions ascribed to deities that are, in the end, imaginary and possess no real power. Because of the status of the Covenant as the cosmic rule that in turn generates countless sub-rules, rule-based reasoning is fundamental to the analysis of divine law.

Chapter 5 highlighted the reasoning that supports particular Qur'ānic laws, both those that stipulate proper devotions (*ʿibādāt*) and those that govern interactions between human beings (*muʿāmalāt*). Because the Qur'ān is the first source of Islamic law, it would be tautologous to use the methods of Islamic law to analyze the Qur'ān, hence the concentration in this chapter upon fundamental legal notions embodied in the text rather than upon the substance of the laws themselves. In the "Excursus on Performatives," I examined a type of utterance that does not describe a legal status but is itself the very act that creates it. Human acceptance of the Covenant is such an act, as is the *shahāda*.

Chapter 6 explored Qur'ānic applications of arguments based upon comparison, including similarity, analogy, and parable. Analysis of apparent comparisons showed that very often such constructions actually mask quite different forms of reasoning, such as legal arguments, categorical arguments, and disjunction.

Chapter 7 demonstrated that the contrast between God and his creation is more fundamental to Qur'ānic reasoning than is comparison, and its range of argument is broader, including, among others, opposition, contrariety, contradiction, and antithesis. This reverses the order of importance of comparison and contrast as found in works of Western classical rhetoric, and for that reason it more truly dramatizes Islamic ontology.

Chapter 8 recapitulated the first part of Ghazālī's unique short treatise on Qur'ānic logic, *al-Qisṭās al-Mustaqīm*, which demonstrates how the first three figures of the categorical syllogism are derived from the Qur'ān. With material from Najm al-Dīn al-Ṭūfī and my own analyses of additional Qur'ānic verses, I was able to identify examples of ten of the nineteen valid moods of the categorical syllogism and leave open the possibility that all nineteen may be found within the sacred text.

In Chapter 9, I considerably amplified Ghazālī's brief presentation of hypothetical and disjunctive syllogisms in the Qur'ān. Discussion of hypotheticals was again augmented with material from Ṭūfī, but, as he considered disjunction a mere rhetorical technique, his contributions here are limited.

Chapter 10, finally, used several extended examples of debates between prophets and their interlocutors to demonstrate how the Qur'ān combines various forms of argument to support its teachings, illustrate debating technique and etiquette, and demolish the counter-arguments of the opposition. Here the forensically-inclined Ṭūfī is indispensable for the connections that he draws between the two vast fields of Qur'ānic exegesis and formal disputation.

Finally, having summarized my findings as presented in the first ten chapters, I shall use the present chapter to suggest further lines of research using the same methods.

One who chooses to focus upon the Qur'ān itself may wish to discover all instances of a given type of argument, such as argument from precedent or the reasoning that supports divine commands, and expand upon the contents of that argument and its possible variants. It is also a common scholarly procedure to focus upon a single Qur'ānic theme, such as the truth of a prophet's message or the importance of prayer, but very often this is done by tracing only textual similarities and variants. Attention to the multiple types of argument that the Qur'ān uses to make the point(s) at issue will add new dimensions to both the analysis of the text and the understanding of the audience's reception.

Clearly, the "audience reception" most accessible to the scholar lies in the massive work of the exegetes. One gauge of the evolution of *tafsīr* is the increasing sophistication with which it engages Qur'ānic argument, and the methods set forth in this book are useful in evaluating the differences between earlier and later works.[5] Some exegeses, such as those of Zamakhsharī and Fakhr al-Dīn al-Rāzī, are known for their "rationalist" tone; and Rāzī in particular has a solid bibliography of works on logic[6] in addition to the content of the extensive methodological preface to *Mafātīḥ al-Ghayb* that appears in his commentary on the *Fātiḥa*. It is all the more instructive, then, to analyze his treatment of Qur'ānic arguments that fall outside the realm of logic as he understood it.

Legal exegeses of the genre *aḥkām al-Qur'ān*, such as the works of Jaṣṣāṣ and Qurṭubī quoted in earlier chapters, deserve far more scholarly attention than they have so far received.[7] I have found that analyzing Qur'ānic argument is particularly useful in understanding works of this type, in that one can begin to discern in a systematic manner how the legal point of a passage is or is not dependent upon time and place, and the circumstances, status, and mental state of the people involved. Perhaps for the same reasons, I have found these methods unexpectedly useful as an aid to scrutinizing the reasoning of extremist Islamists, particularly their use of the Qur'ān to justify the most violent actions and to exclude other Muslims from consideration as brothers and sisters in faith.[8]

I have attempted in my approach to Qur'ānic argument to combine methodological rigor with an understanding of Qur'ānic priorities. Now when I take up any passage from the Qur'ān, any verse chosen at random, I cannot but be aware that the manner in which it argues its own significance is integral to its meaning. I offer the techniques of analysis presented in this book in the hope that others will find them useful additions to the ones that they and other colleagues in the field have developed over so many years.

Najm al-Dīn al-Ṭūfī concludes his section on *tafsīr* with these remarks:

> Know that ... I have mentioned only what is self-evident and well-known (*ẓāhir*^{an} *mashhūr*^{an}) from among instances

> of debate and cases which involve proof (*al-waqā'iʿ al-jadalīya wa-l-qaḍāyā al-istidlālīya*); otherwise, when the Qur'ān is contemplated, much more will be found in it than I have mentioned, because it appeared as a miracle in its entirety and in its details. And the nature (*sha'n*) of a miracle is to confound the opponent and prove the opposite of what he alleges, so know this. And perhaps I have failed to [include] something on the topic that is well known, whether through ignorance, or laziness, or being content with something similar to it that has been repeated, or some other similar reason.[9]

In the same spirit of humility, and with the same reservations about having presented only a sample of the whole, I conclude this book.

NOTES

INTRODUCTION

1 See the works of Toshihiko Izutsu, in particular *Ethico-Religious Concepts in the Qur'ān* (Montreal: McGill University Press, 2002), originally published in 1959 under the title *The Structure of Ethical Terms in the Koran*.
2 Although al-Ghazālī says that the ancient peoples learned them from "the scriptures of Abraham and Moses (*ṣuḥuf Ibrāhīm wa-Mūsā* – Q 87:18–19)." See *al-Qisṭās al-Mustaqīm* (ed. Riyāḍ Muṣṭafā al-ʿAbd Allāh), Damascus: Dār al-Ḥikma, 1406/1986, p. 82.
3 *Iʿjāz al-Qur'ān*, p. 47. He says that he has discussed the matter in his book on *Uṣūl*. Editor A. Ṣaqr attributes two books of this title to al-Bāqillānī, *Kitāb al-Uṣūl al-Kabīr fi al-Fiqh* (no. 9, p. 43 of the Introduction) and *Kitab al-Uṣūl al-Ṣaghīr* (no. 26, p. 47). In addition, at least five other works of his have the word *uṣūl* in the title. All appear to be lost, although Ṣaqr saw a single crumbling volume of *Hidāyat al-Mustarshidīn wa-al-Muqniʿ fi Maʿrifat Uṣūl al-Dīn*, dated 459/1066–67, in the library of al-Azhar.
4 Private interview, June 21, 1996.
5 *Al-Itqān fi ʿUlūm al-Qurān, Cairo, 1370/1951 [repr. Beirut, Dar al-Nadwa al-Jadida, n.d.]* ṣ68, ii, p. 135.
6 Now available in a fine edition by Wolfhart Heinrichs from Wiesbaden: Franz Steiner Verlag, 1408/1987, 30+283 pp. The work is prefaced by an exhaustive list of biographical sources, and editor Heinrichs refers the reader to his "abbreviated" study in ZDMG Suppl. 3, vol. 1, 1977, pp. 463–673.
7 Najm al-Dīn al-Ṭūfi, *ʿAlam al-Jadhal fi ʿIlm al-Jadal*, p. 239. I shall use Ṭūfi's work extensively in Chapters 8, 9, and 10 of this book.
8 Burhān al-Dīn al-Zarkashī, *al-Burhān fi ʿUlūm al-Qur'ān*, Beirut: Dār al-Maʿrifa, 1415/1994, in four volumes.
9 Suyūṭī's lapse is noted by the editor, Dr. Zāhir al-Almaʿi, *Kitāb Istikhrāj al-Jidāl min al-Qur'ān al-Karīm*, Beirut: Mu'assasat al-Risāla, 1400/1980, p. 35.
10 Zāhir b. ʿAwwad al-Almaʿī, *Manāhij al-Jadal fi al-Qur'ān al-Karīm*, Riyad, 1399. His entire third chapter is entitled, "There is no connection between Qur'ānic argumentation (*istidlāl*) and Greek

argumentation." The bulk of his book, however, is devoted to Qur'ānic refutation of "materialists and atheists" and the support of divine unicity, prophecy, resurrection, and a host of other theological positions.

11 Khalīl Aḥmad Khalīl, *Jadalīyat al-Qur'ān*, Beirut: Dār al-Ṭalī'a, 1977, p. 26.

12 In *Myths, Historical Archetypes and Symbolic Figures in Arabic Literature: Towards a New Hermeneutic Approach*, Proceedings of the International Symposium in Beirut, June 25–June 30, 1996; Beirut: Steiner Verlag, 1999, pp. 163–188.

13 See Ibn al-Ḥanbalī, pp. 49–51.

1 THE COVENANT

1 See, for example, W.M. Watt and R. Bell, *Bell's Introduction to the Qur'ān*, Edinburgh, 1970, p. 131; J. Wansbrough, *Quranic Studies*, Oxford, 1977, *passim*.

2 Abraham Katsh, *Judaism in Islam*, New York University, 1954, pp. xiii–xiv.

3 Cf. Andrew Rippin, "Desiring the Face of God," in Boullata, ed., *Literary Structures of Religious Meaning in the Qur'ān*, pp. 119f. "Such are the traps into which many studies of the Qur'ān have fallen."

4 In Merlin Swartz, ed. *Studies on Islam*. Oxford University Press, 1981, pp. 86–98.

5 Fück, "Originality," p. 90.

6 Wansbrough, *Quranic Studies*, Oxford, 1977, p. 100. S.a. pp. 148–52. Auerbach's own term is *Deutungsbedürfnis*. Jane Dammen McAuliffe addresses some of the same points in the context of recent scholarship, particularly "reader-response" theory. See her "Text and Textuality: Q.3:7 as a Point of Intersection" in Boullata, ed., *Literary Structures of Religious Meaning in the Qur'ān,* especially her opening and closing sections. In the same *Qur'ān* collection, see Angelika Neuwirth's description of her own method in "Referentiality and Textuality in *Surat al-Hijr*," p. 145.

7 Erich Auerbach, *Mimesis*, Princeton, 1953, pp. 11–12.

8 Wansbrough, op. cit., p. 100.

9 Bernard Weiss, "Covenant and Law in Islam," in *Religion and Law: Biblical-Judaic and Islamic Perspectives*, Eisenbrauns, 1990, pp. 49–83. The present quotation comes at page 50, n. 2. Weiss's excellent article came to my attention only after this chapter was substantially complete and is in accord with most (but not all) of the conclusions presented here.

10 Cf. Weiss, "Covenant and Law," p. 51, n. 2.

11 Gordon Newby, *The Making of the Last Prophet: A Reconstruction of the Earliest Biography of Muḥammad*, South Carolina, 1989, p. 41.

12 Ṭabarsī, *Majma' al-Bayān fi Tafsīr al-Qur'ān*, Sidon: M. al-'Irfān, 1333 [1914–15], repr. Qomm: Mar'ashī 1403 [1982–83], v, p. 476.

13 Ṭabarī, *Jāmi' al-Bayān fi Tafsīr al-Qur'ān* [sic], Beirut: Dar al-Jīl, n.d., xvi, p. 160.

14 Ṭabarsī, op. cit., iv, p. 32.
15 F.E. Peters, *Muḥammad and the Origins of Islam*, SUNY, 1994, p. 260 and n. 16 with its references to Wansbrough and Rippin. S a.Q 6:25, 8:31, 16:24, 23:83, 27:68, 46:17, 68:15, 83:13.
16 Izutsu, *Ethico-Religious Concepts in the Koran,* Montreal: McGill University Press, 1966, pp. 88–89.
17 Paul Kalluveetil, *Declaration and Covenant: A comprehensive review of covenant formulae from the Old Testament and the ancient Near East,* Rome: Biblical Institute Press, 1982, p. 22.
18 Ibid., p. 90, n. 352.
19 Mendenhall and Herion, "Covenant," *The Anchor Bible Dictionary*, New York: Doubleday, 1992, i, p. 1181, c. 1.
20 Ibid., p. 1182, c. 2.
21 Ibid., pp. 1180ff.
22 Crone and Cook, *Hagarism*, Cambridge, 1977, 19. Cf. B.S. Jackson, *Studies in the Semiotics of Biblical Law*, Sheffield, 2000, Ch. 9, especially pp. 236–243.
23 Weiss, "Covenant and Law," p. 58.
24 Ibid., p. 55.
25 The phrase is Fakhr al-Dīn al-Rāzī's, adopted by Weiss ("Covenant and Law," p. 66). For the non-exclusive character of this covenant, see ibid., pp. 55–59 and his conclusions, pp. 81–83.
26 Mendenhall and Herion, op. cit., pp. 1188ff.
27 Compare these to the four elements in what Bernard Weiss calls the "signs/commandments/promises cluster" – "promise" including both reward and punishment – found in Sura 13:1ff, 24:45–77, and "similar lists found in Sura 23 and 70." "Covenant and Law," p. 53.
28 I am aware that "Recite!" is probably a better translation. I only wish that it had the rhetorical power of the single Anglo-Saxon syllable.
29 See Chapter 4.
30 See the epigraph to this chapter.
31 See Chapter 3.
32 Weiss, "Covenant and Law," pp. 63–64, italics original.
33 Mendenhall and Herion, op. cit., pp. 1192 c. 2–1193 c. 1.
34 See, e.g. Fakhr al-Dīn al-Rāzī, *al-Tafsīr al-Kabīr*, Beirut: Dār Iḥyā' al-Turāth al-ʿArabī, n.d., xxv, pp. 119–120.
35 Ṭabarī, op. cit., vi, p. 95.
36 Cf. Weiss, "Covenant and Law", §7, p. 58, where he does not distinguish between the Covenant with the prophets and that with other human beings, and pp. 80–81, with n. 54, where he does. In Q 20:115, God says: "We had already covenanted to Adam, but he forgot, and we found no resolve in him," making ambiguous Adam's status as a prophet.
37 The Arabic root *b-r-'* is not without difficulty in covenantal contexts. A difference of opinion exists over the word *barā'a* in Q 9:1, which Wansbrough (*Quranic Studies*, p. 11) sees as cognate with the Biblical *berit*, "covenant," hence its common translation as "declaration of immunity" (e.g. A. Yusuf Ali's translation of the Qur'ān). Uri Rubin, however, following the Muslim sources, reads it as the *dissolution* of the existing treaty, which dissolution is reiterated in Q 9:3, where the

word *barī'* means "free from obligation or responsibility" as in Q 8:48, 10:41, 26:216, and the present verse. See Uri Rubin, "*Barā'a*: A Study of Some Qur'ānic Passages," *Jerusalem Studies in Arabic and Islam*, V (1984), pp. 13–15. He explains the difference between the meaning of the word in Q 9:1 and its meaning in Q 54:43 as depending upon the associated prepositions.

38 Mendenhall and Herion, op. cit., p. 1192 c. 2.
39 Ibid., p. 1201 c. 1.
40 See, e.g. al-Fīrūzābādī, *al-Qāmūs al-Muḥīṭ*, iii, p. 321.
41 Both men discuss the point in their exegeses of Q 2:128, in which the word first appears. Moshe Weinfeld notes that sacrifice is absent from the covenant-making Decalogue. See "The Decalogue," in E. Firmage et al., eds, *Religion and Law: Biblical-Judaic and Islamic Perspectives*, Eisenbrauns, 1990, pp. 26ff.
42 Ṭabarī (Beirut ed., ii, p. 172) and Suyūṭī (*al-Durr al-Manthur fī al-Tafsīr bi-al-Ma'thūr*, ed. M.A-F. Ibrāhīm, Cairo: 'Isā al-Bābī al-Ḥalabī, 1384/1964, i, pp. 556–558) relate the verse to the custom of gathering to boast about one's forebears after completing the ḥajj in pre-Islamic times. God, then is to be added to or substituted for the tales of glory. Rāzī quotes Mujāhid as equating *manāsik* with "shedding blood" (op. cit. v, p. 184).
43 Ṭabarī, op. cit., viii, p. 82.
44 Ṭabarsī, op. cit., ii, p. 50.
45 Mendenhall and Herion, op. cit., p. 1182. See §11 and 12 below.
46 F.E. Peters, *Muhammad and the Origins of Islam*, SUNY, 1994, pp. 113, 125–127, 131.
47 Ibid., pp. 119–121.
48 Ibid., pp. 120–121; Patricia Crone and Michael Cook, *Hagarism*. Cambridge, 1977, p. 13.
49 Respectively, i, p. 323, and i, p. 157, both *ad* Q 2:88.
50 Rāzī, op. cit., iii, p. 164.
51 It is beyond the scope of this book to discuss "the punishment of the grave" (*'adhāb al-qabr*): the possibility that some punishment comes before resurrection.
52 Watt and Bell, op. cit., p. 133.
53 But see B.S. Jackson, op. cit., p. 243.
54 See above, §5.
55 See Weiss, "Covenant and Law," p. 80, with the references to Rāzī.
56 To this effect, see Weiss, "Covenant and Law," §2, p. 56.
57 Otto Michel, "*Mimnēskomai, mneia*", *Theological Dictionary of the New Testament* (ed. G. Kittel; transl. and ed. G. Bromiley), iv, p. 675; cf. Mendenhall and Herion, op. cit., p. 1192 c. 1.
58 Mendenhall and Herion, op. cit., p. 1198. *Z-k-r* meaning "to swear" is found in the Code of Hammurapi; "invoke" is the RSV translation of the word in II Samuel 14:11.
59 Ibid., p. 1198, c. 1.
60 Ibid.; Michel, op. cit., iv, pp. 676, 678. The phrase is Michel's, p. 678.
61 *Holy Bible: Revised Standard Version*. Muslims believe that this passage and others foretell the coming of the Prophet Muḥammad.
62 Mendenhall and Herion, op. cit., p. 1188, c. 1.

63 See Ibn Qayyim al-Jawziyya, *al-Tibyān fi Aqsām al-Qur'ān*, (ed. M.H. al-Faqī), Beirut: Dār al-Ma'rifa, n.d., pp. 1, 194, 522.
64 Angelika Neuwirth, "The Makkan sura introductions," in *Approaches to the Qur'ān*, G.R. Hawting and A.A. Shareef (eds). New York: Routledge, 1993, pp. 3–36. S.a. Lamya Kandil, "Die Schwüre in den Mekkanischen Suren," in *The Qur'ān as Text*, ed. Stefan Wild, Leiden: Brill, 1996, pp. 41–57.
65 Neuwirth, op. cit., p. 4.
66 Ibid., p. 11.
67 Ibid., p. 16. Also see Soraya Hajjaji-Jarrah's "The enchantment of reading" in *Literary Structures of Religious Meaning in the Qur'ān*, ed. I. Boullata, Richmond: Curzon, 2000, pp. 228–251, for a discussion of the sequence in Sura 100 *al-'Ādiyāt*.
68 Neuwirth, op. cit., p. 18.
69 Curiously, Weiss ignores these oaths, stating that "God by definition cannot swear to anything" ("Covenant and Law", p. 72). This is in line with theological resistance to the notion of God being under any sort of obligation, but the statement that "divine covenanting may be distinguished from human covenanting" by the absence of an oath (p. 73) is sufficiently refuted by pointing out the presence of oaths – lots of them.
70 Qur'ān 79:35 and 89:23 speak of humans' "remembering" when confronted with the Day of Judgment, but that comes too late to do any good. It is presented as a lesson to humans that they should not forget; it is not a commandment.
71 Ṭabarī, op. cit., i, pp. 142–144.
72 Ṭabarsī, op. cit., i, pp. 69–70.
73 Rāzī, op. cit., ii, p. 147.
74 *Durr*, i, p. 104.

2 SIGNS AND PRECEDENTS

1 See Chapter 4.
2 To the signs and commands Bernard Weiss ("Covenant and Law," p. 53) adds "promises" for a "cluster" of factors characteristic of expositions of the Covenant. See Chapter 1, n. 24. See Q 13:1–29 for an extended example.
3 This is al-Ghāzalī's first example of the categorical syllogism. See below, Chapter 8, p. 158.
4 Ibn Rushd, *Manāhij al-Adilla fī 'Aqā'id al-Milla* (ed. Maḥmūd Qasim). Cairo: Maktabat al-Anglo al-Misriyya, 1964, p. 152. S.a. Ibn al-Ḥanbalī, op. cit., pp. 73–74, n. 3.
5 S.a. Hassan Hanafi, "Method of thematic interpretation of the Qur'ān," in S. Wild (ed.) *The Qur'ān as Text*, pp. 206–207 for a brief exposition.
6 Sometimes identified with an individual, al-Walīd b. al-Mughīra al-Makhzūmī. See al-Fīrūzābādī, *Tanwīr al-Miqbās min Tafsīr Ibn 'Abbās*, Multan: Faruqi Kutubkhaneh, n.d., p. 372.
7 Though the context seems to imply that these "signs" are the previously mentioned bounties, exegetes tend to identify "signs" in a

conventional way: Ṭabarī (op. cit., xxix, p. 154) says that they are "God's proofs (*ḥujaj*) to His creatures in the form of the Books and the Prophets;" Fīrūzābādī, *Tanwīr al-Miqbās*, p. 372, "Our Book and Our Prophet."

8 Ṭabarī, op. cit., xxx, pp. 161–162. A. Guillaume adds this passage in *The Life of Muhammad*, Oxford, 1980 (1955), p. 107.

9 Ibn Hishām, *al-Sīra al-Nabawiyya li-Ibn Hishām*, (ed. T.A-R. Sa'd), Beirut: Dar al-Jil, n.d., I, p. 223. Guillaume, *Life of Muhammad*, p. 107.

10 W.M. Watt and R. Bell, *Bell's Introduction to the Qur'ān*, Edinburgh, 1970, pp. 121–122.

11 See Cartlidge and Dungan, *Documents for the Study of the Gospels*, Philadelphia: Fortress, 1980, p. 92, for this incident as found in *The Infancy Gospel of Thomas*.

12 Anderson, Bernhard. *Understanding the Old Testament*, (2nd edn) Englewood Cliffs, NJ: Prentice-Hall, 1966, p. 366.

13 See Chapter 1, p. 2ff.

14 See, e.g., Q 7:59–102; 11:25–100; 26:70–191.

15 When such terms are used instead to indicate *approval*, they require contextualization if they are not to be misunderstood. For example, current colloquial American usage attaches positive connotations to hitherto negative words, such as "wild", "outrageous", and especially "baaad" (said with a rising intonation and the vowel greatly elongated). Francophones will find that the *Petit Robert*, in its etymological notes to the word *insolite*, describes the word as "pejorative up until the twentieth century; it is a fashionable word, laudatory rather in our day." *Petit Robert*, Paris, Société du Nouveau Littré, 1970, p. 915.

16 Izutsu, *Structure*, pp. 218–219.

17 This is the Lebanese mountain dialect version.

18 This was the late Professor Noury al-Khaledy, of Portland State University, Portland, Oregon, whose teaching, moral guidance, and sense of humor influenced me profoundly. I shall never be able to describe them in a way that does them justice.

19 Al-Farrā', *Ma'ānī al-Qur'ān*, ii, p. 22.

20 The choice of words is A. Yusuf Ali's, *The Holy Qur'an*, p. 533.

21 Al-Farrā', *Ma'ānī*, ii, p. 22.

22 Al-Qurṭubī, *al-Jāmi' li-Aḥkām al-Qur'ān*, ix, p. 43.

23 These may have been his own daughters or all the women of the people to whom he was sent as prophet (e.g. Farrā', ii, p. 23, cf. Q 33:6). Ṭabarī reports virtual consensus that what was offered was marriage with these women, not fornication (xiv, p. 51). Qurṭubī quotes Abū 'Ubayda's view that the intent was not to offer women at all, but to drive away the homosexuals by mentioning something repugnant to them (ix, p. 51).

24 Ṭūfī, *'Alam al-Jadhal*, p. 132.

25 Ṭabarī, op. cit., iii, p. 282.

26 Muqātil b. Sulaymān, *Tafsīr Muqātil b. Sulaymān*, (ed. A.M. Shihāta), Cairo: Mu'ạssasat al-Ḥalabi, 1969, p. 172. Cf. Mark 2:23–28 and 3:1–6.

3 THE *SUNNA* OF GOD

1 I first presented ideas fundamental to this chapter in my paper "The Neglected *Sunna*: The *sunna* of God" delivered at the 203rd meeting of the American Oriental Society, Chapel Hill, North Carolina, April 19, 1993. A version of the paper entitled "The neglected *Sunna*: Sunnat Allāh (The *sunna* of God)" was later published as an article in *The American Journal of Islamic Social Sciences* (AJISS), vol. 10 (Winter 1993), no. 4, pp. 455–463.

2 This is line 81 of the poem. Labīd, *Sharḥ Dīwạn Labīd b. Rabī'a al-'Āmiri* (ed. Iḥsān 'Abbās), Kuwait, Ministry of Guidance and Information, 1961, p. 320.

3 Michael Morony, *Iraq After the Muslim Conquest*, Princeton, University Press, 1984, p. 434.

4 M.M. Bravmann, *The Spiritual Background of Early Islam*, Leiden: Brill, 1972, pp. 123–198.

5 Joseph Schacht, *Introduction to Islamic Law*, Oxford, 1964; *The Origins of Muhammadan Jurisprudence*, Oxford, 1950 (repr. 1967).

6 Bravmann, op. cit., p. 148.

7 Ibid., pp. 164ff.

8 Ibid., pp. 139ff., contra Schacht, *Origins*, pp. 62, 70–72; cf. Schacht, *Introduction*, p. 30.

9 Schacht, *Introduction*, p. 17.

10 Schacht, *Origins*, 350, in an addendum to p. 74.

11 These quotations come respectively at p. 135, n. 2 from *Kitāb al-Umm* (Būlāq ed.), ii, 2; p. 121, 8 ("*sunnat allah*"); pp. 143–144 from *Sīrat Rasūl Allūh* (Wüstenfeld, ed.), p. 595 (Sura 3:131/7); and p. 144 from Bayḍāwī's *Tafsīr* (Fleisher, ed.), i, 176, 16. Bravmann's own citation of Sura 8:39/38 comes at pp. 147–148.

12 Schacht, *Origins*, 77.

13 Data for the second part of the table and for some textual references were taken from three sources: M.J. Fischer and M. Abedi, *Debating Muslims*, Madison: University of Wisconsin, 1990, pp. 445–447 and n. 12, pp. 464–465; W.M. Watt and R. Bell, *Bell's Introduction to the Qur'ān*, Edinburgh, EUP, 1970, pp. 206–213; and N.J. Dawood, *The Koran*, Harmondsworth, England: Penguin, 1974, pp. 5–8.

14 Ṭabarsī, from al-Zuhrī (d. 124/742), op. cit., i, p. 508.

15 In Suyūṭi, *Durr*, ii, p. 329.

16 Muqātil, *Tafsīr Muqātil b. Sulaymān* (ed. A.M. Shihāta), Cairo: Mu'assasat al-Ḥalabī, 1969, p. 195.

17 Ṭabarī, op. cit., iv, pp. 65f, *ad* Q 3:137.

18 Ṭabarsī, op. cit., i, p. 507, *ad* Q 3:137.

19 Op. cit., p. 233.

20 Ṭabarī, op. cit., v, p. 18.

21 Zamakhsharī, *al-Kashshāf*, i, p. 521.

22 Ṭabarsī, op. cit., ii, pp. 35–36.

23 Rāzī, op. cit., x, p. 66. For the passage from Jaṣṣāṣ, see above, pp. 92ff.

24 Ṭabarsī, op. cit., ii, p. 35; ii, p. 542, respectively.

25 See n. 13, above.

26 Ṭabarī, op. cit., xxii, p. 96.

27 Ṭabarsī, op. cit., iv, p. 412.
28 The ellipsis indicates the long passage outlining the legal details of the marriage.
29 See Bravmann, *Spiritual Background*, pp. 166f.
30 E.g. Ṭabarsī, op. cit., ii, p. 188.
31 Or "to be declared an outlaw" (*awwal man kutiba ʿalayhi al-shaqāʾ*).
32 Muqātil, op. cit., i, p. 310.
33 Ibid., i, p. 311.
34 Ibid., i, p. 312.
35 See Chapter 5, pp. 90f, for legal arguments on the basis of equivalence.
36 Ṭabarī, op. cit., vi, p. 125. See Wensinck, *Concordance*, s.vv. *kifl, sanna, qatl*. The two halves of the *ḥadīth* sometimes occur separately, and Ṭabarī quotes the second half in a *khabar* from Ibn ʿAmr. Suyūṭi quotes numerous versions as well; *Durr*, iii, pp. 61f.
37 Ṭabarī, op. cit., vi, p. 127.
38 See Ṭabarī, op. cit., vi, p. 124 for a statement to that effect attributed to Mujāhid but of which Ṭabarī doubts the authenticity.
39 "His second work *Aḥkām al-Qur'ān* ... is another important contribution not only to the science of *tafsīr* but also to the science of the principles of jurisprudence." Saeedullah Qazi, *Principles of Muslim Jurisprudence: Chapters on Qiyās and Ijtihād of ... al-Jaṣṣāṣ*, Lahore: al-Maktabat-el-Ilmiyyah, 1981, p. 39.
40 Jaṣṣāṣ, op. cit., ii, pp. 401–402.
41 Ibid., ii, p. 404. S.a. Ṭabarī, op. cit., vi, p. 127.
42 Jaṣṣāṣ, op. cit., ii, p. 405.
43 See Wensinck, *Concordance*, s.v. It is not in Bukhārī or Abū Dāwūd but is in all the other canonical collections, including the *Musnad* of Aḥmad b. Ḥanbal.
44 Ṭabarsī, op. cit,, ii, p. 187.
45 E.g. Ibn Taghribirdī, *al-Nujūm al-Ẓāhira*, Cairo, 1963–72, iii, p. 189.

4 RULES, COMMANDS, AND REASONS WHY

1 For an example of the first, see the position attributed to ʿAbbād b. Sulaymān (d. 250/864) in al-Ashʿarī's (d. 324/935) *Maqālāt al-Islāmīyīn*, H. Ritter, ed., Wiesbaden: Steiner, 1382/1963, pp. 253 and 390. Fakhr al-Dīn al-Rāzī includes other Muʿtazili positions, along with those of *ahl al-sunna*, in his exhaustive analysis of the logic of their interpretations of the two halves of Q 21:23 (*al-Tafsīr al-Kabīr*, xxii, pp. 155–158).
2 Gidon Gottlieb, *The Logic of Choice: An Investigation of the Concepts of Rule and Rationality*, London: Allen and Unwin, 1968.
3 Georg Henrik von Wright, *Norm and Action: A Logical Inquiry*; New York: Humanities Press, 1963.
4 He excludes purely descriptive "laws," such as the laws of nature.
5 von Wright, op. cit., pp. 12–13. Italics are in the original.
6 Gottlieb, op. cit., pp. 37–38.
7 von Wright, op. cit., pp. 3–16.
8 Gottlieb, op. cit., pp. 17–18.
9 Ibid., p. 20. Italics are original.

10 Ibid., p. 40.
11 Gottlieb calls this the *character-tag* of a rule (p. 40).
12 Ibid., p. 39.
13 Cf. ibid.
14 Ibid., p. 41.
15 Ibid., p. 39.
16 Toshihiko Izutsu, *Language and Magic*, Tokyo: Keio Institute, 1956, pp. 52–53.
17 Nicholas Rescher, *The Logic of Commands*, London: Routledge and Kegan Paul, 1966, contains a long bibliography arranged chronologically.
18 For a representative exegesis on the multiple uses of the imperative, see Ṭabarsī, op. cit., i, p. 69, *ad* Q 2:27. For a juristic treatment, see Jeannette Wakin, "The Divine Command in Ibn Qudamah," *Islamic Law and Jurisprudence: Studies in Honor of Farhat J. Ziadeh*, N. Heer, ed., Seattle: University of Washington, 1990, especially pp. 35ff. and the references therein.
19 Rescher, op. cit., p. 2.
20 von Wright, op. cit., pp. 7–8 and *passim*.
21 Cf. von Wright, op. cit., pp. 13–14.
22 Rescher, op. cit., p. 10, with n. 5.
23 Ibid., p. 6, n. 4.
24 Gottlieb, op. cit., pp. 115–116, quoting no. 199 of Wittgenstein's *Philosophical Investigations* (1953 edn).
25 See n. 21 above.
26 Rescher, op. cit., p. 16.
27 Edwards, Paul. *The Logic of Moral Discourse*, Glencoe, IL: Free Press, 1955, p. 127
28 Rescher, op. cit., p. 16.
29 See e.g. Ibn Hishām, *Al-Sīra al-Nabawīya li-Ibn Hishām*, T.A-R. Sa'd, ed., Beirut: Dar al-Jīl, n.d. i, pp. 220–221; *The Life of Muḥammad*, A. Guillaume, ed. and tr., Oxford, 1955 (1980), p. 106.
30 Ibn Hishām op. cit., i, p. 221, text and n. 1; Ṭabarī, op. cit., p. 251; al-Suyūṭī, *al-Itqān fi 'Ulūm al-Qur'ān*, Aḥmad Sa'd 'Alī, ed., Cairo, 1370/1951 (repr. Beirut, Dār al-Nadwa al-Jadīda, n.d.), §7, p. 23.
31 See, for example, al-Qasṭallānī, *Irshād al-Sārī*, vii, pp. 426–429; Guillaume, op. cit., p. 83.
32 Ibn Kathīr, *Tafsịr al-Qur'ān al-'Aẓīm*, Beirut: Dār al-Fikr, 1400/1980, i, p. 10.
33 Suyūṭī, *Itqān*, §7, pp. 23ff.
34 The *basmalah* is the first verse of Sura 1, whereas in Sura 96 it precedes the first verse.
35 Izutsu, *Language and Magic*, pp. 52ff. See above, p. 67.
36 Suyūṭī, *Itqān*, §7, p. 24. He explains that it may have been called "the first" because it was the first to be revealed in its entirety, unlike Sura 96, or because it was the first to be revealed after the long hiatus following the command to "Read!"
37 This is Abū Bakr M. b. 'Abd Allāh al-Ma'āfirī (d. 543/1148), not to be confused with the great mystic Abu 'Abd Allāh M. b. 'Alī Muḥyī al-Dīn Ibn [al-] 'Arabī (d. 638/1240). The passage in question comes in the

entry for Sura 96, iv, p. 1942. Neither Ṭabarī nor the Shīʿī Ṭabarsī mentions ʿAlī's purported dating of the passage.

38 See W.M. Watt and Richard Bell, *Bell's Introduction to the Qur'ān*, Edinburgh, 1970, pp. 115 and 176.

39 Watt and Bell, *Bell's Introduction*, pp. 112, 174–175, and 212–213. Sir William Muir, *The Life of Mahomet*, London, 1894 (Repr. New Delhi: Voice of India, 1992), pp. 38–46.

40 Muir, op. cit., p. 38.

41 Ibid., p. 40.

42 Ibid., p. 38.

43 See below, p. 81f.

44 Muir, op. cit., p. 47. Italics and capital letters are original.

45 Watt and Bell, *Bell's Introduction*, pp. 112 and 176.

46 A good English account is to be found in Mahmoud Ayoub, *The Qur'ān and Its Interpreters, Volume 1*, Albany: SUNY Press, 1984, pp. 137–138. Also see the notes to A. Yusuf ʿAli's and Muhammad ʿAli's renditions of the Qur'ān, as well as the *Tafsirs* of Mujāhid (d. 104/722), ed. A-R. al-Surati, Islamabad: Majmaʿ al-Buḥūth al-Islāmīya, 1966, p. 85; Muqātil b. Sulaymān (d. 150/767), ed. A.M. Shihāta, Cairo: Halabi, 1969, i, p. 59; and Sufyān al-Thawrī (d. 161/777), ed. Imtiyaz A. ʿArshi, Rampur, 1385/1965, ad loc.; Ṭabarī, op. cit., Cairo: Halabi, 3rd edn, 1388/1968, i, pp. 469–474.

47 Tāshköprüzādeh, *Miftāḥ al-Saʿāda* , ii, 442. S.a. al-Baghdādī, *Uṣūl al-Dīn*, Lahore: al-Maktaba al-ʿUthmānīya, n.d., pp. 215f.

48 I have counted some ninety occurrences of this phrase in the Qur'ān.

49 There is a curious divergence in the early exegetical treatment of the two parallel participles *muzzammil* and *muddaththir*. One description of Muhammad's fear following the first revelation has him saying to Khadīja "*daththirūnī, daththirūnī*," and this version of his plea is duly recounted in the exegesis of the word *muddaththir* in Sura 74: see Mujāhid, op. cit., ii, p. 703; Ṭabarī, op. cit., xxix, p. 90; Qasṭallānī, op. cit., vii, p. 403. The same is not true of *muzzammil*: although the more common version of Muḥammad's cry has him saying "*zammilūnī, zammilūnī*", it is not mentioned in the exegesis of Sura 73 *al-Muzzammil* but in that of Sura 96. See Ṭabarī, op. cit., xxx, p. 161; Qasṭallānī, op. cit., vii, p. 427–429. Ṭabarsī conflates the two but the fuller account is under *al-Muddaththir*: op. cit., v, p. 377 and especially p. 384.

50 Mujāhid, *Tafsīr*, ii, p. 766, text and n. 4.

51 Ṭabarī, op. cit., xxx, p. 150. Presumably "Abu Nadrah" was the Baṣrī al-Mundhir b. Mālik al-ʿAbdi. See Ibn Saʿd, *al-Ṭabaqāt al-Kubrā*, Beirut: Dār Ṣādir, 1377/1958, vii, p. 208, and al-Nūrī, *al-Jāmiʿ fī al-Jarḥ wa-al-Taʿdīl*, Beirut, ʿĀlam al-Kutub, 1412/1992, iii, p. 169, no. 4482.

52 Thus Mujāhid, op. cit., ii, p. 794; Fīrūzābādī, *Tanwīr al-Miqbās*, p. 398.

53 Ibn Khālawayh, *Iʿrāb Thalāthīn Sūra min al-Qur'ān al-Karīm*, Beirut: Dār Maktabat al-Hilāl, 1985, p. 228. Jeffery notes that the codex of Ubayy also lacked *qul*. See *Materials for the History of the Text of the Qur'ān*, Leiden: Brill, 1937 (repr. AMS Press, 1975), p. 113.

5 LEGAL ARGUMENTS

1 See Chapter 4, pp. 63ff.
2 Mendenhall and Herion, op. cit., i, p. 1180, col. 1.
3 See Chapter 1, p. 9f.
4 Qurṭubī, op. cit., i, p. 227.
5 In my experience, the recipient usually responds in a way that preserves the triangular relationship, asking God to bless the giver rather than thanking her/him directly.
6 The verb is *iʿtadā*, with related participle.
7 The difficulties of translating this word are notorious. Some attempts: "tumult and oppression" (A. Yusuf Ali), "idolatry" (N.J. Dawood), "persecution" (Pickthall and Arberry).
8 Qurṭubī, op. cit., ii, pp. 237–238.
9 See note 7, above, for suggested translations of this word. The translation does not affect the rule under consideration, namely, that there are things worse than killing.
10 See Jaṣṣāṣ, op. cit., i, pp. 133–158; Qurṭubī, op. cit., i, pp. 164–172.
11 In the summer of 1990 I was sitting with His Eminence the Grand Mufti of Yemen, Aḥmad Muḥammad Muḥammad Yaḥyā Zabāra, when he received a petition from a man who was attempting to use his absence "in a foreign country" (Saudi Arabia!) as a circumstance that would limit his obligation to send financial support to his wife in Yemen. The Mufti found for the wife.
12 Qurṭubī, op. cit., i, p. 225 *ad* Q 2:187.
13 S.a. above, p. 91.
14 Qurṭubī, op. cit., i, p. 170.
15 The word *Allāhu* is in the nominative case.
16 The usual understanding is that this prohibits simultaneous but not sequential marriage to sisters.
17 See, e.g. al-Dhahabī (d. 748/1348), who ranks it eighth among the great sins: *Kitāb al-Kabā'ir*, Aleppo: Dār al-Waʿy, pp. 41–49. Cf. Q 2:83, 4:36, 6:151, 17:23; and A.J. Wensinck, *Concordance et Indices de la Tradition Musulmane*, Leiden: Brill, 1936, s.v. *birr.*
18 Bernard Weiss, "Exotericism and objectivity in Islamic jurisprudence," in N. Heer, ed., *Islamic Law and Jurisprudence: Studies in Honor of Farhat J. Ziadeh*, Seattle, University of Washington, 1990, pp. 65–66.
19 See Chapter 9, "Conditional and Disjunctive Arguments."
20 Ṭabarsī, op. cit., iii, p. 388. A Shīʿī, he describes as *taqīya* the mental state of the believer who is forced to reject his faith outwardly.
21 But cf. his position on forced conversion and declaration of divorce, in the "Excursus on Performative Utterances," below.
22 Jaṣṣāṣ, op. cit., iii, p. 192.
23 George A. Kennedy, *Aristotle: On Rhetoric: A Theory of Civic Discourse*, Oxford, 1991, p. 109, n. 247.
24 Edward P.J. Corbett, *Classical Rhetoric for the Modern Student*, Oxford, 1971, p. 34.
25 Certain passages may have been revealed following incidents of torture. Q 16:106, for example, is said to have been revealed when the young ʿAmmār b. Yāsir verbally renounced his faith after seeing his

parents tortured to death but remained faithful internally. Such actions were perpetrated on Muslims, not by them. See, e.g. Qurṭubī, op. cit., x, pp. 118ff.

26 Kennedy, op. cit., pp. 110–111.
27 Ibid., p. 113.
28 Ibid.
29 A useful summary can be found in Mustansir Mir's *Dictionary of Qur'ānic Terms and Concepts*, New York: Garland, 1987, s.v. "witness."
30 See Chapter 1, especially pp. 12–13.
31 Three different vowelings for the last phrase have been proposed; see Ṭabarsī, op. cit., iii, p. 299.
32 See the next section, "Contracts."
33 Kennedy, op. cit., p. 114.
34 Ibid., p. 115.
35 Jaṣṣāṣ, op. cit., i, 487. Also see above, Chapter 4, pp. 80–81.
36 See above, p. 80.
37 Cf. Ṭabarī, iii, p. 116.
38 Legal scholars qualify this as applying only if no others are present who could do the job equally well. It is also questionable whether a fee can be paid for what is in the first instance a religious duty, whereas it is usual to charge a fee for copying a document. See Qurubī, op. cit., iii, p. 248.
39 See Jaṣṣāṣ, op. cit., i, p. 482. His argument against the occurrence of abrogation in verse 283 runs as follows: if the hypothesis were true, it would mean that the abrogated and abrogating verses were revealed at the same time; but "it is inadmissible that a rule should be abrogated before it goes into effect." There is no evidence that the verses were revealed at different times. Therefore, the "trust" clause renders the locution a recommendation and not a commandment. Jaṣṣāṣ's exegesis of the verse occupies 42 large pages of fine print.
40 Kennedy, op. cit., p. 117.
41 Mir, op. cit., s.v. "Oaths."
42 Op. cit., i, p. 1182, col. 1.
43 Cf. Jaṣṣāṣ, op. cit., ii, pp. 454, 457.
44 Ibid., ii, pp. 489–494.
45 To wit, in Q 2:133, 3:52, 3:64, 3:84, 5:111, 6:163, 10:90, 27:42, 28:53, 41:33, and 46:15 (declarations); in Q 2:136, 10:72, 27:91, 29:46, and 39:12 (commands); and in Q 2:131, 3:20, and 27:44 (verbs), respectively.
46 This rough and ready definition must suffice, as full treatment is beyond the scope of this book. Performatives occur at the junction of logic, language, and law; they may be pursued in the works of the Oxford logician J.L. Austin and the linguist Jan Andersson (*How to Define Performative*, Uppsala, 1975), *inter alia*. I am indebted to my colleague at the University of Tennessee, the linguist and lawyer Bethany Dumas, both for introducing me to performatives and for recommending to me what she considers the best description of them, "How Performatives Work," by Berkeley philosopher John Searle (*Tennessee Law Review*, vol. 58/1991, pp. 371–392), q.v. with its credits and bibliography.

47 The difficulties of translating the verb are well known. "Submit" seems closer to the unequal relationship between man and God, yet "commit" also conveys that relation, as one can learn from an etymologically complete dictionary. "Commit" more clearly denotes the element of discrimination pointed out by Muḥammad Abdul Rauf, "Some Notes on the Qur'ānic Use of the Terms *Islam* and *Iman*", MW, vol. 57 (1967), pp. 94–102. He equates *islām* with "monotheism," basing his argument upon the root *s-l-m* as indicating "the absence of something undesired or abhorred, implying at the same time the existence or fulfillment of the desired or required opposite" (p. 94). Also cf. the King James rendering of Psalm 37:5: "Commit thy way unto the Lord; trust also in him; and he shall bring it to pass."
48 Jaṣṣāṣ, op. cit., i, pp. 452–454.
49 Ibid. iii, p. 193. See above, pp. 97–98.
50 Andersson, op. cit., pp. 5 and 115ff, with the references therein.
51 Ayoub, op. cit., i, p. 5.

6 COMPARISON

1 See the next chapter.
2 See the previous chapter.
3 Edward P.J. Corbett, *Classical Rhetoric for the Modern Student*, Oxford, 1971, p. 116.
4 See above, Chapter 5, pp. 84–87 and 90–91, respectively.
5 This is called *antanaclasis*; see Corbett, op. cit., p. 482.
6 See e.g. Ṭabarsī, op. cit., i, p. 288. S.a. Chapter 5 above, p. 85
7 See above, Chapters 1, 2, and 3, and below in the present chapter.
8 See Chapter 5, pp. 86–87.
9 See my article, "Impotence," in the *Encyclopaedia of the Qur'ān*, Jane Dammen McAuliffe, ed., Netherlands: Brill, ii, pp. 507–508.
10 Dagobert Runes, *Dictionary of Philosophy*, Ames: Littlefield, 1955, p. 11.
11 Ibn Ḥazm, *Mulakhkhaṣ Ibṭāl al-Qiyās wa-al-Ra'y wa-al-Istiḥsān wa-al-Taqlīd wa-al-Ta'līl*, Sa'īd al-Afghānī, ed., Damascus University Press, 1379/1960, p. 70. He and Wensinck ascribe it to the *Sunan* of al-Dārimī, who credits it to Ibn Sīrīn. Wensinck cites it as §22 of al-Dārimi's *Muqaddima*: *Qāsa Iblīs wa-hwa awwal man qāsa* (*Concordance et Indices*, v, p. 503, c. 2).
12 Corbett, op. cit., p. 116.
13 *Webster's Dictionary of Synonyms*, Springfield, MA: Merriam, 1951, p. 40, col. 2., s.v. "allegory."
14 The phrase *Allāhu a'lam* occurs many times in the Qur'ān but not as an absolute, that is, it is always used with an object, e.g. "God knows best what they are hiding" (Q 3:167, 5:61, cf. 60:1). Popular usage of the phrase, of course, implies the superlative.
15 Suyūṭī quotes Qatāda to the effect that these ranks depend upon their deeds in this life. To this he adds a remark by al-Ḍaḥḥāk that precludes the possibility of jealousy in Paradise: "The higher one sees his preference over the one lower than he in rank, while the lower one does not see that there is anyone above him." A *hadīth* from Salmān quotes the Prophet: "There is no one who wants to ascend a rank in

this world and succeeds but God lowers him in the Hereafter by a greater and longer rank. Then he quoted, 'And the Hereafter is greater in ranks and greater in preference'." (Suyūṭī, *Durr*, v, pp. 256–257.)

16 This wording is borrowed from Pickthall's translation, with minor changes. See *The Meaning of the Glorious Koran*, Mentor, 1953, p. 428.

17 See Chapter 5, pp. 89–90.

18 *Afʿal* is of course the pattern for both the elative adjective and the adjective of color or defect, so another construction must normally be used for making an elative of a defect – "more blind." However, there are precedents for using *afʿal* as the elative of an elative: in Chapter 10 of *al-Kitāb*, Sībawayh uses the word *awwal*, "first," in the phrase *awwal minhu*, where it can only mean "prior to" (*al-Kitāb*, ed. H. Derenbourg, Paris: Imprimerie Nationale, 1881 (repr. Hildesheim), i, p. 11). Zamakhsharī says that some have considered the second *aʿmā* in this verse as possibly elative and that Abu ʿAmr read it in such a way as to distinguish the two (*Kashshāf*, ii, p. 460).

19 See, e.g. Ibn Rushd (d. 595/1198), *Bidāyat al-Mujtahid*, i, "*Kitāb al-jihād*", §5, p. 283.

20 See my article, "The *a fortiori* argument in *fiqh*, *naḥw*, and *kalām*," *Studies in the History of Arabic Grammar II: Proceedings of the 2nd Symposium on the History of Arabic Grammar, Nijmegen, 27 April–1 May, 1987*, Amsterdam/Philadelphia: Benjamins, 1990 (Published as Vol. 56 of the series Studies in the History of the Language Sciences), pp. 165–177.

21 See, e.g. L.S. Stebbing, *A Modern Introduction to Logic*, New York: Humanities Press, 1933, p. 113; P.F. Strawson, *Introduction to Logical Theory*, London: Methuen, 1952 [repr. University Paperbacks, 1971], pp. 207–210.

22 Ralph Eaton, *General Logic*, New York: Scribner's, 1931, pp. 220–222.

23 Al-Shāfiʿī *al-Risāla*, Muḥammad Kaylānī, ed., Cairo: Muṣṭafā al-Bābī al-Ḥalabī, 1403/1983, §1482–83 and 1489–90, pp. 223–224.

7 CONTRAST

1 Angeles, op. cit., s.v. "opposites (metaphysics)."

2 Corbett, op. cit., 129.

3 Note that Sura 63 is called *al-Munāfiqūn*, "The Hypocrites."

4 See below, pp. 145–147.

5 The canonical collections quote it in relation to belief, marriage, divorce, freeing slaves, legal fictions (*ḥiyal*), jihād, ritual purity (*ṭahāra)*, and asceticism (*zuhd)*. See Wensinck, *Concordance et Indices*, vii, p. 55, c. 2.

6 See above, p. 131.

7 E.g. *a-m-n* and *k-f-r*. See the explanation of these two concepts below, p. 143.

8 See Chapter 5 above.

9 *Iʿjāz al-Qur'ān*, ed. Aḥmad Ṣaqr, Cairo: Dār al-Maʿārif, 1963, p. 87. In the terms of classical rhetoric, some of these figures are examples of *antimetabole*, others of *chiasmus*; see Corbett, op. cit., pp. 477–478.

10 This may also be construed as "contrariety," especially if a third state (neither creating nor being created) is admitted, a logical but not a Qur'ạnic possibility. See below, pp. 144–145, and Corbett, op. cit., pp. 129f.
11 See Chapter 5, "An excursus on performative utterances," pp. 105–109.
12 In Q 12:89, Joseph uses the two when asking his brothers if they knew what they did to him. In Q 46:22, Hūd tells his people who persist in ignoring his warnings (*tajhalūn*) that only God knows the Day of Judgment. Goldziher and others, of course, have long since expanded the connotation of *Jāhilīya* beyond mere ignorance.
13 Toshihiko Izutsu, *God and Man in the Koran*, Tokyo: Keio Institute, 1964, pp. 59–62; cf. Corbett, op. cit., pp. 56ff.
14 Particularly *God and Man in the Koran* and *Ethico-Religious Concepts in the Koran*, a reworking of *The Structure of Ethical Terms in the Koran*. See Bibliography. Also note our remarks *passim*, but especially in Chapter 6.
15 *Ethico-Religious Concepts*, pp. 121–131.
16 See my article "Hell and hellfire," *Encyclopaedia of the Qur'ān*, Jane Dammen McAuliffe, ed., Leiden: Brill, 2001, ii, pp. 414–420.
17 The phrase is the title of Chapter VIII in his *Structure of the Ethical Terms in the Koran*, Tokyo, 1959.
18 See Izutsu, *Ethico-Religious Concepts*, p. 107 and above, Chapter 5, p. 105.
19 See above, Chapter 6, p. 123.
20 Izutsu, *Ethico-Religious Concepts*, p. 108.
21 Ṭabarsī, op. cit., i, p. 88, *ad* Qur'ān 2:37.
22 *Logic and Rhetoric*, New York: Macmillan, 1962, p. 122.
23 Ibid., p. 120
24 See Chapter 9 below.
25 E.g. Corbett, op. cit., p. 465.
26 See Chapter 6, pp. 115–117.
27 *Ghill*, in A. Yūsuf 'Alī's translation.

8 CATEGORICAL ARGUMENTS

1 See Introduction, p. viii.
2 *The Book on the Scandals of the Esotericists Dedicated to the Caliph al-Mustaẓhir bi-Llāh (r. 487/1094–512/1118)*, A-R Badawi, ed., Cairo: Dār al-Qawmīya lil-Ṭibā'a wal-Nashr, 1383/1964, written at the order of the caliph. Ghazālī composed at least five works on the subject; see Bouyges, *Essai de Chronologie des Oeuvres de Al-Ghazali*, M. Allard, ed., Beirut: Imprimerie Catholique, 1959, nos. 22 and 42.
3 *Faḍā'iḥ* exposes the methods allegedly used by agents of the Hidden Imām, whom Ghazālī accuses of entrapping gullible students in heresy by promising them secret teaching (*al-ta'līm*) that in the end is nothing less than abolition of all the rules of religion (*al-sharā'i' – Faḍā'iḥ*, p. 12.)
4 See pp. xii–xiii.
5 Najm al-Dīn al-Ṭūfī, *'Alam al-Jadhal fī 'Ilm al-Jadal*, Wolfhart Heinrichs, ed., Wiesbaden: Franz Steiner, 1987, p. 60.
6 Ṭūfī, op. cit., p. 41.

7 Ibid., at pp. 4 and 53.
8 See below, Chapter 9.
9 Bouyges, op. cit., nos. 19 and 20, p. 25.
10 To my knowledge, there are three treatments of this book in Western languages. The first is by Victor Chelhot, "'Al-Qisṭās al-Mustaqīm' et la Connaissance Rationelle Chez Ġazālī," *BEO* 15 (1955–57), pp. 7–42, which includes a French translation. The second is by Angelika Kleinknecht, "*Al-Qisṭās al-Mustaqīm*: eine Ableitung der Logik aus dem Koran," *Islamic Philosophy and the Classical Tradition*, S. Stern et al., eds, South Carolina, 1973, pp. 159–187. The third is Richard McCarthy's translation, published as Appendix III to *Freedom and Fulfillment: An Annotated Translation of al-Ghazālī's 'al-Munqidh min al-Ḍalāl' and Other Relevant Works of al-Ghazālī*, Boston: Twayne, 1980, pp. 287–332.
11 Bouyges, op. cit., no. 42.
12 McCarthy, op. cit., p. 287. Chelhot (op. cit., p. 12) calls it "un genre littéraire 'sui generis'," Goldziher "le plus intéressant de ces ouvrages [de polémique] pour la forme et le fond" (*Le Dogme et la Loi de l'Islam*, Paris: Geuthner, 1958, p. 295, n. 156).
13 Ghazālī, *Qisṭās*, e.g. pp. 42, 43, 78; s.a. n. 55 below.
14 Cf. Ghazālī, *Mi'yār al-'Ilm*, pp. 177ff.
15 Ghazālī, *Qisṭās*, p. 28.
16 Chelhot, op. cit., p. 11.
17 Ghazālī, *Qisṭās*, pp. 93 and 99.
18 Ibid., p. 19.
19 Ibid., pp. 19–20. All translations are my own, but see n. 10 above for full Western language versions.
20 Ibid., pp. 23–24. Cf. Q 24:11–12, and 16.
21 Ghazālī, *Qisṭās*., pp. 24–25.
22 Ibid., pp. 27–30.
23 Ibid., p. 26.
24 Ibid., p. 69.
25 Ibid., pp. 101–102.
26 Ibid., p. 41.
27 Ibid., p. 42.
28 This verse actually concludes a passage that contains another type of syllogism, the second-figure syllogism that is Ghazālī's "Middle Scale" (see pp. 162–167).
29 Square brackets indicate the parts of arguments implicit in the Qur'ānic text.
30 Ibid., p. 42
31 Ibid., p. 44. There is a misprint in the edition cited – for *adhin* read *azin* (from *w-z-n*, cf. *mīzān*.)
32 Ibid., pp. 44–45.
33 Ibid., pp. 46–47.
34 Ibid., pp. 47–48.
35 Celestine Bittle, *The Science of Correct Thinking: Logic*, Milwaukee: Bruce, 1935–37, p. 186. The Jesuit Bittle's examples would be of great interest to Muslims, as they are syllogisms that prove that God is One and Eternal.

36 Bittle, op. cit., p. 189 (italics removed).
37 Bittle, op. cit., p. 185–186.
38 Ghazālī does the same in one of his technical treatises on logic, *Kitāb Miḥakk al-Naẓar fi al-Manṭiq*, M.B.D. al-Naʿsānī, ed., Beirut: Dār al-Nahḍa al-Ḥadītha, 1966, pp. 41–44.
39 Bittle, op. cit., p. 166.
40 Ṭūfī, op. cit., p. 193.
41 Ṭūfī, op. cit, p. 199.
42 My rewording of the verse as a syllogism avoids having to assign a precise meaning to the word *tamannā*, which is notoriously obscure. Without the second half of the verse, one would ordinarily translate it and its cognate noun as "hope" or "aspiration." Yet the verse is cited to prove the integrity of the Qur'ānic text and its freedom from any misreading caused by Satan. One compromise that avoids a circular definition is that it means *ḥaddatha*, "relating ḥadīth" or "conversing," including the Prophet's "conversation with himself." See e.g. al-Qurṭubī, op. cit., xii, pp. 53–57.
43 See Chapter 1 for the importance of the notion of "witness" in the Covenant between God and humankind.
44 See the "Excursus on Performative Utterances" in Chapter 5, pp. 105–109.
45 Bittle, op. cit., p. 192.
46 Ghazālī, *Qisṭās*, pp. 55–56.
47 Ibid., p. 59.
48 Ibid., p. 58.
49 Ibid., p. 62.
50 Ṭūfī, op. cit., p. 121.
51 Bittle, op. cit., pp. 117–118, 210.
52 Ṭūfī, op. cit., p. 127–128.
53 The charge that the source of the Qur'ān was not God but a human being who was not an Arab appears in various versions throughout the literature. According to al-Wāḥidī (*Asbāb al-Nuzūl*, p. 159), it was attributed to two Christian slaves called Yasār and Khayr. Ṣuyūṭī (*Durr*, v, pp. 167–168) gives no fewer than eight alternative versions: a Persian named Balʿām, ʿAbdah b. al-Ḥaḍramī (from four sources, one calling him Abū al-Yusr), a Persian slave named Mqys, Salmān al-Fārisī, and an unnamed secretary.
54 Ghazālī, *Qisṭās*, p. 65. Ghazālī quotes the verse piecemeal, interspersing it with elements of the argument.
55 Ibid., pp. 66–67. Thus in *Qisṭās* Ghazālī combines two conceptions of the enthymeme: (1) that it is a logical syllogism in which premises and conclusion are necessary but one or more is understood by all parties and hence suppressed for greater overall effectiveness, and (2) that it is a rhetorical figure in which these are only probable, as in Aristotle's *Rhetoric*, Book I, Chapter 1. S.a. p. 153 above in the present chapter.
56 Bittle, op. cit., pp. 194–195; italics removed.
57 Ghazālī, *Qisṭās*, p. 68.

9 CONDITIONAL AND DISJUNCTIVE ARGUMENTS

1 Benson Mates, *Stoic Logic*, Berkeley, 1953 (repr. 1961), p. 67.
2 Mates, op. cit., pp. 69–71.
3 Thus Victor Chelhot gets them backwards in his article "'Al-Qisṭās al-Mustaqīm' et la connaissance rationelle chez Ġazālī," *BEO*, xv (1955–57), pp. 7–42. The mistake in question is at p. 13.
4 Irving Copi, *Introduction to Logic* (4th edn), New York: Macmillan, 1972, p. 233.
5 Ibid., p. 234.
6 Chelhot, "règle de concomitance," p. 13. In *Mi'yār al-'Ilm*, Ghazālī calls it the "conditional conjunctive syllogism" (*al-qiyās al-sharṭī al-muttaṣil*), pp. 151ff.
7 Ghazali, *Qisṭās*, p. 75.
8 Ibid., p. 76. Note that in Riyāḍ Muṣṭafā al-'Abd Allāh's edition there are many misprints and omissions in this passage. I have checked it against that of Muḥammad 'Afīf al-Zu'bī, Beirut: Mu'assasat al-Zu'bī, 1392/1973, pp. 33–34.
9 Ghazālī, *Qisṭās*, p. 76.
10 Celestine Bittle, op. cit., pp. 227–229, contains a complete list of the valid forms of both the "constructive" and "destructive" moods. Qur'ān 2:120 is in the fourth form, 41:52 in the first.
11 Ghazālī, *Qisṭās*, p. 74.
12 The first section of Ṭabarsī's commentary on the passage fills in the argument in a characteristically useful way. See *Majma' al-Bayān* ii, pp. 379ff. A possible problem in the English wording comes from the fact that the verb *shā'a* in these verses does not have an explicit object. One might therefore render the English as follows: If God had exercised His will, we would not believe in many gods. We do believe in many gods. Therefore, God did not exercise His will.
13 See Chapter 1.
14 Ṭūfī, op. cit., p. 120.
15 This is the implication as understood by "most exegetes" according to Ṭabarsī, and as understood by R.M. al-'Abd Allāh in his edition of *Qisṭās*; see p. 71, n. 3. Mujāhid and Qatāda, along with the modern A. Yūsuf 'Alī, interpret it as the lesser deities' desire to profit from God's power. Ṭūfī opts for the first interpretation, and it seems likely that Ghazālī does as well, as the other might not have an effect visible on earth. See Ṭabarsī, op. cit., iii, p. 417.
16 "A necessary implication follows, which is the negation of one of the two gods." *Qisṭās*, p. 73. S.a. Ṭūfī, op. cit., p. 47.
17 Ghazālī, *Qisṭās*, p. 73–74.
18 That is, not available for scrutiny or not yet in existence, such as a future crop.
19 Ghazālī, *Qisṭās*, p. 74.
20 Ṭụfi, op. cit., p. 94.
21 Ibn al-Jawzī, *Kitāb al-Muntaẓam*, Hyderabad: Dā'irat al-Ma'ārif al-'Uthmānīya, 1357, vi, pp. 102ff. S.a. A.A. al-A'sam, *Tārīkh Ibn al-Rīwandi al-Mulḥid*, Beirut: Dar al-Āfāq al-Jadīda, 1395/1975, pp. 159ff. and other references s.v. *Dāmigh*.

22 Ṭūfī, op. cit., pp. 108ff.
23 This form is attributed to Aristotle's pupil Theophrastus, not to the Stoics. See Czeslaw Lejewski, "Ancient Logic," *Encyclopedia of Philosophy*, iv, p. 518.
24 See above, p. 177.
25 Note the use of the performative. See the "Excursus on performative utterances" in Chapter 5, pp. 105–109.
26 Rāzī, op. cit., xiv, p. 227.
27 E.g. the Shīʿī Ṭabarsī, op. cit., ii, p. 475.
28 Rāzī, op. cit., xiv, p. 233–234.
29 Copi, pp. 258–259. Copi's own example is, "If State loses the Homecoming Game, then I'll eat my hat."
30 See, for example, Ṭabarsī, op. cit., ii, pp. 100–101.
31 So the "vanished nations" stories. See Richard Martin, "Structural analysis and the Qur'an," *JAAR* 47, no. 4S, pp. 670–671.
32 Mates, op. cit., p. 71.
33 Ṭūfī notes, "It is as though he expected them to say that 'Every one whom we killed was a liar and his prophethood was not established with us.'" Op. cit., p. 99.
34 Mates, op. cit., p. 72.
35 Ibid., p. 73.
36 *"Mabnāhu ʿalā al-ḥadhf wa-l-ījāz,"* *Qisṭās*, p. 42.
37 Ṭūfī, op. cit., p. 103.
38 Ghazālī, *Qisṭās*, p. 78.
39 S. a. Ṭūfī, op. cit., p. 100.
40 Calling both types "conditional" as is done in both Arabic and English (and, presumably, Latin) seems unnecessarily confusing. Apparently it began with Galen, who equated the meaning of the disjunction "Either it is day or it is night" with that of the conditional "If it is not day then it is night." See Mates, op. cit., pp. 55ff.
41 Or "restricted" and "unrestricted," or "complete" and "incomplete" (McCarthy, op. cit., p. 305); or "proper" and "improper" (Bittle, op. cit., pp. 231ff.)
42 Ghazālī, *Qisṭās*, p. 79. The entire eighth chapter is entitled *Mīzān al-Shayṭān*.
43 See above, p. 145.
44 Ṭūfī, op. cit., p. 193.
45 But compare this with the punishment visited upon the weak who have followed the strong into Hell (Q 14:21; see Chapter 6 above, p. 114).
46 Ghazālī, *Qisṭās*, pp. 97ff.

10 TECHNICAL TERMS AND DEBATING TECHNIQUE

1 Here theology and English grammar part company, in that a plural verb sounds correct but implies an unacceptable plurality of subject. I have followed A. Yūsuf ʿAlī, M.M. Pickthall, and N.J. Dawood and used the singular. In Arabic, of course, the construction is an equational sentence with no verb.
2 Ṭūfī, op. cit., p. 13, with n. 1.

3 *Kitāb Istikhrāj al-Jidāl min al-Qur'ān al-Karīm*, pp. 49ff.
4 Ṭūfī, op. cit., pp. 155–156. The word here translated as "the human being" is, of course, *al-insān* – grammatically definite, as is proper Arabic for a generic term. But the presence of the definite article in a Qur'ānic reference often led exegetes, especially early ones, to refer the word to a specific person. Ṭabarsī notes that Ibn ʿAbbās held *al-insān* to be al-Naḍr b. al-Ḥārith, al-Kalbī that it was Ubayy b. Khalaf (op. cit., iv, p. 477). Suyūṭī (*Durr*, v, p. 406) cites the story from Bukhārī, Muslim, Ibn al-Mundhir, and Ibn Abī Ḥātim, on the authority of ʿAlī himself. Naturally enough, the Shiʿi Ṭabarsī leaves it out.
5 There is more than one possible construction of this verb. See Zamakhsharī, *Kashshāf*, iii, p. 325.
6 S.a. Robert Brunschvig's article "Simples remarques négatives sur le vocabulaire du Coran," *SI*, v (1956), pp. 19–32. *Dalīl* here is a "sign" of the sun's motion, or a "guide" like those used by travelers. The combination of sun and shadow is a "sign" of God's unicity. See Ṭabarsī, op. cit., iv, p. 173.
7 See above, pp. 36–37; and Ibn al-Ḥanbalī, op. cit., p. 115.
8 Ṭūfī, op. cit., p. 161.
9 Ibid., p. 162.
10 Ibid.
11 Ibid., p. 163.
12 *Mā waqqaraka kabīr*[an] *man ʿarafaka ṣaghīr*[an] (Ṭufi, op. cit., p. 174); cf. Aristotle's inclusion of the "maxim" (*gnōmē*) among his "common modes of persuasion" (*koinai pisteis – Rhetoric*, ii, Chapter 21).
13 Ṭūfī, op. cit., p. 174.
14 Ibn al-Ḥanbalī observes that Moses does not answer the unanswerable question about the nature (*māhīya*) of God or expose its invalidity (*fasād*) but characterizes God by his creation. Op. cit, p. 70.
15 Loc. cit.
16 Ṭūfī, op. cit., p. 175.
17 *ʿAqluhu*. The editor notes (though I see no need for such an emendation) that perhaps this is a mistake for *ʿadluhu,*"his sense of justice".
18 Ṭūfī, op. cit., p. 175.
19 Ibid.
20 See above, Chapters 2 and 3.
21 Ṭūfī, op. cit., p. 197. See Ibn al-Ḥanbalī, op. cit., p. 113, for a brief description of this technique.
22 See Chapter 6, pp. 126–129, for analysis and discussion of *a fortiori* arguments.
23 See Chapter 1, pp. 6–7 and Chapter 2, pp. 30–33.
24 Ṭūfī, op. cit., p. 195.
25 See Chapter 6, p. 118.
26 See Chapter 9, p. 177.
27 *Asbāb al-Nuzūl*, p. 60.
28 See above, pp. 13–14 and 16–17.
29 See A. Katsh, *Judaism in Islam*, NYU, 1954, p. 64, ad Qur'ān 2:58. It is closer in tone to the "Constitution of Medina," with its attention to communal rights and responsibilities and not individual ones. See

M Hamidullah, *The First Written Constitution in the World: An Important Document of the Time of the Holy Prophet*, 2nd rev. edn, Lahore: Sh. Muḥammad Ashraf, 1968, based on Ibn Isḥāq's biography of the Prophet. See A. Guillaume, *The Life of Muḥammad*, Oxford, 1955; Ibn Hishām, *al-Sīra al-Nabawīya* (ed. Ṭāhā T.A-R. Saʿīd), Beirut: Dār al-Jīl, n.d., ii, pp. 106–108.

11 CONCLUSIONS

1 This from al-Suyūṭī. See M. Ayoub, op. cit., p. 5.
2 From Ibn Abī Uṣaybiʿa, *ʿUyūn al-Anbāʾ*, ii, p. 27. See G.C. Anawati, "Fakhr al-Dīn al-Rāzī," EI, vol. xx, pp. 751–755.
3 *Qisṭās*, p. 126.
4 *Al-Itqān fi ʿUlūm al-Qurʾān*, Cairo, 1370/1951 [repr. Beirut, Dār al-Nadwa al-Jadīda, n.d.] §68, part ii, p. 135. As Jane Dammen McAuliffe points out, here Suyūṭī "both incorporates and expands upon" a chapter from Burhān al-Din al-Zarkashī's *al-Burhān fi ʿUlūm al-Qurʾān*. See McAuliffe, "Debate with them in a better way," in *Myths, Historical Archetypes and Symbolic Figures in Arabic Literature,* Beirut: Steiner, 1999, pp. 184f.
5 For a clear and accessible summary of the field of *tafsīr*, see Andrew Rippin's article "*Tafsīr*" in *The Encyclopaedia of Religion*, M. Eliade, ed., New York: Macmillan, 1987, xiv, pp. 236–244; reprinted in Andrew Rippin, *The Qurʾan and Its Interpretive Tradition*, Aldershot: Ashgate Variorum, 2001, x, pp. 1–24.
6 See H. Djavad Falaturi, "Fakhr al-Dīn al-Rāzī's critical logic," in *Yādnāme-ye Īrānī-ye Minorsky*, M. Minovi, ed., Tehran, 1348/1969, pp. 51–79.
7 See Andrew Rippin, "The present status of tafsīr studies," *The Muslim World*, lxxii (1982), reprinted in Rippin, *The Qurʾan and Its Interpretive Tradition*, xi, pp. 224–238.
8 See my draft article "Al-Qāʿida and al-Qurʾān: The '*Tafsir*' of Usamah bin Ladin," online at http://web.utk.edu/~religion/faculty.html or at http://web.utk.edu/~warda/bin_ladin_and_quran.htm currently being revised for publication.
9 *Jadal*, p. 209.

BIBLIOGRAPHY

The Holy Qur'ān (ed. and tr. A. Yusuf Ali), American Trust Publications, (2nd edn), 1977 (Lahore, 1938).

The Koran (Tr. N.J. Dawood), Harmondsworth, England: Penguin, 1974.

The Meaning of the Glorious Koran (tr. M.M. Pickthall), Mentor: New American Library, 1953.

al-Qur'ān al-Karīm, Cairo: Maktabat al-Ahrām al-Tijarīya, 1392/1972.

The Quran: Translated, with a Critical Re-arrangement of the Surahs (ed. and tr. Richard Bell), Edinburgh: Clark, 1937.

The Holy Bible: Revised Standard Version, New York: Thomas Nelson and Sons, 1952.

'Abd al-Bāqī, Muḥammad Fu'ād, *al-Mu'jam al-Mufahras li-Alfāẓ al-Qur'ān al-Karīm*, Beirut: Khayyāṭ, 1945.

Abdul Rauf, Muḥammad, "Some notes on the Qur'anic use of the terms *islām* and *īmān*," *Muslim World*, 57 (1967), pp. 94–102.

Abu 'Ubayda, *Majāz al-Qur'ān* (ed. F. Sezgin), Cairo: al-Khānjī, 1979.

Abelson, Raziel, "Definition," *Encyclopedia of Philosophy*, New York: Macmillan, 1972, ii, pp. 314–324.

Āl Yāsīn, M, *Fī Riḥāb al-Qur'ān*, Baghdad: Maṭba'at al-Ma'ārif, 1388/[1968–69].

al-Alma'ī, Zāhir A., *Manāhij al-Jadal fī al-Qur'ān al-Karīm*, Riyadh: Maṭābi' al-Farazdaq al-Tijārīya, 1984.

The Anchor Dictionary of the Bible (ed. D.N. Freedman), New York: Doubleday, 1992.

Anderson, Bernhard, *Understanding the Old Testament* (2nd edition) Englewood Cliffs, NJ: Prentice-Hall, 1966.

Andersson, Jan, *How to Define Performative*, Uppsala: Philosophical Society and Dept of Philosophy, University of Uppsala, 1975.

Andrae, Tor, *Mohammed, the Man and His Faith* (tr. T. Menzel), New York: Harper, 1955 (1960).

Angeles, Peter, *Dictionary of Philosophy*, New York: Barnes and Noble, 1981.

Aristotle, *Aristotle 'On Rhetoric': A Theory of Civic Discourse* (ed. and tr. George A. Kennedy), New York: Oxford University Press, 1991.

—— *The Rhetoric of Aristotle* (ed. and tr. J.E.C. Welldon), London and New York: Macmillan, 1886.

'Arjūn, M. al-Ṣādiq, *Al-Qur'ān al-'Aẓīm: Hidāyatuhu wa-I'jāzuhu fī Aqwāl al-Mufassirīn*, Cairo: Maktabat al-Kullīya al-Azharīya, 1386/1966.

al-A'sam, A.A., *Tārīkh Ibn al-Rīwandi al-Mulḥid*, Beirut: Dār al-Āfāq al-Jadīda, 1395/1975.

Askari, Hasan, "The Qur'ānic conception of apostleship," in D. Cohn-Sherbok (ed.), *Islam in a World of Diverse Faiths*, New York: St Martin's, 1991.

Auerbach, Erich, *Mimesis*, Princeton: Princeton University Press, 1953.

Austin, J.L., *How To Do Things With Words* (2nd edn), Harvard, 1975.

Ayoub, Mahmoud, *The Qur'an and Its Interpreters, Vol. 1*, Albany: SUNY Press, 1984.

al-Baghdādī, 'Abd al-Qāhir, *Uṣūl al-Dīn,* Lahore: al-Maktaba al-'Uthmānīya, 1978–1979.

al-Bāqillānī, Abū Bakr M. b. al-Ṭayyib. *I'jāz al-Qur'ān* (ed. Aḥmad Ṣaqr), Cairo: Dar al-Ma'ārif, 1963.

—— (See von Grünebaum).

al-Bayhaqī, Aḥmad b. al-Ḥusayn, *Kitab al-Asmā' wa-al-Ṣifāt*, Beirut: Dār al-Kutub al-'Ilmīya, 1405/1984.

Bell, Richard, *The Origin of Islam in Its Christian Environment*, London: Frank Cass, 1926 (repr. 1968).

—— S.a. Watt, W. Montgomery.

Bijlefeld, W., "A prophet and more than a prophet?", *Muslim World*, 59 (1969).

Birkeland, Harris. "The legend of the opening of Muhammad's breast," *Norske Videnskapsa* Akademie I Oslo. II Hist.-Filos. Klasse, 1955, no 3. Oslo: Dybwad, 1955.

—— *The Lord Guideth: Studies on Primitive Islam*. Oslo: Nygaard, 1956.

Bittle, Celestine, *The Science of Correct Thinking: Logic*, Milwaukee: Bruce, 1935–1937.

Bosworth, C.E., "*Mīthāḳ*," *Encyclopaedia of Islam* (2nd edn), v, pp. 187–88.

Boullata, Issa, ed., *Literary Structures of Religious Meaning in the Qur'ān*. Richmond: Curzon, 2000.

Bouyges, Maurice, *Essai de Chronologie des Oeuvres de Al-Ghazālī* (ed. M. Allard), Beirut: Imprimerie Catholique, 1959.

Bravmann, M.M., *The Spiritual Background of Early Islam*, Leiden: Brill, 1972.

Brunschvig, R., "Simples remarques négatives sur le vocabulaire du Coran," *Studia Islamica* 5 (1956), pp. 19–32.

Buhl, F., "Koran," Encyclopaedia of Islam (1st edn).

al-Bukhārī, M. b. Ismā'īl, *Al-Jāmi' al-Ṣaḥīḥ* (M.D. Bugha, ed.), Beirut, 1990.

Burton, John. *The Collection of the Quran*. Cambridge, 1977.

Calder, Norman, "*Ḥinth, birr* . . . ; an inquiry into the Arabic vocabulary of vows," *Bulletin of the School of Oriental and African Studies* 51 (1988), pp. 214–239.

Cartlidge, David and Dungan, David, *Documents for the Study of the Gospels*, Philadelphia: Fortress, 1980.

—— *Documents for the Study of the Gospels* (revised edn), Philadelphia: Fortress, 1994.

Chelhot, Victor, "'Al-Qisṭās al-Mustaqīm' et la connaissance rationelle chez Gazālī," *Bulletin d'Études Orientales*, xv (1955–57), pp. 7–42.

Conley, Thomas M., "The enthymeme in perspective," *Quarterly Journal of Speech*, May, 1984, pp. 168–187.

Copi, Irving, *Introduction to Logic* (4th edn), New York: Macmillan, 1972.

Corbett, Edward P.J., *Classical Rhetoric for the Modern Student*. New York: Oxford University Press, 1971.

Crone, Patricia and Cook, Michael, *Hagarism: The Making of the Islamic World*. Cambridge: Cambridge University Press, 1977.

Denny, Frederick M., "The meaning of *umma* in the Qur'ān," *History of Religions* 15 (1976), pp. 34–70.

al-Dhahabī, Shams al-Dīn M., *Kitāb al-Kabā'ir*. Aleppo: Dar al-Wa'y, 1396/[1976].

Eaton, Ralph, *General Logic: An Introductory Survey*, New York: Scribner's, 1931.

Edwards, Paul, *The Logic of Moral Discourse*, Glencoe, IL: Free Press, 1955.

Falaturi, A. Djavad, "Fakhr al-Dīn al-Râzî's critical logic," *Yādnāme-ye Īrānī-ye Minorsky* (M. Minovi, ed.), Tehran: Publications de l'Université de Tehran, 1348/1969, pp. 51–79.

al-Farrā', Abu Zakarīyā Yaḥyā b. Ziyād, *Ma'ānī al-Qur'ān* (I.D. 'Abd al-'Azīz and A-S. Shāhīn, eds), Cairo: Markaz al-Ahrām li-'l-Ṭibā'a wa-'l-Nashr (Taqrīb al-Turāth), 1409/1989.

—— *Ma'ānī al-Qur'ān* (M. 'A. Al-Najjār, ed.). Cairo: al-Dār al-Miṣrīya li-al-Ta'līf wa-'l-Tarjama, n.d.

Fearnside, W.W. and Holther, W., *Fallacy: the Counterfeit of Argument*, Englewood Cliffs, NJ: Prentice-Hall, 1959.

Firmage, E. et al. eds, *Religion and Law: Biblical-Judaic and Islamic Perspectives*, Winona Lake: Eisenbrauns, 1990.

al-Fīrūzābādī, Majd al-Dīn Muḥammad b. Ya'qūb, *al-Qāmūs al-Muḥīṭ*, Cairo: Mu'assasat al-Ḥalabī, 1306/[1888–89].

—— *Tanwīr al-Miqbās min Tafsīr Ibn 'Abbās*, Multan: Faruqi Kutubkhaneh, n.d.

Fischer, M.J. and Abedi, M., *Debating Muslims*, Madison: University of Wisconsin, 1990.

Fück, Johann, "The originality of the Arabian prophet," in *Studies on Islam* (Merlin Swartz, ed. and tr.), New York: Oxford University Press, 1981, pp. 86–98.

Fūdah, ʿAbd al-ʿAlīm al-Sayyid, *Asālīb al-Istifhām fī al-Qur'ān*. Cairo: al-Majlis al-Aʿlā li-Riʿāyat al-Funūn wa-al-Ādāb wa-al-ʿUlūm al-Ijtimāʿīya, 1975(?).

Gardet, Louis., "al-Asmā' al-ḥusnā," *Encyclopaedia of Islam* (2nd edn), I, pp. 714–717.

—— "*Dīn*," *Encyclopaedia of Islam* (2nd edn), ii, pp. 293–296.

—— "*Īmān*," *Encyclopaedia of Islam* (2nd edn), iii, pp. 1170–1174.

—— "*Islām*," *Encyclopaedia of Islam* (2nd edn), v, pp. 171–174.

Ghāzī, Muḥammad J.A., *Asmā' al-Qur'ān fī al-Qur'ān*. Cairo: al-Mu'assasa al-Saʿūdīya bi-Miṣr, 1975.

al-Ghazālī, Abu Ḥāmid, *Kitāb Miḥakk al-Naẓar fī al-Manṭiq* (M.B.D. al-aʿsānī, ed.), Beirut: Dār al-Nahḍa al-Ḥadītha, 1966.

—— *Miʿyār al-ʿIlm* (Sulayman Dunyā, ed.), Cairo: Dār al-Maʿārif bi-Miṣr, 1379/1960.

—— *al-Qisṭās al-Mustaqīm* (Muḥammad ʿAfīf al-Zuʿbī, ed.), Beirut: Mu'assasat al-Zuʿbī, 1392/1973.

—— *al-Qisṭās al-Mustaqīm* (Riyāḍ Muṣṭafā al-ʿAbd Allāh, ed.), Damascus: Dār al-Ḥikma, 1406/1986.

Gibb, H.A.R., "Pre-Islamic monotheism in Arabia," *Harvard Theological Review*, 55 (1962), pp. 269–280.

Gimaret, Daniel, *Les Noms Divins en Islam*, Paris: Éditions du Cerf, 1988.

Goitein, S., "The birth-hour of Muslim law," *Studies in Islamic History and Institutions*, Leiden: Brill, 1966, pp. 126–134.

Goldfeld, Isaiah, "The illiterate Prophet (*nabī ummī*): an inquiry into the development of a dogma in Islamic tradition," *Der Islam* 57 (1980), pp. 58–67.

Goldziher, Ignaz, *Muslim Studies* (S.M. Stern, ed.; S.M. Stern and C.R. Barber, trans.), Chicago: Aldine, 1967 (vol. I) and 1971 (vol. II).

Gottlieb, Gidon, *The Logic of Choice: An Investigation of the Concepts of Rule and Rationality*, London: Allen and Unwin, 1968.

Graham, William, *Divine Word and Prophetic Word in Early Islam*, Paris: Mouton, 1977.

—— "Qur'ān as Spoken Word," *Approaches to Islam in Religious Studies* (Richard C. Martin, ed.) Tucson: University of Arizona Press, 1985.

von Grünebaum, G., *A Tenth-Century Document of Arabic Literary Theory and Criticism: The sections on poetry of al-Bāqillānī's 'Iʿjāz al-Qur'ān,' translated and annotated*. University of Chicago, 1950.

Guillaume, A., *The Life of Muḥammad: A Translation of Ibn Isḥāq's 'Sīrat Rasūl Allāh,'* Karachi: Oxford University Press, 1980 (1955).

Gwynne, Rosalind, "The *a fortiori* argument in *fiqh, naḥw,* and *kalām*," *Studies in the History of Arabic Grammar II* (K. Versteegh and M. Carter, eds), Philadelphia: John Benjamins, 1990.

—— "Hell and hellfire," *Encyclopaedia of the Qur'ān*, Jane Dammen McAuliffe, ed., Leiden: Brill, 2001, ii, pp. 414–420.

—— "Impotence," *Encyclopaedia of the Qur'ān*, Jane Dammen McAuliffe, ed., Netherlands: Brill, ii, pp. 507–508.

—— "The neglected *sunnah*: Sunnat Allāh (the *sunnah* of God)," *American Journal of Islamic Social Sciences*, 10 (1993), no. 4, pp. 455–463.

—— *The Tafsīr of Abū 'Alī al-Jubbā'ī* (unpublished doctoral dissertation, University of Washington), 1982.

Haddad, Yvonne, "The conception of the term 'dīn' in the Qur'ān," *Muslim World* 64 (1974), pp. 115–123.

Hajjaji-Jarrah, Soraya, "The enchantment of reading," in I. Boullata (ed.) *Literary Structures of Religious Meaning in the Qur'ān*, Richmond: Curzon, 2000, pp. 228–251.

Ḥammūsh, A.R., *Kunūz al-Bāḥithīn: al-Tarājim wa-'l-Fahāris al-Tafṣīlīya li-Kitāb Riyāḍ al-Ṣāliḥīn*, Beirut: Dār al-Fikr, 1413/1992.

Hawting, G.R. and Shareef, A.A., eds, *Approaches to the Qur'ān*, New York: Routledge, 1993.

Haykal, Muḥammad Ḥusayn, *The Life of Muḥammad*, North American Trust, 1976.

Hourani, George, "The Qur'ān's doctrine of prophecy," *Logos Islamikos* (R. Savory and D. Agius, eds), Toronto: Pontifical Institute, 1984, pp. 175–181.

Ibn al-'Arabī, Abu Bakr M. b. 'Abd Allāh al-Ma'āfirī, *Aḥkām al-Qur'ān* (A.M. al-Bajawī, ed.), Cairo: 'Īsā al-Bābī al-Ḥalabī, [1967–68].

Ibn al-Ḥanbalī, *Kitāb Istikhrāj al-Jidāl min al-Qur'ān al-Karīm*, ed. Z. al-Alma'ī, Beirut: Mu'assasat al-Risāla, 1400/1980.

Ibn Hazm, *Mulakhkhaṣ Ibṭāl al-Qiyās wa-al-Ra'y wa-al-Istiḥsān wa-al-Taqlīd wa-al-Ta'līl* (Sa'īd al-Afghānī, ed.), Damascus University Press, 1379/1960.

Ibn Hishām, *Al-Sīra al-Nabawīya li-Ibn Hishām* (T.A-R. Sa'd, ed.), Beirut: Dār al-Jīl, n.d.

Ibn Isḥāq, *The Life of Muḥammad* (A. Guillaume, ed. and tr.), Karachi: Oxford University Press, 1955 (1980).

Ibn al-Jawzī, *Kitāb al-Muntaẓam*, Hyderabad: Dā'irat al-Ma'ārif al-'Uthmānīya, 1357/[1938–39].

Ibn Kathīr, *Tafsīr Ibn Kathīr*, Beirut: Dār al-Fikr, 1400/1980.

Ibn Khālawayh, Abū 'Abd Allāh al-Ḥusayn, *I'rāb Thalāthīn Sūra min al-Qu'rān al-Karīm*, Beirut: Dār Maktabat al-Hilāl, 1985.

Ibn al-Nadīm, *al-Fihrist*, (Reza Tajaddod, ed.), Tehran, n.d.

—— *The Fihrist of al-Nadīm* (Bayard Dodge, ed. and tr.). New York: Columbia, 1970.

Ibn Rushd, Abū al-Walīd Muḥammad. *Bidāyat al-Mujtahid wa-Nihāyat al-Muqtaṣid*, Beirut: Dār al-Fikr, n.d.

—— *Manāhij al-Adilla fī 'Aqā'id al-Milla* (Maḥmūd Qāsim, ed.), Cairo: Maktabat al-Anglo al-Misrīya, 1964.

Ibn Sa'd, *al-Ṭabaqāt al-Kubrā*, Beirut: Dar Ṣādir, 1380/1960.

Ibn Salāma, Abū al-Qāsim Hibat Allāh, *al-Nāsikh wa-al-Mansūkh* (published with al-Wāḥidī's *Asbāb al-Nuzūl*), Cairo: Maktabat al-Mutanabbī, n.d.

Ibn Qayyim al-Jawzīya, *al-Tibyān fi Aqsām al-Qur'ān* (ed. M.H. al-Faqī), Beirut: Dar al-Ma'rifa, n.d.

Ibn Taghribirdī, *al-Nujūm al-Ẓāhira*, Cairo, 1963–1972.

'Iṭr, Nūr al-Dīn, *Mu'jam al-Muṣṭalaḥāt al-Ḥadīthīya*, University of Damascus, 1397/1977.

Izutsu, Toshihiko, *Ethico-Religious Concepts in the Koran*, Montreal: McGill University Press, 1966.

—— *God and Man in the Koran: Semantics of the Koranic Weltanschauung*, Tokyo: Keio Institute, 1964.

—— *Language and Magic*, Tokyo: Keio Institute, 1956.

—— *The Structure of the Ethical Terms in the Koran*, Tokyo: Keio Institute of Philological Studies, 1959.

Jackson, B.S., *Studies in the Semiotics of Biblical Law*, Sheffield, UK: Sheffield Academic Press, 2000.

al-Jaṣṣāṣ, Abū Bakr Aḥmad b. 'Alī, *Aḥkām al-Qur'ān*, Beirut: Dār al-Kitāb al-'Arabī, 1986/1406. (Photocopy of 1335/[1916–17] ed., Maṭba'at al-Awqāf al-Islāmīya).

Jeffery, Arthur, *The Foreign Vocabulary of the Quran*, Baroda: Oriental Institute, 1938 (repr. Lahore: al-Bīrūnī, 1977).

—— *Materials for the History of the Text of the Qur'an*, Leiden: Brill, 1937 (repr. AMS Press, 1975).

—— *The Qur'ān as Scripture*. New York: Russell F. Moore, 1952.

—— "Was Muhammad a prophet from his infancy?", *Muslim World* 20 (1930), pp. 226–234.

Johnson, James William, *Logic and Rhetoric*, New York: Macmillan, 1962.

Jomier, Jacques, "*Le nom divin 'al-Raḥmān' dans le Coran*," in *Mélanges Massignon* (Damascus) 2 (1957), pp. 361–381.

Juynboll, G.H.A., *Muslim Tradition*, Cambridge: Cambridge University Press, 1983.

Kalluveetil, Paul, *Declaration and Covenant: A comprehensive review of covenant formulae from the Old Testament and the ancient Near East*, Rome: Biblical Institute Press, 1982.

Kandil, Lamya, "Die Schwüre in den Mekkanischen Suren," in S. Wild (ed.), *The Qur'ān as Text*, Leiden: Brill, 1996, pp. 41–57.

Katsh, Abraham, *Judaism in Islam*, New York: SUNY, 1954.

Khalīl, Khalīl Aḥmad, *Jadalīyat al-Qur'ān*, Beirut, Dār al-Ṭalī'a, 1977.

Kittel, G. (ed.), *Theological Dictionary of the New Testament*, Grand Rapids: Eerdmans, 1964–1976.

Kleinknecht, Angelika, "Al-Qisṭās al-Mustaqīm: eine Ableitung der Logik aus dem Koran," *Islamic Philosophy and the Classical Tradition* (S. Stern, et al., eds). South Carolina, Columbia: University of South Carolina Press, 1973, pp. 159–187.

Labīd, *Sharḥ Dīwān Labīd b. Rabīʿa al-ʿĀmiri* (Iḥsān ʿAbbās, ed.), Kuwait, Ministry of Guidance and Information, 1961.

Leemhuis, F., "About the meaning of *nabba'a* and *anba'a* in the Qur'ān," *Akten des VII. Kongresses für Arabistik und Islamwissenschaft*, Gottingen, 1974.

Lejewski, Czeslaw, "Ancient Logic," *Encyclopedia of Philosophy*, New York: Macmillan, 1972, iv, pp. 513–520.

Locke, John, *An Essay Concerning Human Understanding* (ed. A.D. Woozley), New York: Meridian, 1964.

McAuliffe, Jane Dammen, "'Debate with them in the better way': the construction of a Qur'ānic commonplace," in *Myths, Historical Archetypes and Symbolic Figures in Arabic Literature: Towards a New Hermeneutical Approach* (A. Neuwirth et al., eds), Beirut: Steiner, 1999.

—— *Qur'ānic Christians: An Analysis of Classical and Modern Exegesis*. Cambridge, 1991.

McCarthy, Richard J., *Freedom and Fulfillment: An Annotated Translation of al-Ghazālī's 'al-Munqidh min al-Ḍalāl' and Other Relevant Works of al-Ghazālī*, Boston: Twayne, 1980.

Madkour, Ibrahim. *L'Organon d'Aristote dans le Monde Arabe*. Paris: J. Vrin, 1934.

Martin, Richard, "Structural analysis and the Qur'ān: Newer approaches to the study of Islamic texts," *Journal of the American Academy of Religion Thematic Issue*, vol. 47 (Dec. 1979), no. 4S, pp. 665–683.

Mates, Benson, *Stoic Logic*, Berkeley: University of California Press, 1953 (repr. 1961).

Mendenhall, G. and Herion, G. "Covenant," *The Anchor Bible Dictionary* (D.N. Freedman, ed.), New York: Doubleday, 1992.

Michel, Otto, "*Mimnēskomai, mneia*", *Theological Dictionary of the New Testament* (G. Kittel, ed.; and G. Bromiley, tr. and ed.), iv, pp. 675–683.

Mir, Mustansir, *Dictionary of Qur'ānic Terms and Concepts*. New York: Garland, 1987.

Morony, Michael, *Iraq After the Muslim Conquest*, Princeton: Princeton University Press, 1984.

Muir, William, *The Life of Mahomet*, London, 1894 (repr. New Delhi: Voice of India, 1992).

Mujāhid, Abū al-Ḥajjāj b. Jabr al-Tābiʿī, *Tafsīr Mujāhid*. (A-R. al-Sūratī, ed.), Islamabad: Majma' al-Buḥūth al-Islāmīya, 1966.

Muqātil b. Sulaymān, *Tafsīr Muqātil b. Sulaymān* (A.M. Shihāta, ed.), Cairo: Mu'aṣsasat al-Ḥalabī, 1969.

Muslim b. al-Ḥajjāj *Al-Jāmiʿ al-Ṣaḥīḥ,* Beirut: al-Maktab al-Tijārī, n.d.

al-Nawawī, Abu Zakarīyā Yaḥyā b. Sharaf. *Riyāḍ al-Ṣāliḥīn min Kalām Sayyid al-Mursalīn* (M.M. ʿAmāra, ed.). Beirut and Damascus: Maktabat al-Ghazālī, n.d.

Neuwirth, Angelika, "The Makkan sura introductions," in *Approaches to the Qur'ān* (G.R. Hawting and A.A. Shareef, eds), New York: Routledge, 1993, pp. 3–36.
Newby, Gordon, *The Making of the Last Prophet: A Reconstruction of the Earliest Biography of Muhammad*, Columbia, South Carolina: University of South Carolina Press, 1989.
al-Nīsābūrī, Niẓām al-Dīn al-Ḥasan b. M. al-Qummī, *Tafsīr Gharā'ib al-Qur'ān wa-Raghā'ib al-Furqān* (on the margins of al-Ṭabarī, *Jāmiʿ al-Bayān fī Tafsīr al-Qur'ān*), Beirut: Dar al-Jil, n.d. (reprint of the Bulaq edition).
al-Nūrī, al-Sayyid Abū al-Maʿātī, et al., *al-Jāmiʿ fī al-Jarḥ wa'l-Taʿdīl*, Beirut, ʿĀlam al-Kutub, 1412/1992.
Ogden, C.K. and Richards, I.A., *The Meaning of Meaning* (8th edn), New York: Harcourt, Brace, 1923, 1946.
Peters, F.E., *Muhammad and the Origins of Islam*, New York: SUNY, 1994.
al-Qasṭallānī, Ahmad b. M., *Irshād al-Sārī li-Ṣaḥīḥ al-Bukhārī*, Cairo: Būlāq, 1887.
Qatāda, *Kitāb al-Nāsikh wa-'l-Mansūkh* (Ḥ.Ṣ. al-Ḍāmin, ed.), in *al-Mawrid*, ix, no. 4, Baghdad, 1985/1401, pp. 479–506.
Qazi, Saeedullah, *Principles of Muslim Jurisprudence: Chapters on Qiyās and Ijtihād of Abū Bakr... al-Jaṣṣāṣ*, Lahore: al-Maktabat-el-Ilmiyyah, 1981.
al-Qurṭubī, M. b. A., *al-Jāmiʿ li-Aḥkām al-Qur'ān*, Beirut: Dār al-Kutub al-ʿIlmīya, 1408/1988.
Rabin, C., *Ancient West-Arabian*, London: Taylor, 1951.
al-Rāzī, A. b. M. b. al-Muẓaffar, *Kitāb Ḥujaj al-Qur'ān* (A. ʿUmar al-Maḥmaṣānī, ed.), Beirut: Dār al-Kutub al-ʿIlmīya, 1406/1986.
al-Rāzī, Fakhr al-Dīn Abū ʿAbd Allāh M. b. ʿUmar, *al-Tafsīr al-Kabīr.* Beirut: Dār Iḥyā' al-Turāth al-ʿArabī, n.d.
al-Rāzī, Muḥammad b. Abī Bakr, *Mukhtār al-Ṣiḥāḥ* (ed. M. Dīb al-Bughā), Damascus and Beirut: al-Yamāma, 1405/1985.
Rescher, Nicholas, *The Logic of Commands*, London: Routledge and Kegan Paul, 1966.
Ringgren, H., "The root SDQ in poetry and the Koran," *Ex Orbe Religionum: Studia Geo Widengren*, Leiden: Brill, 1972, pp. 134–142.
Rippin, Andrew, "Desiring the face of God," *Literary Structures of Religious Meaning in the Qur'ān*, (I. Boullata, ed.) Richmond: Curzon, 2000, pp. 117–124.
—— "The present status of tafsīr studies," *The Muslim World*, lxxii (1982), reprinted in Rippin, *The Qur'an and Its Interpretive Tradition*, xi, pp. 224–238.
—— *The Qur'an and Its Interpretive Tradition*, Aldershot: Ashgate Variorum, 2001,
—— "*Tafsīr*," *The Encyclopaedia of Religion* (M. Eliade, ed.), New York: Macmillan, 1987, xiv, pp. 236–244; reprinted in Andrew Rippin, *The*

Qur'an and Its Interpretive Tradition, Aldershot: Ashgate Variorum, 2001, x, pp. 1–24.
Robinson, Richard, *Definition*, Oxford: Clarendon Press, 1954 (1965).
Rodinson, Maxime, *Muḥammad* (Anne Carter, tr.), New York: Pantheon, 1980.
Rubin, Uri, "*Barā'a*: A Study of Some Qur'ānic Passages," *Jerusalem Studies in Arabic and Islam*, V (1984), pp. 13–32.
—— *The Eye of the Beholder: The Life of Muḥammad as Viewed by the Early Muslims*, Princeton, NJ: Darwin Press, 1995.
—— "*Iqra' bi-smi rabbika*," *Israel Oriental Studies* 13 (1993), pp. 213–230.
Ryle, Gilbert, *The Concept of Mind*, New York: Barnes and Noble, 1949.
Saiyidain, K.G., "The Quran's Invitation to Think," *Islam and the Modern Age*, 4 (1973), no. 2, pp. 5–27.
Schacht, Joseph, "*'Ahd*," *Encyclopedia of Islam* (2nd edn).
—— *Introduction to Islamic Law*, Oxford: Clarendon Press, 1964.
—— *The Origins of Muhammadan Jurisprudence*, Oxford: Clarendon Press, 1950 (repr. 1967).
Searle, John, "How Performatives Work," *Tennessee Law Review*, vol. 58, 1991, pp. 371–392.
al-Shāfi'ī, M. b. Idrīs, *Aḥkām al-Qur'ān* (M.Z. al-Kawtharī, ed.), Beirut, Dār al-Kutub al-'Ilmīya, 1400/1980.
—— *Kitāb al-Umm*, Beirut: Dār al-Fikr, 1400/1980.
—— *al-Risāla* (ed. Muḥammad Kaylānī). Cairo: Muṣṭafā al-Bābī al-Ḥalabī, 1403/1983.
Shahid, Irfan, "Two Qur'ānic suras: *al-Fīl* and *Quraysh*," *Studia Arabica et Islamica* (W. al-Qadi, ed.), Beirut: American University of Beirut, 1981, pp. 429–436.
Shehaby, Nabil, *The Propositional Logic of Avicenna*, Dordrecht: Riedel, 1973.
Sībawayh, *Kitāb Sībawayh* (A-S.M. Hārūn, ed.), Beirut: 'Ālam al-Kutub, 1403/1983.
—— *al-Kitāb* (H. Derenbourg, ed.), Paris: Imprimerie Nationale, 1881 [repr. Hildesheim].
Stebbing, L.S., *A Modern Introduction to Logic*, New York: Humanities Press, 1933.
Strawson, P.F., *Introduction to Logical Theory*, London: Methuen, 1952 [repr. University Paperbacks, 1971].
Sufyān al-Thawrī, *Tafsīr al-Qur'ān al-Karīm* (I.A. 'Arshī, ed.), Rampur, 1385/1965.
al-Suyūṭī, Jalāl al-Dīn. *Bughyat al-Wu'āt fi Ṭabaqāt al-Lughawīyīn wa-'l-Nuḥāt* (M.A-F. Ibrāhīm, ed.), Cairo: 'Īsā al-Bābī al-Ḥalabī, 1384/1964.
—— *al-Durr al-Manthūr fī al-Tafsīr bi-'l-Ma'thūr*, Beirut: Dār al-Fikr, 1414/1993.

—— *al-Itqān fī 'Ulūm al-Qur'ān*, Cairo, 1370/1951 [repr. Beirut, Dār al-Nadwa al-Jadīda, n.d.].

al-Ṭabarī, *Jāmi' al-Bayān 'an Ta'wīl Āy al-Qur'ān*, Cairo: M. al-Bābī al-Ḥalabī, 1388/1968.

—— *Jāmi' al-Bayān fī Tafsīr al-Qur'ān* [sic], *wa bi-Hāmishihi Tafsīr Gharā'ib al-Qur'ān wa-Raghā'ib al-Furqān li-'l-'Allāma Niẓām al-Dīn ... al-Nīsābūrī,* Beirut: Dār al-Jīl, n.d. [reprint of the Bulaq edition].

al-Ṭabarsī, *Majma' al-Bayān fī Tafsīr al-Qur'ān*, Sidon: M. al-'Irfān, 1333/[1914–1915] [repr. Qomm: Maktabat al-Mar'ashī, 1404/1983].

Tashköprüzadeh, Aḥmad b. Muṣṭafā, *Miftāḥ al-Sa'āda*, (K. Bakrī and 'A-W Abū al-Nūr, eds). Cairo: Dār al-Kutub al-Ḥadītha, 1968.

al-Tirmidhī, *al-Jāmi' al-Ṣaḥīḥ wa-huwa Sunan al-Tirmidhī* (A.M. Shākir, M.F. 'Abd al-Bāqī, and I.'A. 'Awaḍ, eds), Beirut: Dar 'Imrān, n.d.

al-Ṭūfī, Najm al-Dīn *'Alam al-Jadhal fī 'Ilm al-Jadal* (W. Heinrichs, ed.), Wiesbaden: Franz Steiner Verlag, 1408/1987.

al-'Ukbarī, Abū al-Baqā', *Imlā' Mā Manna Bihi al-Raḥmān fī Wujūh al-I'rāb wa-'l-Qirā'āt fī Jāmi' al-Qur'ān*, (ed. I. Awaḍ), Lahore, n.d.

al-'Ulaymī, Qāḍī Mujīr al-Din al-Ḥanbalī *al-Uns al-Jalīl bi-Tārīkh al-Quds wa-al-Khalīl*, Najaf, 1388/1968.

Vahiduddin, S., "Richard Bell's study of the Qur'ān: (A critical analysis)," *Islamic Culture*, July, 1956, pp. 263–272.

Waardenburg, J., "Un débat Coranique contre les polythéistes," *Ex Orbe Religionum: Studia Geo Widengren*, Leiden: Brill, 1972.

—— "Faith and reason in the argumentation of the Qur'an," *Perennitas: Studi in Onore di Angelo Brelich*, Rome: Edizioni dell'Ateneo 1980, pp. 619–633.

Wagtendonk, K., "Muḥammad and the Qur'ān: criteria for Muḥammad's Prophecy," *Liber Amicorum: Studies in Honour of Prof. Dr. C.J. Bleeker,* Leiden: Brill, 1969, pp. 254–268.

al-Wāḥidi, Abū al-Ḥasan 'Alī, *Asbāb al-Nuzūl*, Cairo: Maktabat al-Mutanabbī, n.d.

Wakin, Jeannette, "Interpretation of the divine command in the jurisprudence of Muwaffaq al-Dīn Ibn Qudāmah," *Islamic Law and Jurisprudence: Studies in Honor of Farhat J. Ziadeh* (Nicholas Heer, ed.), Seattle: University of Washington, 1990.

Waldman, Marilyn, "The development of the concept of *kufr* in the Qur'ān," *Journal of the American Oriental Society* 88 (1968), pp. 442–455.

Wansbrough, John, *Quranic Studies: Sources and Methods of Scriptural Interpretation*, Oxford: Oxford University Press, 1977.

Watt, W. Montgomery, "Conversion in Islam at the time of the Prophet," *Journal of the American Academy of Religion Thematic Issue*, 47 (Dec. 1979), no. 4S, pp. 721–731.

—— "Early discussions about the Qur'ān," *Muslim World* 40 (1950), pp. 96–105.

Watt, W.M. and Bell, Richard, *Bell's Introduction to the Qur'ān*, Edinburgh: Edinburgh University Press, 1970.

Weinfeld, Moshe, "The Decalogue," in E. Firmage, et al., eds, *Religion and Law: Biblical-Judaic and Islamic Perspectives*, Winona Lake: Eisenbrauns, 1990.

Weiss, Bernard, "Covenant and Law in Islam," in E. Firmage, et al., eds, *Religion and Law: Biblical-Judaic and Islamic Perspectives*, Winona Lake: Eisenbrauns, 1990, pp. 49–83.

—— "Exotericism and objectivity in Islamic jurisprudence," *Islamic Law and Jurisprudence: Studies in Honor of Farhat J. Ziadeh* (Nicholas Heer, ed.), Seattle: University of Washington, 1990.

Welch, Alford, "Allah and other supernatural beings: the emergence of the Qur'ānic doctrine of *tawḥīd*," *Journal of the American Academy of Religion Thematic Issue*, 47 (Dec. 1979), no. 4S, pp. 733–758.

—— "*al-Ḳur'an*". *Encyclopedia of Islam* (2nd edn).

—— "Muḥammad's understanding of himself: the Koranic data." *Islam's Understanding of Itself* (R. Hovannisian and S. Vryonis, eds), Malibu: Undena, 1983, pp. 15–52.

Wensinck, A.J. *Concordance et Indices de la Tradition Musulman*. Leiden: Brill, 1936.

—— *The Muslim Creed*, London: Frank Cass, 1965.

Wild, Stefan (ed.), *The Qur'an as Text*, Leiden: Brill, 1996.

Winnett, F.V., "Allah Before Islam," *Muslim World* 28 (1938), pp. 239–248.

Wright, W. *A Grammar of the Arabic Language*. Cambridge (1859) (3rd edn), (rev. by W. Robertson Smith and M.J. de Goeje), Cambridge: Cambridge University Press, 1964.

al-Zabīdī, Abū al-ʿAbbās Aḥmad, *Mukhtaṣar Ṣaḥīḥ al-Bukhārī: al-Tajrīd al-Ṣarīḥ li-Aḥādīth al-Jāmiʿ al-Ṣaḥīḥ* (K. al-Abyānī, ed.), Beirut: Mu'assasat al-Kutub al-Thaqāfīya, 1413/1993.

al-Zajjāj, *Tafsīr Asmā' Allāh al-Ḥusnā* (A.Y. al-Daqqāq, ed.). Damascus: Dār al-Ma'mūn li-'l-Turāth, 1983.

al-Zamakhsharī, Abū al-Qāsim Jār Allāh Maḥmūd, *al-Kashshāf ʿan Ḥaqā'iq al-Tanzīl* (M.S. Qamḥawī, ed.), Cairo: Muṣṭafā al-Bābī al-Ḥalabī, 1392/1972.

al-Zarkashī, Badr al-Dīn M. b. ʿAbd Allāh, *Al-Burhān fī ʿUlūm al-Qur'ān* (M.A-F. Ibrāhīm, ed.). Cairo: ʿĪsā al-Bābī al-Ḥalabī, 1376/1957.

Zwettler, Michael, "A mantic manifesto: the sura of 'The Poets' and the Qur'anic foundations of prophetic authority," *Poetry and Prophecy* (James Kugel, ed.), Ithaca: Cornell University Press, 1990.

INDEX TO QUR'ĀNIC VERSES

INDEX

CPSIA information can be obtained at www.ICGtesting.com
Printed in the USA
LVOW11s0029171014

409129LV00001B/46/P

9 780415 554190